DANGEROUS PLACES

Travels on the Edge

Rosa Jordan

Pottersfield Press
Lawrencetown Beach
Nova Scotia, Canada

Copyright © 1997 by Rosa Jordan

All rights reserved. No part of this publication may be reproduced or transmitted in any form or by any means, electronic or mechanical, including photocopying, or by any information storage or retrieval system, without permission in writing from the publisher.

Canadian Cataloguing in Publication Data

Jordan, Rosa
    Dangerous Places
    ISBN 1-895900-05-0

1. Jordan, Rosa – Journeys – Central America. 2. Jordan, Rosa – Journeys – South America. 3. Central America – Description and travel. 4. South America – Description and travel. I. Title

G465.J67 1997   917.204'83   C97-950015-X

Credits:
Cover photo by Larry Doell
Author's photo by Larry Doell
Maps by Derek Choukalos

Pottersfield Press gratefully acknowledges the ongoing support of the Nova Scotia Department of Education, Cultural Affairs Division, as well as the Canada Council of the Arts and the Department of Canadian Heritage.

Printed in Canada

Pottersfield Press
Lawrencetown Beach
83 Leslie Road, East Lawrencetown
Nova Scotia, B2Z 1P8, Canada

DEDICATION

To Derek
my best trip so far
and only true home

PROLOGUE: No Destination	7
LEAVING HOME (1960)	15
DOMESTIC TRAVEL	
Mecca in a Mercedes	26
Motorcycle Nights	36
LEAVING HOME (1970)	41
MEXICO OF OUR IMAGINATION	
La Paz	48
Cabo San Lucas	51
San Miguel de Allende	55
Wildcat Crossing	61
LEAVING HOME (1973)	64
TRAVELING WITH A MAN	
Argentina Mornings	72
Death in Bolivia	76
Unbeaten Paths in Peru	82
Prisoners in Ecuador	88
LEAVING HOME (the 'Seventies)	103
TRAVELING WITH MY DAUGHTER	
Guyana – The Lion	112
Brazil – Monkeys	119
Quintana Roo – Memories	123
Belize – Jaguars	125
Guatemala – Margays	132
LEAVING HOME (the 'Eighties)	139
TRAVELING ALONE	
Presidential Whim	152
Beyond Predictability	162
End of a War Beginning	167
The Training of a Touroist	180
Rambos and Realities	187
Finca Ixobel	198
LEAVING HOME (1993)	205
TRAVELING THROUGH TIME	
Cancun to Chiapas	210
Cuba Journal	218
LEAVING HOME (the 'Nineties)	232
EPILOGUE: The Rainforest	239

PROLOGUE

No Destination

It is midnight and raining in Villahermosa. I am drenched to the skin.
"Is there a flight?" I ask. "To anywhere?"
The ticket agent shakes his head. "Come back tomorrow."
I continue to stand there, dripping a pool of warm tropical rainwater onto the cool tile floor.
"*Mañana, Señorita.* We are closing. You must go."

Go where? Two months ago I had come for what was meant to be a working vacation to San Miguel de Allende, Mexico's mecca for artists and writers. But I had produced nothing; had sat on a sun-drenched terrace collecting depression by the pound. Perhaps I was tired. Perhaps I was lazy. Or perhaps things had become too easy. All I knew was that an existence I had felt to be ever-expanding had in this, my thirty-fifth year, reversed itself and begun to spiral inward. I felt myself slipping into a narrower and narrower space.

It wasn't my work as a writer which, although not wildly successful, I did enjoy. The same could be said about my relationship. Without being trapped in any definable way, I felt just that. They say that when a person freezes to death it begins with a numbness in the extremities. This was where mine had begun, in the extremities of my imagination. My days had become predictable, my activities repetitive. Movement, physical and psychological, was becoming increasingly difficult.

Repeatedly I packed to go home, either to the small town in British Columbia where I had recently bought a house, or to California, where I rented a one-room writing studio at the beach. I packed without knowing where I was going, with a resolve that took me no further than the San Miguel bus station. There I sat as buses arrived and departed, swamped with indecision.

It might have been my third or fourth trip to the bus station, sitting there on a hard wooden bench between an Indian woman with a burden of pottery and an affluent Mexican woman with a caged bird, that I saw the notice: *Woman with van wants someone to share expenses to Guatemala.*

Driven to desperation by my inability to make a decision, I phoned the number and was told by a woman with a California accent that she would be heading south the following morning. I said I'd like to go and told her where to pick me up. I didn't care where the trip took me, as long as it was away from the lung-squeezing boredom of another predictable day.

Sandy was a dropped-out psychiatric social worker who supported herself by buying Indian fabrics in Guatemala and reselling them to tourists in San Miguel. I could have tolerated the odor of her unwashed body, but her two large dogs were even smellier. For three days I claimed carsickness and rode with my head hanging out the window. Then, blessedly, the van broke down.

Sitting outside a VW shop in Chiapas, the last state in Mexico before the Guatemalan border, I fell into conversation with three Mexican professors. They were renting a jeep for a trip over the Sierra Madre to the ruined Mayan ceremonial center of Palenque. They sympathized with my plight and invited me to come along. Mild-mannered and middle-class as they were, joining their party did not strike me as reckless. At worst the trip would be dull, but hardly duller than hanging around a VW garage for a week until the van was repaired, and pressing on with Sandy. I got my small bag from the van and told her I wouldn't be back.

Professor Aldana turned off the highway onto the new road that had just been cut through the mountains. "How long is the drive to Palenque?" he asked an Indian.

The man looked away, as if contemplating an unanswerable question. Finally he replied, "Four hours, with good luck."

Aldana nodded thanks and slipped the jeep into gear. The Indian raised a hand. "With bad luck, eight hours." As we pulled away, he pointed to the sky and called after us, "A week if it rains."

We thought his answer amusing. The road was not paved but smooth enough to make good time. The teachers consulted their map, confident that we would be in Palenque by early afternoon. The little Safari jeep climbed steadily up the spine of the Sierra Madre mountains and started the long twisting descent down to the jungle floor. We didn't notice the massing clouds until thunderheads collided above us. Within seconds, the Indian's reply took on the clarity of a lightening bolt. A torrent of rain transformed the road into a river of mud. The Safari, unsteerable and unbrakable, moved down the slope like a log in a current. It came to a halt with one front wheel poised on the brink of a precipice that dropped away to a canyon so deep that in the rain we could not see its bottom some hundreds of feet below. We climbed out into ankle-deep mud. No one asked how long we might be here. If it took a week for the rain to stop and the road to dry, we knew we would be here a week.

A group of Indian men wearing only wide-blade machetes and polyester trousers rolled to the knees passed without speaking. We followed them, assuming that wherever they were going, we would find food and a place to stay.

When we arrived at their camp, the Indian men fell into hammocks or sat around a long table drinking some local brew. We edged under the thatched roof to get out of the still-driving rain. They did not acknowledge our presence, and offered us nothing. The women, busy in a communal kitchen, likewise ignored us. The children followed their example. We stood around feeling awkward, unable to imagine what abuses these Chiapas Indians had suffered at the hands of outsiders that would cause them to resist our intrusion by pretending we were invisible.

Sometime after dark the men were fed, and one by one wandered off to individual huts. When the last man had gone the women sat down, ate, and fed their children. Their meal finished, one woman motioned that we were welcome to what remained. Neither the teachers nor I had eaten breakfast; our last meal had been dinner the previous night. We ate the leftover beans and few tortillas gratefully, leaving nothing for the skeleton dogs nosing about our legs. I wondered, guiltily, whether we had been given their share.

We slept there under the thatch, I on a hard wooden bench, the teachers on the dirt floor. At daybreak the rain stopped. We hiked back up the mountain beneath a blistering sun. By the time we reached the jeep, the heat had steamed all moisture from the mud and left behind a navigable surface of hard dry earth. We traveled the remaining distance to Palenque in silence, all suffering from too little sleep and too many mosquito bites. I scratched at the bites with a certain perverse satisfaction; small badges of discomfort that proved I had spent a night beyond the walls of a familiar room.

When we arrived in Palenque the professors looked for a hotel where we could clean up and get some sleep. I said goodbye and followed a flow of tourists out to the ruins. Within an hour I had expended most of my curiosity and all my energy, so I came back to town and sought refuge from the sun in the patio of a dusty café. Food was a long time coming. When it arrived I nibbled slowly, made drowsy by the warm air and soft Spanish conversations.

A couple suffering from sunburn came in on a different beat. Their New York voices were bigger and quicker than anything else around. The man muttered annoyances about the slow service until the woman interrupted with a complaint of her own.

"How could the Mayans have built temples in this heat?"

Snappishly he replied, "They worked at night."

I got up and moved away. It annoyed me that they were here in this fascinating place by choice, yet (like me) lacking enthusiasm for it. Why had they chosen to be here? Had they chosen? Hadn't I? Chosen what?

As I stepped into the street, a Canadian couple pulled up to the curb and asked directions to the main highway. I pointed the way and with no forethought whatever, asked for a lift as far as the intersection north of town. When they dropped me off ten minutes later, I saw the glance that passed between them. Once out of hearing distance, one would say and the other would agree that if that tired-looking woman had any sense at all, she'd be looking for a bath and a good night's sleep, not setting out alone on a long road across the Yucatán peninsula.

But I was traveling on instinct, not common sense. As their car pulled away, I moved to the opposite side of the highway and stuck out my thumb. I knew in my heart if not my head that I needed to get to a place where patterns ceased to be discernible. Some would call that chaos. To me it felt like hope.

The first ride was with an old man whose heavy sedan stank of unrefrigerated shrimp which he delivered to small cafés across the Yucatán. The next day I traveled with a bee keeper who periodically bounced off the highway into the jungle to tend his hives. Often he would point to a barely-visible path and tell me to follow it. Picking my way through tangled undergrowth I would eventually emerge at a pile of hewn stones or a small temple, some ancient Mayan ruin too minor for exploration or restoration. They were strangely peaceful places, seeming both more abandoned and more sacred than the great temples of Palenque and Chichén Itzá where one rarely has the luxury of being alone.

Next I traveled with a veterinarian, bouncing along dusty roads of powdered white limestone that ran arrow-straight through the Yucatán jungle to Mayan villages where he would explain to subsistence farmers why their chickens were dying or their goats not giving enough milk. The children, having learned Spanish in school, were sent out by their parents to greet us. One child would stand between farmer and vet, translating questions from Mayan to Spanish and answers from Spanish to Mayan, while the other children circled around me. Sometimes one would slip a hand into mine. We would stand there, the small person accepting my smile like a gift and I feeling inexplicably blessed by the delicate touch of those tiny fingers.

When I reached Quintana Roo, that part of the Yucatán peninsula that borders the Caribbean, I no longer felt compelled to keep moving. I bought a hammock, hung it between two palms at water's edge, and lost track of time. I did a lot of walking along a mostly empty beach, fending off the heat with hourly plunges into the bath-warm sea. Flurries of physical activity ended with a collapse in the hammock. For hours I would lie there, one bare foot resting on the sand, pushing just enough to sustain a gentle motion, and watch the ocean.

Mostly it was the horizon that fascinated me, not so much what I could see as what lay beyond. Maybe it was this same kind of dreaming that got those ancient mariners going, dreams of riding the predictable currents of wind and water to some unpredictable destination. The search for trade routes and gold was just an excuse. What they really wanted, and I as well, was the unholy thrill of dancing with the unknown. But one would need courage to take risks like that, either courage or some kind of obsession. I felt neither, nor any stirring of the can-do, must-do chemistry that had shaped my life thus far. So I lay there in my still-damp swimsuit with sand in the crotch, under a feathery bit of palm-frond shade, and watched the horizon.

Once, walking along the beach, I came upon a hammock occupied by a middle-aged man reading Dostoyevsky. He said he was a Missouri farmer and had been spending his winters like this for years, during which time he had worked his way through most of the classics. I walked on without offering any information about myself. What could I have told him anyway — that I was a writer, mother, lover sometimes? A single glance would have informed him that they were no more than labels sewed into various parts of my past.

I avoided thinking about what I was now, where I was going, or where I'd been. The only evidence that I thought about anything at all was a poem I scrawled in the back of my address book. It was bleak, and not particularly personal.

> *Tulum's temples squat here still,*
> *So still, above the sea.*
> *Their ruined arches frame empty space*
> *And tourists, face after face.*
> *Only the iguanas meditate*
> *But I do not think they pray*
> *To gods long gone.*
> *On the beach below*
> *Americans are laughing, consuming*
> *Fresh-speared lobster from the reef*
> *And drugs from a legless*
> *Now godless*
> *Vietnam war survivor.*

I had not had a poem published for at least two years, but envisioned this one as the first in a collection called *To My Country*. Then the notion vanished, washed away like a shallow footprint by the soft lap-lap of the sea.

Every other day I packed up my hammock and walked to the village for food and fresh water. Usually I went in the cool of the morning, but one day I dawdled too long, and found myself plodding along the sandy road in noonday sun. Tanned though I was, I could feel my face reddening and my head throbbing from the heat. As I reached the main highway, an air-conditioned bus ground to a stop to let someone off. The door swung open and cool air wafted over me. I looked up at the driver. He motioned me aboard. Eight hours later I was in the rain-drenched city of Villahermosa.

"You can't stay here," the ticket agent repeats. "This airport closes from midnight to dawn."

"I can't find a room. I've looked all over town."

A taxi driver confirms my dilemma. "All the hotels are full, from the best to the worst."

A small circle of men gather — ticket agent, taxi driver, night watchman, runway guard. I have lived in Mexico before and am familiar with this flip side of Latin chauvinism. It is a chivalry older than Don Quixote, wherein a man does for a woman because she is a woman, and without reward, because he is a man. They confer. I wait.

At last the ticket agent says, "All right. You can stay, but the doors must be locked. You'll be safe. Call the watchman if you need anything."

With their honor protecting me, from each other if necessary, I string my hammock between two metal railings and sleep.

The watchman wakes me a dawn and tells me to take down my hammock quickly and conceal it so no one will know that I have spent the night here. Still half-asleep I stumble into the rest room, and recoil from the wall of silver mirrors. I have not seen my reflection in weeks, do not want this reminder of how old I am. But already the glass has captured my likeness and flung it back at me.

I stare. It is not the image of sagging middle age I have carried in my mind in the months since my thirty-fifth birthday. This body is slim from irregular meals, and firmed by miles of walking. There are still wrinkles at the corners of my eyes, but a worn look I had thought part of the aging process has disappeared. I feel, for the first time in months, a sense of elation. I brush my straight brown hair, put on a clean blouse and denim shorts, and go out into the lobby.

During my twenty minutes in the rest room, the airport has changed from an empty cavern to a terminal swarming with men in formal tropical attire. I squeeze through the crowd to the coffee shop. It is jammed with people whose equipment and air of importance identify them as media. A man sitting alone, holding his head in the universal manner of someone with a hangover, offers me a seat at his table.

"Journalist?" he asks.

A journalist is sometimes what I am. But before I can reply he turns his attention to the waitress and shouts for a beer. A press pass clipped to his pocket identifies him as Julio Rodrigriz, photographer for one of Mexico City's leading newspapers. I gather from fragments of conversation around us that they are covering some activity of the president of Mexico. There is a final call for the press helicopter, and a dash for the door just as the waitress arrives with his beer.

"*Momentito!*" Julio yells. He squeezes lime into the beer downs it in one long gulp. Outside, the chopper lifts off. Swearing, he rushes out onto the runway. Too late. He shouts to a man leaning against a small plane. The pilot nods.

Julio comes back into the coffee shop and orders another beer. He seems surprised that I am still there. "You missed it, too? Well, come on. There's room in my plane."

My spirits soar. I shoulder my bag and follow him out onto the runway. In the company of an absolute stranger and about to board a plane whose destination I do not know, I sense that I have arrived, finally, at a place I need to be. The pilot shouts to hurry and we begin to run.

This is how it has always been: me, running. I've always thought of it as running away. But the light has shifted. I see that what started with running away has become, or perhaps always was, running toward something. Toward danger, my friends would say, and they may be right. But it's not the danger that draws me. What draws me are those unexpected revelations that seem to flower in dangerous places.

Sometimes the places aren't even dangerous, merely unpredictable to a degree that causes me to imagine them so. And sometimes a place I thought was safe is mined with dangers I never meant to face. Either way, what I once knew instinctively and now know from experience is that when faced with real or imagined danger, truths about life, other people, and myself are revealed; truths that remain hidden from me as long as things are predictable and I feel safe.

In a few hours Julio will pass out of my life; I will never see him again. My next flight will be with the President of Mexico, and from there I'll go on to others. Eventually this traveling to the edge of predictability and stepping off into events I cannot even imagine will become a habit, a way of life. I am sometimes inclined to call it a dangerous addiction. But more often it comes to me like a gift, and with it a feeling that some part of me, long caged by named and unnamed fears, is free.

LEAVING HOME

Florida — 1960

I sit in a booth at Woolworth's sharing a banana split with my four-year-old daughter Jo. I'm fretting about the sorts of things that might pass for thought in the mind of any twenty-one year old divorcee. Can I afford a baby sitter this weekend? Will whimpering to my boss that I don't like his sexual innuendos cost me my raise? Will the chocolate dribbling down the front of Jo's sunsuit wash out? I lean over to wipe away the syrup.

A sudden hush causes my skin to prickle. Then the shouts come like staccato barks, followed by thuds and crashes. My head swivels around and I see young black men trying to seat themselves at the lunch counter, being jerked off the stools by white men. The black men are struggling to stay on their feet, but one by one they are knocked down, and then are on the floor being kicked.

Jo whiffs the excitement and tries to stand up in the booth. I jerk her down. "Sit still. Finish your ice cream!"

As I speak, a man named Manucy, whose sister works in the same office I do, walks by, his big hand tangled in the hair of a black man he is dragging. He grins at me over the top of the booth. "Ain't had so much fun since my sister's wedding," he chuckles.

There are at least fifty local men out on the sidewalk, and quite a few black ones, uncommon in St. Augustine, which still has a "colored town." I cannot bear to watch the uneven fight. I slide down in the booth next to Jo, babble to her about the "banana boat," and encourage her to do what she wanted to do all along, which is play in the ice cream rather than eat it. Five minutes pass. A store employee hurries over, tells us to leave by the back way, and escorts us out into the alley.

I drive out to St. Augustine Beach to see Sylvia, a woman with whom I work. She is only a little older than I, but being from New

England, views the South through different eyes. She subscribes to numerous publications and seems to understand world events which are barely on my mental map. I don't know that she really likes me, but she tolerates me, and I have come to rely on her for interpretations of things that I don't understand.

Sylvia answers the door with an interrupted look, finger marking her place in a book. This is our only day off; I should have called. She takes a look at my trembling mouth guesses that this isn't an ordinary drop-by visit.

"So. Is it time to hit the beach?"

I nod. We change into our swim suits and walk down to the water. While Jo builds sand castles, I tell Sylvia what happened at Woolworth's.

"Good old St. Augustine — cradle of civilization in the New World."

Sylvia's way of saying something in a tone that implies something else confuses me. "Oh well, I guess it's all over by now."

"Over? No, Rosa, just beginning. You're crazy to raise a child here. You ought to get out of the South, at least for a while."

She says it as if it were easy, the way I might say to Jo, "Go outside and play a while." Resentfully, I ask, "Where would I go?"

Sylvia picks up a bottle of suntan lotion and begins to smooth it over her already smooth tan. "Didn't your mother move back to Texas, or wherever it was you came from?"

"Yes, but I was so young when we came to Florida, I don't even remember — anyway, she's not there now. She's sharecropping fruit up in Utah."

"Ever been to Utah?"

"No."

"Wouldn't you like to travel?"

"Well, you know I wanted to go to Cuba this spring, when I had that week off, but everybody said how dangerous it was."

Sylvia tosses her auburn hair the way she does when she's a little bit annoyed. "There is a whole world out there, you know."

"I know. There's that poster that says, 'Join the Army and see the world.' I used to think about it. Before Jo was born."

"That is *so* Southern. You want to travel, haven't got the money, so let the military buy you a ticket."

"What's wrong with that?"

"Nothing, I suppose. A way out is a way out. Look at that black kid at Tastee-Freeze, the dishwasher. The day he got his high school diploma, he joined the Air Force and was out of here."

I know what she is saying: that if a black teenager has the gumption to leave, so should I. I'm pleased that she thinks I can do it, but wish she'd stop pushing.

"Don't you think things will settle down once these outsiders leave?"

"Outsiders? Like other Americans?" Sylvia laughs, as she often does, without humor. "No. Things are going to get worse. That's not what I think; it's what I know. What's wrong with Utah?"

I squint at the sand, trying to remember from fifth grade geography exactly where Utah is. "It's a long ways from here."

She picks up a stick and sketches a rough map in the sand between our two beach towels. "Let's see, you'd cross northern Florida, Alabama, and Mississippi in one day, maybe make it all the way to New Orleans. Then there's Texas, New Mexico, and Colorado — they'll take longer. I'd say a week altogether."

"I don't have any friends out there."

She pushes her sunglasses up among the auburn curls and looks at me with a kind of pity. "And what do you have here?" Her throaty voice is softer than usual. "It's not just the racism, Rosa. As long as you don't read and you don't travel and you've got no education, you're going to keep on thinking the same ignorant thoughts and making the same dumb mistakes and doing the same dull things day in and day out."

I swallow an unexpected mouthful of sobs. "That's what I hate about my life."

"It's your choice. Either you keep pacing back and forth in the cage or, first chance you get, you climb out and run like hell."

"I thought we're not supposed to run away from things."

Sylvia laughs her strange, mirthless laugh. "Who made that rule?"

I shrug.

"Don't ever let anybody tell you running is a dirty word, not if it gets you where you want to go, or away from where you don't want to be."

* * *

Once I am on my way, it is exactly as Sylvia said it would be. By dusk of the first day I am in Mississippi, driving slowly, thinking I should find a motel but not sure how to pick one.

Perhaps it is the fading light that causes me to imagine that the young hitchhiker in an airman's uniform is the dishwasher from the Tastee Freeze where Sylvia and I used to work on weekends. I have already stopped, and he is at the car window before I see that he is a stranger.

"Thankya ma'am," he gasps, out of breath from running. "I 'preciate ya stoppin. I thought I was gonna get stuck out theah in the dark."

Jo pulls up the door lock and scoots over next to me on the seat. The young man flings his duffle bag into the back and gets in beside her.

"Are you going far?" I ask nervously.

"New O'leans," he grins. "You so kind to gimme a ride, I'll be gettin' theah on time to catch some jazz on Bourbon Street."

"We're going to see my gramma," Jo informs him. "In Utah."

"My word! Now that's a long way!"

Gradually I relax. He may be a stranger, but he is just a boy. His polite, diffident drawl is reassuring.

"How long you been in the Air Force?" I ask.

"A year, ma'am."

"Do you like it?"

From the corner of my eye I see his jaw tighten and work a bit before he answers, "Why, yes ma'am. Only I was kinda hopin' to get into flying school — that's what I was wantin' to do."

"You sound just like Jo's daddy. Wanting to be a pilot so much he joined the Air Force when he was only seventeen. Then found out they don't take married men into cadets."

"So your husband didn't get pilot training?"

"Well yes, but not from the Air Force. He went to flying clubs — you know, they have them on all the bases — and started taking lessons. He spent so much on lessons..." My voice trails off. There is no reason to tell a stranger that my boy husband abandoned us so he could afford to fly. "Anyway, he's a pilot now. Soon as he got out of the service, he got a job with Eastern Airlines."

"Gee, that's a great idea. I never thought —"

As we speak, Jo stands in the seat between us. Suddenly she reaches out, wipes her hand across the airman's cheek, and looks at her fingers.

"Jo!" I exclaim, mortified.

But the airman only grins. "People just like puppies, Missy. They come in lotsa different colors. You one color, I'm another, and see there, your mama's another. Looks like she's been out in the sun and got herself a tan."

At his reference to my body, I glance sharply at him to see whether it was meant to convey something more. But no. He is holding out his hand to Jo, who inspects it solemnly, then examines her own.

"I'd druther be silver," she announces.

"Silver? Like the Lone Ranger's horse?"

"Like that." Jo points to a piece of chrome on the dash. "That way I could look at my hand and see my face."

His surprised laughter and my own explodes the tension. Jo sits between us, looking smug. "You know any songs?" she asks.

"Sure, Miss Silver, I know a lotta songs." He begins to sing, and then teach her, the words to *Alouette*.

"Is that Spanish?" I ask doubtfully, Spanish being the only foreign language I have ever heard, and very little of it.

He gives me an astonished look. "No, ma'am. That's French. Spanish go like this: *La cucaracha, la cucaracha...*" He soon has Jo singing along with him, clapping her hands as he is clapping his, trying to keep the rhythm.

It is nearly 10 p.m. when we reach New Orleans. I tell him I have never been here before, and don't know how to get through the city. He offers to stay in the car until we get past the most confusing part.

"Just stay on this road," he says finally. "It'll take you right on out. Or if you want to stop, there are motels all along."

As I pull over to the curb, he adds, "I sure appreciate the ride. If ya'll hungry, I'd be happy to take you to supper in the French Quarter."

My mouth opens in surprise, but it is a second before I can think of anything to say. "Uh, thanks, but it's pretty late. I ought to be getting my little girl to bed."

I see that I have offended him — not my answer but that instant of astonished silence. Already he has reached for his duffle bag and is swinging his long legs out of the car. He touches his hand to his cap in an almost-military salute, and walks away.

I sit there in a jumble of emotion, wanting to call after him, to explain that it's just because he sprang it on me so suddenly and not because ... but I am afraid. How do I know how people are around here? My mouth opens, but none of the skittering words come out.

He is perhaps twenty steps away when he turns suddenly and calls, "By the way, thanks for the information about flying clubs. I'm going to give it a try."

"Good luck," I yell back. As I ease the car into gear, it registers that he was no longer speaking in a black accent. It wasn't even Southern.

In the motel room there are brochures advertising clubs featuring famous musicians and mouth-watering restaurants in the French Quarter. Long after Jo has gone to sleep I am kept awake by a grumpy feeling that something has been taken — no, hidden — from me about how things are in other places. If I went to a restaurant in this French Quarter would I be expected to speak French? Would they actually let black and white people sit down at a table together? That airman was younger than me and black besides, but he knew what to expect and I didn't. Somebody or something had somehow kept it from me. And that wasn't the worst. The worst was that I'd had a chance to find out for myself, and lacked the courage.

West Texas is the place of my birth; I have relatives here. But I do not remember them, and do not like the flat emptiness, nor the way my skin cracks in the dry wind, nor the smell of gas given off by oil wells. I drive steadily until Jo begins to fret, then wheel into a motel which has a pool where we can frolic, and an oasis of greenery to soothe my eyes.

In eastern New Mexico I stop to visit my brother Alan, the sibling nearest my age. Like me, Alan married young; he now has two little daughters. But where I dropped out of high school, he graduated and is working his way through college. I toy with the idea of settling near him, hoping that his example might show me a way to further my own education. But that hope vanishes within hours of my arrival in the dusty little college town. Between demands of school and supporting wife and children, Alan is seriously overburdened. The last thing he needs is the distraction of another family member. Friendship with this brother, though neither of us know it, lies decades in the future. I drive west in the shimmering heat knowing only that this place is too flat for me anyway, too dry, too colorless.

Somewhere around Albuquerque, when the first mountain peak looms up, I am overcome with wonder. Each time we round a curve and see another one silhouetted like the pyramid of some ancient god against the sky, I feel a sense of reverence. Then we are in Colorado, where the mountains are more than awesome. Now they are not only high but green, so to my eyes, infinitely beautiful. Not yet, but soon, they will come to mean almost as much to me as the ocean.

By the end of the week we are in Utah, on a road that follows a river through red stone canyons. Jo wants to play in the strange red dirt, but I will not stop, not here where we are hemmed in by high red walls. I must keep moving until geography allows for the many possibilities of direction I have been made aware of since our trip began.

As we continue over the Wasatch Mountains and down into the Great Salt Lake Valley to the small town where my mother lives, the openness returns. Not since I was a child on horseback galloping across the mucklands of Southern Florida have I felt so unrestrained. I'm sorry the trip is ending.

* * *

I rent a furnished apartment and my life quickly falls into a familiar routine: off to work (another low-paid clerical position) in the morning, pick up Jo in late afternoon, and dating (somewhat more of this now that there is family around to babysit) on weekends. My widowed mother, struggling to support a houseful of younger children, is helpful in caring for Jo, and my Mormon landlady cheerfully absorbs us into her own family.

If there is a difference between where I was in Florida and where I am here in Utah, it is that in St. Augustine I was firmly assigned to an unobtrusive niche reserved for poor white divorced women with no family. In Brigham City I find myself floating between two cultures, with what appears to be an open door into both.

At work I am one of several thousand newcomers involved in the production of the Minuteman missile. Other secretaries and young engineers become my weekend social circle. At every opportunity we gather for sports and parties. Water skiing, which I had learned in Florida, transfers easily to Utah's lakes, and by winter I am more than ready for snow skiing.

My feeling for snow is like my feeling for the mountains: pure wonderment. Were I childless and had the money, I would channel all my time and twenty-one years of pent-up frustrations to skiing. Riding a chairlift up a mountain and winging down at speeds I can barely control give me a sense of absolute release. As often as I can afford it, I buy myself a Saturday of this transcendental experience.

The other half of the weekend, which I endeavor to spend with Jo, requires a cultural leap of some proportion. My mother, who had come to Utah to sharecrop fruit, has now, as a matter of economic necessity, taken her younger children and gone back to the West Texas prairie where she grew up, where despite the distances between farms and ranches, she feels a sense of community. My landlady seeks to compensate for my mother's absence by integrating Jo and me into her groaning Sunday dinners. Along with four big sons and her double-sized daughter, we pile our plates with meat, potatoes, and gravy, topped off with homemade pies and hand-whipped cream.

The only mental effort required of me is learning the lingo of the Latter Day Saints so that I can follow the boys' conversations about their "missions" to foreign countries. Having grown up with the intense and often intolerant fundamentalism of the South, I am intrigued by the Mormons' more relaxed approach to proselytizing.

"It's not our responsibility to convert anyone," explains the eldest son, whose mission was to Canada. "We only have to carry the truth to people."

"Once you hear it, you'll accept it," agrees the second oldest, who has just returned from New Zealand. "Maybe immediately, maybe on your death bed. We don't have to worry about when. It'll come."

It gradually dawns on me that in their view I have been exposed to "the truth" during our Sunday dinner conversations. This explains their acceptance; I am as good as one of them already. This may also explain why, with increasing frequency, other returned missionaries are invited to dinner, and afterwards have a pressing desire for me to take a walk with them through the cherry orchard. I go, but with Jo along to keep a distance between myself and the serious, sandy-haired young man of the day. It's not that I object to their country-boy looks or even their religion so much as an almost-universal lack of imagination. I try to make conversation about whatever foreign country they visited. They want to talk about the future, and in this, Jo is their ally.

"Hold my hand and people will think you're my daddy," she says, sidling in between us.

How many times she says this, or something like it, I cannot precisely recall, but it invariably provides the opening the young man is waiting for to launch his three-pronged proposal: (1) Will I marry him? (2) Will I convert to Mormonism? (3) Am I willing to work and support him through college? The questions are put to me in varying orders, and I am never quite sure which, in their mind, is most important. I do understand that, possibly because of their heritage of polygamy, virginity is not the prize it seemed to be in the South, nor does my having been previously married create the problem it did in Catholic St. Augustine. I appreciate and need their acceptance, but the predictable future they paint scares me to death. What they see as comfortable I see as confining.

As my sense of unease grows, I look for a way out. I haven't the courage to go forward, so I go back. Not back to St. Augustine, which as Sylvia predicted, now seethes with racial violence, but to Palm Beach. It is familiar in the sense that it is not so far from the subsistence farm in southern Florida where I grew up, yet the name has a sophisticated ring that suggests a place a young woman could escape small town pressures.

I have a friend in Palm Beach, a telephone operator with two small sons about the age of my daughter. She encourages me to come and share an apartment with her and, well, why not?

What direction my life might have taken if I had stayed in Florida I will never know, because ten days after my arrival, Jo and I are on the road again, returning to Utah.

The cause of this abrupt reversal is as simple as the Woolworth violence. It occurs on a night when my girlfriend and her beau invite me to go dancing with them.

I have no date, but at the club, catch the attention of an attractive young man who tells us he is on the Palm Beach police force. After dancing several times with me, he courteously asks my girlfriend to dance. When she accepts, her boyfriend flies into a rage. Grabbing her by the arm, he drags her outside. I trail behind, protesting. Ignoring me, he slaps her and shoves her into the car. As he marches around to the driver's side, I jerk open her door.

"Get out!" I plead with her. "Don't go with him. He might hurt you."

He reaches across to the door and slams it in my face. With a shriek of tires on pavement, the car spins away.

I do not know anyone else in the city, and have very little money in my purse, not enough for a taxi back to the apartment, which is clear across town. I look around for help and see that the policeman has followed us.

"Looks like you need a ride home," he offers politely.

Relief wells up in me. "Yes, please!" I follow him to his car, still trembling. "This is so nice of you," I babble.

"No problem," he says reassuringly. "Where do you live?"

I give him the address. He leans across to lock my door, then opens the glove compartment. I gasp when I see the gun.

"It's just my service revolver," he says calmly, as he snaps the glove compartment shut. "It's necessary."

Minutes later he turns off the main highway onto a dark road leading to the beach. When he stops and kills the engine, I understand what he meant when he said, "It's necessary."

All he says now is, "You know what's there. Don't make me use it."

When it's over he drives to the address I gave him and lets me out at the curb. I walk to the door of my friend's duplex still not knowing if he intends to let me live. The gun is within his easy reach, or perhaps in his hand, aimed at my terror-stiffened spine. I fumble the key into the lock and when the door opens, slip inside and slam it shut.

I listen to the car pull away and think that I should have gotten his licence plate number; that is what one is supposed to do when a crime has been committed. But I am a newcomer to this town, last seen in a nightclub dancing with this man. Who could I tell, and who would believe me? And what would I say when they asked if I'd been hurt? There must have been pain, for I am bleeding. But in truth, I hadn't felt it. It had been blotted out by terror, all my senses gripped by the anticipation of my death.

Now alone in the apartment, huddled on the side of the tub waiting for a bath to run, terror gives way to trembling rage. Pounding in my temples and engulfing my mind, it is the only thing I feel. It is this rage, and not the terror, that I will relive again and again and again.

I bathe, douche, wash my hair, and brush my teeth. Then pack my things into the car and double-check the apartment to be sure that no trace remains of my having been here. Although it's now four in the morning, I walk next door to the babysitter's house and get my daughter.

With Jo half-awake and fretting, then falling asleep on the seat beside me, I drive out of Palm Beach, out of Florida, out of the South.

DOMESTIC TRAVEL

MECCA IN A MERCEDES

I return to Utah, to a life made up of working the job, raising the child, playing the mating game. Now and again I receive a tentative proposal, but marriage is not what I want. Young men who deserve better are sent on their way with rejections that range from gentle to cruel, depending on my mood. I struggle to pit my intelligence against my biology and figure out what I really need, but cultural certainties are much louder than my own inner whisper. There's no way to hold onto an independence that I haven't completely won. Friends tell me and I truly believe that my daughter is being shortchanged. Everyone assures me that her best destiny as well as my own is a proper marriage. If this is not a dream I'm dreaming, it's one I should. And so I do.

The man to whom I eventually say yes is neither the one I love nor one who shares my deeper values; he is simply available at the moment I let go of the fragile bit of self I have. As I am washed into the main current of thought regarding the necessity of marriage, he, seeing I am there to be caught, fishes me out.

* * *

I am twenty-six and traveling west. I sit in the back seat playing chess with nine-year-old Jo, or up front next to Frank, who does all the driving. He is a tall New Yorker, recently divorced. I hadn't really wanted to marry, not him, and not now. But he insisted that this was the logical conclusion to our four-month affair. He has a job offer in California, and wants to arrive there with the complement of a family rather than the stigma of divorce. I want what I believe is best for my child.

We cross the remainder of the continent Holiday Inn to Holiday Inn. With my daughter and the dog, a boat towed behind and furniture following by van, we are the typical American family moving from

Point A to Point B and taking our lifestyle with us. This time there is no heady sense of self-sufficiency, no loosing of myself from old ways, no stretching to learn new ones. I watch the scenery through the car window as if it were on a TV screen. Each day's drive brings us to a near-replica of where we have already been. I have reached the mainstream and am learning a fundamental characteristic of that milieu: motion without movement.

Frank is an engineer and drives a Mercedes. I am a wife and do not work. We spend our winter holidays at destination ski resorts, and weekends sailing across well-charted waters to nearby islands. Mostly I take dramamine and fall into spirals of vertigo. There is no matching this motionless motion with a voice in my inner ear which whispers that the horizon is not where it appears to be.

Jo gets seasick on the boat and carsick in the Mercedes, but takes her dramamine as I take mine. At school she passes from fourth grade to fifth to sixth. In our clean suburban neighborhood, every kid beyond seventh grade is into illegal drugs except the twelve-year-old girl at the end of the block who has flipped out, been institutionalized, and now gets her mood-altering chemicals by prescription.

I cling to the notion that this is mecca, if not for me at least for Jo. Whenever she becomes withdrawn (we call it sulky), I remind her that she now has what she always wanted: a housewife mother waiting with cookies and milk when she comes from school.

In fact, Jo arrives from school at the onset of the most tense hour of my day. Cookies and milk are flung on the table along with a hurried "How was your day?" She eats in silence as I rush around the house trying to bring it up to Frank's rather strict level of order, and simultaneously start cooking dinner.

Frank will arrive home to an aura of calm. Jo will have gone out to play, or be in her room doing homework. The house is as near to perfect order as my almost-is-good-enough philosophy will permit. Dinner reaches the table when expected, at precisely the last sip of his second martini. Only my insides are churning.

Relaxation comes after supper, when Jo and I engage in a ritual that started when she was born: our nightly bath. On weekend evenings, when we usually go out to dinner, we plop into the tub beforehand.

On this particular Saturday I sit quietly unwinding in the rose-scented water while Jo, facing me, sculpts soap bubbles into fantastic shapes. She is talking about her current crush, the junior high boy across the street. He and his friends are experimenting with drugs I've never heard of.

"What about you? Have you tried anything?"

"I would if everybody else wasn't doing it. But I can't stand being one of the herd."

"Um," I murmur approvingly. And after a bit, "I think it's time you had braces."

"I don't want braces."

"Oh. Why not?"

"I like the way my teeth go crooked in the front. It makes me unique."

The door swings open and Frank pokes his head in. "We're going to be late." As he snaps the door shut, we hear him mutter, "When are you going to stop squeezing into the tub with that big lug?"

Jo gets out of the bath. Tracking water and soap bubbles across the floor, she goes to the door and locks it. Then slides back into the tub.

"Late for what?" she asks.

"Didn't I tell you? It's dinner with the Hamptons tonight."

Her expression hovers between tension and relief. Relief, because Grace and Phil Hampton, friends of Frank's from his college days, are our favorites among the couples whom we "date," as she puts it, on weekends. Tension, because they live a half hour away — far enough to get carsick, not far enough to take dramamine.

When we arrive, Jo sprawls her already-developing body in front of the color TV alongside the Hamptons' daughter, Wendy. I go into the kitchen and watch Grace, who is serving up a gourmet meal on Haviland china with the same ease I would pop a tuna salad sandwich on a paper plate, while discussing cultural geography, which she is currently studying at a local university.

After dinner we (mostly Phil and I) argue politics, he being a thoughtful conservative, and I struggling to articulate my reasons for opposing the Vietnam war. Grace contributes in a moderating way, while Frank downs another drink or two.

Frank's view of the conversation will not be voiced until we are in the Mercedes on our way home. His focus is not on ideas aired, but on my stubborn refusal to avoid controversial topics. In the back seat, Jo is getting quietly carsick. Sometimes I accept his criticism in silence. Sometimes I argue. We might or might not make it home before Jo throws up.

Day by day Jo turns more inward. She doesn't like school, doesn't like sailing, doesn't like skiing. I sometimes nag her to get her nose out of that book and go get some exercise, but don't really notice the degree to which she has retreated. I myself am moving in the opposite direction; not inward but outward. Under the guise of housewife-with-time-on-hands-takes-classes-to-kill-time, I enroll at a community college.

The science fiction writer, Les Cole, who lives across the street, tutors me (shouts at me) hour upon impatient hour until I grasp the basics of writing. In American history class, a Mr. Shibley introduces me to the concept of analytical reading. With these skills in hand, I transfer to UCLA. It has a student population of 30,000. Before moving to L.A. I'd never even lived in a town that big.

"The classes are enormous," I fret. "My professors won't even know my name."

"Sure they will," Les smirks. "All you have to do is sit on the front row, wear mini-skirts, and make A's."

The Cole formula works. With a few exceptions, every professor knows my name before the end of the quarter. I am happier and feel more successful in university than anywhere or anytime else in my life. Only the political divisions take me by surprise. I am shocked by what is being said about the government by students, and incredulous at what is being said about students by my husband's friends in aerospace. By the time Phil and I start driving Frank mad with our evening-long political debates, I have switched from history to political science in an effort to make sense of it all.

One day walking across campus I find myself in a large group of students protesting ROTC. They are saying that military training does not belong on university campuses. I do not agree with this. I think that young men being trained to fight, probably in foreign places, are likely to be more thoughtful if they have been exposed to the broader world of a university than if they are ghettoized in a military academy like West Point. The crowd is going the same way I am, so I walk with them until I see, up ahead, a row of black-booted policemen. I move quickly to the fringes, not wanting any part of this confrontation.

The marchers, several hundred strong, stare defiantly at the police. The police make a quick, stomping dash forward, and stop. The students rush backward, falling over one another. Then surge forward again, but stop short of the police line. This dare/double-dare is repeated twice more. A soda can sails through the air and falls among the police. At this the police charge in among the students, laying about with their clubs.

A skinny girl, blood streaming from her nose and mouth, staggers past me and falls on the sidewalk. "The bastard broke my braces," she wails. "My mother will kill me!"

I help her into the rest room of a nearby building, and tell her to give me a phone number so I can call her mother. Between sobs, she gasps out the number. I phone and tell the woman who answers where to pick up her daughter. When I get back to the bathroom the girl is vomiting. She says it is from all the blood she has swallowed.

"Stay with me," she begs. "Tell Mom it wasn't my fault."

The mother arrives half hour later, a high-strung blonde in a cream-colored Buick. I tell her what happened, but she is too upset to listen.

"I can't imagine you getting mixed up in something like this, Stephanie! What on earth were you doing there? For God's sake, use a Kleenex. You're dripping on the upholstery."

"Not *there*," I say. "She was *here*, on campus. What were the police doing *here?*"

"Well, I'm sure I don't know," the woman snaps.

"I don't know either," I retort. "But it's a cold day in hell I'd let the police come to school and beat up on my little girl."

Maybe it was unfair to expect the woman to understand something she hadn't witnessed and which most Americans couldn't yet even imagine, but I was in no mood to be tolerant. The way she blamed her daughter for being beaten did more to politicize me than campus teach-ins, feminist forums, and images of Vietnam under siege.

By the time I'm a senior at UCLA, my academic/activist life is far more real than endless repetitions of up-in-the-morning-at-7:05-three-minute-eggs-Dagwood-Blondie-kiss-goodbye-hello-dear-how-was-your-day-dinner-on-the-table-at-the-last-sip-of-that-second-martini. I'm so distracted that even Jo, now deeply retreated into herself, has become less real to me. One morning as she is dawdling and I am trying to hurry her off to school so I can begin what feels like "my real life," I catch a fleeting expression of pain in her eyes that stops me cold.

"Are you okay?" I ask.

She scoops breakfast cereal into her mouth, the full mouth giving her a reason to not answer. It dawns on me that not answering has been her most frequent response for a disturbing length of time. I stand there searching for what it was I saw in her eyes. The word "abandoned" comes to mind. How long has it been since she had a classmate over to visit, or asked to go somewhere with friends?

"Why don't you invite some friends to go sailing with us on Saturday?" I suggest brightly.

"Haven't got any," she mumbles, jamming another spoonful of Cheerios into her mouth.

"Oh, that's not true! But I know what you mean. Sometimes a person just feels lonely."

Her blue eyes flash up to meet mine. She swallows without chewing and says with quiet intensity, "I've never been so lonely in my life."

I drop into the chair next to her and my lips part to reveal something I hadn't even known. "Me too."

Jo gives me an indignant look. "You've got Frank. I've got nobody." Suddenly she is crying, tears spilling over dark lower lashes and dripping into her cereal. "At least I used to have you."

Her pain hits me like a blow to the chest. "But you're the one who kept asking for a daddy! I only married him because I wanted you to have — everything. I never felt— " I can't go on. The truth is too shameful.

Jo is looking at me in astonishment. "I thought people only got married because they were in love."

"I wanted to be, but ... oh, Jo, why didn't you tell me you were unhappy?"

"I didn't want to spoil it for you."

"And I didn't want to spoil it for you."

We stare at each other and into ourselves, trying to cope with this crushing double-revelation of love, deception, and prices paid.

"What are we going to do?" Jo asks finally.

"I don't know." My mind is muddled with almost unbearable guilt for the mess I seem to have made of our three lives.

"We could divorce him."

"It's not that simple. You don't remember how it was when we were poor, and I was working all the time just to feed us and pay the rent. If we go out on our own again, it'll be hard. It was *so hard*."

Jo picks up a pencil that has fallen out of her notebook, and begins to doodle on the white formica table top. "I do remember," she says quietly. "And I know how it will be. Like this." The pencil sketches a roller coaster.

By the image I see that she does understand. Neither of us like roller coasters. Their plunges nauseate us. They make us throw up.

She dips her napkin into the leftover milk in her cereal bowl and wipes away the roller coaster. "If we stay with Frank it'll be like this." The pencil moves across the formica in a dead straight line. "Till we come to the end." Her hand drops limply over the edge of the table.

Goose bumps prickle the back of my neck as the image of a roller coaster life is replaced by an even more terrifying vision of an existence in which there are no lows or highs, just flat, emotion-deadening predictability.

Jo drops the pencil into her notebook and zips it shut. "I'm going to be late. You, too." Her voice is dull; she has moved back into herself.

"Wait!" I can't bear to see her disappear like that. "I'll think of something. As soon as finals are over, okay? I need some time to think."

Her small smile wrenches my heart. She is holding back spontaneity, not daring to allow herself to hope.

For me the question is not what to do but how. How can I push this knowledge and guilt aside long enough to get through finals and make it to graduation? How can I find a job and start supporting us again? How can I leave a man who hasn't done anything to precipitate it and, whatever his limitations, deserves better?

One thing at a time, I decide. There's no other way. Study first. Write the exams. Wait for graduation. Read the job ads. Make time for Jo. Don't let her slip away from me again.

I have no reason to suppose that Frank has any inkling of what's going on. He was never one to delve into my feelings, which in any case I would have done my best to conceal. But I have underestimated him. He must have registered my emotional absence long ago. The day after my last exam he asks for a divorce, explaining that he has fallen in love with another woman.

Apart from a whisper of shame, knowing that I am about to be cast into that category of supposedly flaky women twice-divorced, my feeling is one of enormous relief. "Do you intend to marry her?"

"Of course. We'll probably leave the area."

"Well then, why don't you take the portable stuff — the car, the boat, the bank account — and I'll keep the house. We don't have much equity in it anyway. There's the $5,000 we borrowed from your parents for the down payment. I could pay that back."

"I don't want to do it that way."

"Oh. What do you want?"

"I want you to disappear." There is a fury in his voice I don't understand. Maybe my relief is evident; maybe that's what has made him so angry. Whatever it is, I know that the pretenses we've cheated each other with these four years past are no more. We are now adversaries, and will remain so until the legalities of separation are done and our relationship can become what it should have been: a brief then forgotten affair.

Days pass. I have spoken to a lawyer who says I am crazy for offering to repay the loan to Frank's parents. Frank has spoken to a lawyer who told him I don't know what. We have not spoken to each other again on the subject, but like robots follow the patterns which Frank long ago established as appropriate daily routine. We have just finished a quiet dinner of non-consequential conversation. I am at the kitchen sink washing dishes, listening to the shrill voices of children having a last romp across neatly-trimmed lawns before being called in for the evening. Jo is sitting on the curb, hoping that Les Cole's teenage son will notice her.

Frank enters the kitchen and comes to stand beside me. He raises his hand and cold metal presses against my temple. Although I had not turned to look at him, my peripheral vision registers the shape of a gun. It will be the .32 he keeps on the top shelf in our closet. I never liked having a gun in the house, and long ago took the clip out and hid it in the freezer. He would have noticed that it is missing, so this cannot be a threat. It's just an ugly game, one of his meaner practical jokes.

"I found the clip," he says.

The slanting sun flows through Jo's hair, creating a halo effect. The Cole boy sits down on the curb beside her. They smile at each other. Tears trickle off the end of my nose and into the dishwater. I don't know whether they're tears of fear or anger or sadness. I only know that my suburban dream wasn't supposed to end like this.

"What do you want?"

"I want you to disappear."

I am voiceless, no sound even to my weeping. Seconds pass. Frank lowers the gun and goes out to the garage. The Mercedes backs out of the driveway and disappears down the street.

I finish the dishes, the warm soapy water a soothing antidote to the icy spot I still feel where the gunbarrel touched my temple. Gradually the moment becomes comprehensible; I understand why he is so angry. He doesn't want his life disrupted, doesn't want to remove his underwear from the drawer, or have to commute to work from a different address. He wants to bring the woman here, and continue his daily routine with as little change as possible. Had he been able to tell me this, guilt-ridden as I am, I might have been persuaded. But not now. Now I am afraid, and fear makes me defiant. I will not go.

The dishes finished and counters wiped, I dig a fruit pop out of the freezer and loosen it from the mold. The clip is still there, frozen in the fruit juice. I drop it into the garbage just as Jo comes bounding in.

"I didn't know there were any of those left." She reaches for one of the remaining pops. "Can I have one?"

"Take out the garbage first," I tell her.

The next morning I ask Jo if she'd like to skip the last few weeks of school and spend the summer with my mother.

"What's up?" Jo asks.

"Frank and I are divorcing. I think you'd be better off with Grandma until it's over."

"You're saying I can ditch the last month of school, spend all summer in Texas, and Frank won't be here when I come home?" Jo's smile is dazzling. "Is this a dream?"

"No. It's for real."

"When can I leave?"

"Whenever you like."

"How about today?"

"You need a plane ticket, and we have to call Grandma. How about tomorrow?"

The last weeks of spring find Frank living on his boat, Jo in West Texas breaking green horses to the saddle under her grandmother's tutelage, and I in my walled garden working on an all-over tan. The full economic responsibility for myself and Jo will soon settle on my shoulders, but has not yet. I have never been so alone and so unrestricted. An inclination to lie here luxuriating in this unaccustomed liberty is prodded aside by restlessness. I want recognition for my newly-acquired graduate status, and have an itchy desire to prove that I'm a "liberated woman."

I pick up the phone and start to call friends. It's easier than I imagined. A French poli-sci professor is followed by a Welsh sociology instructor, an Ethiopian teaching assistant, a Japanese grad student, and a Jamaican singer I met at an anti-war rally. My (unadmitted) shame at having been found lacking as a wife is quickly replaced by a sense of power. But it is a contingent sort of power that rises on a man's response like a kite riding the wind. When I'm alone and becalmed in my garden, I am again powerless, and fearful, able to do nothing, it seems, except lie there and wait.

On one such day, rubbing suntan lotion into my warm skin, the smell of cocoa butter recalls Sylvia's voice as clearly as if it were coming to me out of the moment rather than from a Florida beach ten years ago. "If you don't read and you don't travel you're going to keep on thinking the same ignorant thoughts and making the same dumb mistakes ..."

Why is that echo coming back to taunt me? Books scattered through the house and around me even here in the garden attest to the fact that if university did nothing else, it has made a reader of me. What ignorant thoughts and dumb mistakes? Where's the mistake in being a free woman? Aren't I?

Suddenly the truth comes with such awful clarity that I fling the suntan lotion across the yard. It hits the fence and slides down to dribble out among the roses. The truth is that I have become one more in a sea of suburban women supported by husband or ex, who imagine ourselves free because we're flitting from one man to another. The truth is that I'm going nowhere, nowhere at all.

Travel, Sylvia said, but how can I? We were a one-car family. Frank took the boat, the bank account, and the Mercedes. All I have is a Honda mo-ped used for shuttles to and from campus. Jo and I couldn't get far on that. A chill creeps over me in the midday sun. Somehow I've lost my way, and now we're stranded. It's middle class nuclear family suburban mecca as far as the eye can see.

MOTORCYCLE NIGHTS

It is Les Cole's wife Esther who rescues me, guiding me to a job interview in downtown Los Angeles. The mo-ped is not much, but as she points out, it is adequate for the fourteen-mile commute from our suburb to inner-city L.A.

The work consists of helping high school dropouts improve their reading, writing, and arithmetic skills. My students are bruised and broken teenagers, almost all in pain and many beyond recovery: poor white girls raised on welfare and middle-class runaways heavy into drugs, black power-tripping girls from the West Coast and choir-singing "colored girls" from the Deep South, Latinas from East L.A. shooting up smack, and recently arrived immigrants raised like nuns, Hawaiian girls from rural enclaves and others from Honolulu gangs, culture-shocked Samoans and reservation Indians experiencing their first immersion in white society. Between the ages of sixteen and twenty-one, they are a cross-section of every girl child in America that has fallen through the cracks. Before coming to board and study at "the Center," they have been neglected, segregated, abandoned, beaten, raped, pregnant, drunk, and drugged.

Their lives have been more difficult than mine ever was, but I identify with their poverty and their dream of attaining the mecca of middle class. I dreamed that dream myself, and might be longing for it yet if I hadn't so recently been there. But there's no point in harping on its limitations. My job is to help them get there, and if it works for them, well, so much the better. Middle class reality is — or can be — better than where they are now.

At first the job seems easy: just give them a chance. Laverna, a homely sixteen-year-old who suffered continuous abuse before coming home one day to find that her mother had moved and left no forwarding address, looks over our list of career options, (nursing, cosmetology, secretarial, food service), rejects them all, and asks for photography training. Later she joins the military as staff photographer, and becomes a favorite with General Haig and other brass. Josefina, a lively Latina from East L.A., passes her high school equivalency exams within a month and enrolls at a local junior college with the goal of becoming a psychiatric social worker.

While these and a handful of others portend success, we cope with dozens who are damaged in all the ways America allows its children to be damaged: a charismatic eighteen-year-old from Arkansas, the only black child in a newly-integrated elementary school, who was rendered invisible by her teachers and never taught to read. A barely-sixteen Puerto Rican army brat, body scared by parental beatings, who spends her weekends hooking on Hollywood Boulevard. A nerve-shattered nineteen-year-old who was the only white child in a Chicago ghetto school who writes just one sentence, over and over on all assignments: "I am a human bean; I am a human bean."

A month after Josefina leaves our "basic education" program, we meet for coffee on her junior college campus. I tell her I've heard a rumor that she is sleeping with the lesbian director of the Center. She grins at my naivety. "You just found out? I thought you knew."

"But why, Josie? You've got everything going for you!"

She pushes up the sleeve of her jacket and reveals the needle tracks. I must have gasped, because she pulls it down again and says, with a grin that holds no happiness, "I thought you knew."

This is how it goes, day after day, month after month. Successes are counted on the fingers of one hand, and then half of them are eliminated. We try to find meaning in doing what little we can, forget what it's like to not feel drained, and show up next morning to try again.

By "we" I mean six teachers, plus our soft-voiced supervisor, Barbara. Barbara's favorite device is the "case conference" which she holds after work on those worst days, days of drug overdoses, fights, earthquakes, and sheer despair, in the corner booth of the corner pub. There, with cold beer and warm words, she untangles our snarls of tension.

Barbara herself vanishes at a designated witching hour, six, I think, when rush-hour traffic thins. Otherwise I suppose her husband would turn into a pumpkin and spit Jack-o-lantern faces at her as she rolls into the drive. Dave would have left earlier, after one quick beer, to pick up his wife at work. Then Diana, a light-skinned black woman with a great halo of rust-colored hair, is off to rehearsals with an inner city theater troupe. That leaves me alone with the three single men: Jeff, John and Steve.

Being a non-drinker, I would have left early, too, but Jo is still in Texas with her grandmother. Unless I have a date or a craving for solitude, there is nothing to compel me home. Thus, one or two evenings a week my little white mo-ped remains outside the pub with Jeff's motorcycle and John's, and Steve's rusting, unwashed Chevy.

The men are unmarried and slightly my junior. John, the youngest, is a sensitive skeleton of a boy who has grown up thinking of himself as the "exceptional" child, not from a family point of view but in context of the species. He distrusts me from the first, perhaps imagining some challenge to his inexperience from what he called to my back my "used" look. Most of his arrogances I forgive on the grounds that he is barely twenty-five. Steve is six-foot-four, yet has about him a gentle vagueness that causes us all to feel protective toward him. Jeff is dark-eyed and restless, more than a little mistrustful of both women's motives and ones they might ascribe to him. I find this offensive but reassuring, for as long as his defenses are up, mine needn't be. His social ease and love of companionship often holds the group together after Barbara has gone.

"Anybody like blues guitar?" Jeff asks with an enthusiasm that is infectious. "Lightnin' Hopkins is at the Ash Grove."

So we are off to listen to blues guitar, which seems an appropriate way to end a day that began with being told that a girl who had just passed the academic levels she needed to get into the nursing program and gone home for the weekend to celebrate had quarreled with her boyfriend and been stabbed to death.

For convenience's sake we often go together, Steve on the back of John's cycle, I on Jeff's, to whatever novelty the night affords. The city feels exotic, yet the most foreign-scented neighborhood has its air of familiarity. We feel confident of our ability to interpret nuances; we know, for example, whether a burning odor comes from food, garbage, hash, somebody's fireplace, or a low-rider's hotrod. Another thing that distinguishes these novel experiences from the truly foreign is the certainty that from any point in the city I can, in a matter of minutes, be in the privacy of my own home, initiating bedtime routines as predictable as the movement of hands on a clock face.

Roaming about Los Angeles is to travel as learning the basics of surfboard balance in a swimming pool is to hanging ten. It is not adventure I gain this summer, but the rudiments of balancing myself on new planes. I learn to judge the safety of a thing, whether a stranger's stare on the street or the movement of the motorcycle beneath my body. I learn to relax when sharing, even with semi-strangers, so intimate a place as sleep. I learn to wake not knowing where I am, and to hold back panic until the place recalls itself to me. I learn to accept the isolation and liberation that comes with knowing that I can stay or go, laugh or weep, without having to explain why. Slowly but surely I am regaining what may be the first impulse of life — a sense of physical freedom.

The Center's program requires teachers to attend a monthly group psychiatric counseling session. The doctor in charge of ours has recently become a minor celebrity by playing the part of an incompetent shrink in a popular movie. Overwhelmed by what I don't know about dealing with my students, I attend the first session willingly. We sit in a circle in Barbara's office. Most of the teachers are cracking jokes, but I see nothing funny in the problems we face, and need all the help I can get. The psychiatrist tilts his chair back on two legs, chats about inconsequential things for ten minutes, then asks, "Anything in particular bothering you?"

"The girls on reds," I venture. "If they sleep through class, that's not such a problem, but it's scary when they're coming down. They're always fighting. That Cherokee girl, Shilo, she tested higher than any student I've ever had, but she started a fight in class so I sent her back to the dorm..." My voice trails off and I struggle to hold back tears.

Somebody in the group finishes. "She ODed. They didn't find her till it was too late."

"Hmmm." The doctor fingers his chest hairs thoughtfully. "These are girls on barbiturates?"

"Yes."

"Do you have any starch eaters?"

"Starch eaters?" A blank look goes around the circle. Teachers shake their heads, no.

"A lot of the Southern girls are addicted to starch. Eat it right out of the box." He discourses at length on starch-eating, with a side discussion on children who eat dirt. I can't bring him back to the original question, and when my frustration starts to show, he offers some platitudes on the importance of "insulating" ourselves from becoming too emotionally involved. I leave the meeting in a rage.

Jeff catches up to me in the parking lot. "I'm never going to one of those damned meetings again!" I yell.

He shrugs. "Ah, he's harmless. How about dinner at that Greek restaurant on Melrose?"

"I'm not hungry."

"Sure you are. It's your birthday."

"How did you know?"

He grins, and kicks the starter on his bike. "Barbara told me. Come on; the others are meeting us there."

L.A. is far-flung, and our nightly forays often take us twenty miles or more from home. We live in different parts of the city, so as the evening winds down, we head for whoever's abode is closest. John will put on some music and Steve might open a six-pack while Jeff lights up a joint. Conversation always turns to the girls. Tonight it's about how much we miss the Hawaiians who resigned *en masse* and demanded to be sent home after the earthquake. Steve is imagining the terror they felt when their bunk beds on the fourteenth floor overturned and someone's arm was broken and the elevator jammed and one girl fell to her death trying to climb out. Jeff remembers what a great pool player "Willy" Kalamalama was. John remarks on how the small tough street girls from Honolulu protected the bigger gentler girls from the outer islands, and I remember, with a lump in my throat, one of those tough little cookies, said to have killed a man when she was fourteen. She had wanted to become a physical therapist and I thought she had what it took to make it through training. By tomorrow she'll be back on the street, and after that, who knows?

We go on talking and listening to music until it's too late to go home. We often sleep right where we are, on a lumpy sofa or carpet in need of vacuuming, and wake in the morning hoping to find our spirits less rumpled than our clothes.

It is on such a night, when the others have gone but I have stayed, that Jeff eventually takes me to bed. Though it may have been sympathy or masculine ego on his part, and need or recklessness on mine, the feeling is of no real motivation on either part; just that on this particular night in this particular summer, sharing bed and body is a natural thing to do.

Friends from the past now perceive me as having crossed a line, undefined yet definite, into the counterculture. Jokes are made about the length of my hair, motorcycles parked in the driveway, and marijuana smoke wafting from the window. I'm not a smoker myself, and don't feel that I've changed. I've only inhaled the culture of late-sixties California. It has made me more thoughtful and, I confess, a little high.

LEAVING HOME

California 1970

When Jo returns in the fall, she accepts the divorce with relief and Jeff as my lover with equanimity. We have a long heart-to-heart in which I explain that I am in the process of throwing off old, restrictive modes and adopting freer forms which I believe, regardless of what social judgments may be passed, are healthier.

Jo is little concerned with convention and extremely original. I can tell by the way her tumbled blonde curls swing forward with each affirmative nod that she understands the transition I'm trying to make. My guilt is just beginning to subside when she adds that as a matter of fact, she is planning something along the same lines herself. As a step toward eliminating restrictions, she does not intend to return to school; grade nine, she is certain, holds nothing of value for her. And surely I won't object if by way of expressing her own freedom, she takes a lover?

I can't believe she means it, yet why would I suppose she doesn't? I am no sheltered Victorian parent living with the illusion that young girls lack sexual drive. Virginity is ancient history for all my teenage students; many were pregnant and some had children before they walked into my class. Nor is there any reason to believe that passion is the exclusive domain of lower-class girls, not if statistics about thirteen- and fourteen-year-old pregnancies in suburban junior highs are any indicator. I myself was married at fifteen, and roused with fantasies (not to mention some passionate petting) for at least a year before that. I have no illusions and even if I had, how could I foist them onto my daughter, who towers above me by a good six inches and wears a size 36-C bra?

What staves off panic is her coolness, which allows me to hope it's all hypothetical, and she hasn't really moved beyond my control.

The truth is that Jo has known, probably since she could talk, that the way to get her way is not by sulk or tantrum but with quietly reasoned arguments. Pretending not to notice the discordant music of tensions building, she engages me in a dance of words, leading me toward her own conclusions step by rational step.

It's easy enough to support her decision on school. Dealing every day with basket cases from the public education system, I hardly need my own daughter to tell me that any kid who keeps off the streets and applies herself even moderately can outshine a high school graduate. I am a qualified teacher and have friends willing to help. If Jo chooses to forgo the society of her peers (whom she deems "immature" and barely acknowledges) there is no reason why she can't be tutored at home.

But sexual activity is a Pandora's box, I tell her; better the lid stays shut. I admit I have often asserted that, "My daughter won't be forced to have her first sexual experience in the back seat of a car. When the time comes, she has every right to her own bed." But that time, I had imagined, would be at the blossoming age of eighteen, give or take six months. Consideration of same at sixteen would have put me in an uproar. Fourteen, I tell her, isn't even in the ballpark.

She fixes me with a blue-eyed gaze, slightly amused. "You mean four more years of making out at movies and school dances before you'll consider me mature enough to do what comes naturally?"

I counter with a rap about the social implications, possible consequences, responsibilities to self and others.

"Look, Rosa —" She always calls me by name when she's pushing for a peer relationship. "Don't judge me by how dumb you were when you got married. In the first place, I'm not getting married. And in the second place, I don't plan to get pregnant. There is such a thing as family planning, you know."

Whereupon she launches into a detailed discussion of the physical, social, and psychological aspects of various types of birth control methods that leaves me feeling like a ten-year-old rocket builder trying to take notes on a lunar launch.

I have no doubt, after that conversation, that Jo will sleep with the person she chooses when she chooses. I want to rise to the occasion and say yes, physical freedom is your birthright; take it. But just because I am beginning to feel the good of it for myself doesn't mean I can bless my daughter to follow the same road, landmined as it is with social disapproval. Only vaguely do I grasp the central issue, which has to do with two women on the threshold of independence, one with a decision as to how much restriction she should, would or could exercise, the other with the decision of how much she should, would or could accept.

Jo ignores my unease and forges ahead. Having achieved the goal of extracting herself from school, she sets about locating a man who meets her rather lengthy list of "must bes." I attempt to delay the inevitable by hurrying home after work and providing diversions that keep her under my watchful eye. I regularly invite co-workers to join us for dinner. Their presence relieves both tedium and tension, and creates an informal forum for Jo's home education beyond what I alone can give her.

Three or four nights a week, around a coffee table littered with take-out Chinese food or ordered-in pizza, mock battles rage and alliances form over the virtues of one composer compared to another, what historical waves have churned up our current political climate, and which writers are truly first-rate.

"*Young Torless* is an adolescent novel," Jeff scoffs in response to John's praise of same.

"If *Torless* is adolescent, what do you call Philip Roth?" John shoots back. "All the American writers, for that matter."

"The only thing harder than being an adolescent in America is to stop being one," Jeff quips.

"Take a look at this." John tosses a copy of *Sons and Lovers* to Jo. "D.H. Lawrence — now there's a first-rate writer for you."

"If that isn't the work of an adolescent!" Jeff needles, knowing John would give years off his life to write as well. "Who wants this last piece of pizza? How about you, Jo?"

Steve drains the wine bottle into his, Jeff, and John's glasses. The debate goes on, with the men taking equal pleasure in the challenges they pose one another, our rapt attentions, and hearing themselves hold forth. I find the intellectual stimulation more exciting than any of our previous diversions, and Jo is electrified. We are in love with life and, just a little, with each other.

Yet beneath the easy sociability is an undercurrent of moodiness. As we listen to music, argue politics, and discuss books, we are each searching for ways to face or avoid new realities. Central is Jo's sexuality, now a matter of group concern, for she has set her sights on John. Steve is non-committal, but Jeff cannot imagine himself as a friend of any man who would sleep with a fourteen-year-old, even if that man admittedly has no more experience in such matters than the nymph in question.

John is jumpiest of all, doubly terrified by the intensity of their mutual attraction and its unconventionality.

"I'm not denying the physical," he tells me, when he can finally bring himself to admit it. "But that's not what this is about. I've had young girls throwing themselves at me ever since I started teaching at the Center. You've never seen me take advantage of one. I never would. But Jo ... you know as well as I do what kind of mind she's got. There's a clarity there, and a kind of originality that's damn near irresistible."

"But at her age? Surely it's better to wait."

He gnaws at a fingernail like a boy being scolded. "To a point, Rosa. But only to a point. Too much frustration and she'll start playing some bad games. We both will."

One evening when Jo and I are alone, and have squeezed into the tub together as we still sometimes do, she asks, "What's most important to you, Rosa? Apart from people, I mean."

"Freedom."

"For me, too?" She blows a soap bubble through the air to make the question seem casual.

"Of course I want you to be free. But also safe," I add, to remind her of limits.

"That's what I'll be with John, you know."

"No, I don't know. And neither do you."

She lifts her busty woman's body out of the water and reaches for a towel. "Well, no. But I'm pretty sure." She tosses me the towel to dry her back. "How can anybody be *completely* certain?"

While we stew in the far-from-certain, other potions are added to the pot. The neighbors are gossiping about my having let Jo drop out of school. Sometimes a parent of one of her former classmates, encountered in grocery store or post office, asks questions we'd rather not answer. State laws related to home schooling are stringent, and my way of educating Jo does not meet many of them. Strangers on our street make me watchful, and nervous. We are vulnerable.

Things have changed at work, too. Barbara is no longer among us, having been spirited away by her Othellian husband to the outer reaches of suburbia. On the few occasions we visit, he is fiercely courteous to us, oppressively possessive of her. We who had been her knights all cringe and depart, not one of us having the wherewithal to rescue a lady whose distress is not yet revealed, even to herself.

Without Barbara to protect us from the upper administrative echelons, work is pure frustration. As if its emotional content and impossible goals aren't burden enough, we now chafe under bureaucratic pharaohs who want pyramids built of paper. Our muttering grows. Maybe it's time to think about calling a few plagues down on them and plunging into the Red Sea.

Restlessness overtakes us, and talk of faraway places. Barbara, we know, once lived in France. Steve spent two years with the Peace Corps in Ecuador, and Jeff taught school in Cameroon. I have never been out of the United States, but their travel stories remind me of something I learned on that trip from Florida to Utah ten years ago: that when you leave a place, some problems go with you, but others are left behind.

One evening I clear away the debris of our meal and, more as an imaginary possibility than anything like a plan, spread a map of Mexico across the coffee table.

"Ah yes," Steve muses. "A little fishing village where I can live out my old-man-and-the-sea fantasies."

Jeff says, "I've always fantasized about a woman who'd get on the back of my bike and go with me to Mexico."

"I will," I flip back. "Let's go."

Jo kneels on the floor and points to the approximate center of the map. "There," she proclaims. "Away from cities."

John leans over Jo's shoulder to study the map. One hand slides under her hair and rests there on the curve of her neck.

Jo leans back against his legs and looks at me with a triumphant smile. She knows I ran away from home and married at age fifteen for no better reason than that my mother insisted I come in from dates at a reasonable hour, and knows that my ever-growing fear is that I will be repaid in kind. She knows, without it ever being discussed, that I'll allow John to come with us as her lover rather than lose her like that.

At first it is just a game, a grown-up fantasy of the five of us mounted on snow-white and silver cycles, cruising south to strains of *Vaya Con Dios*. But little by little that playful pastime evolves into serious plans. If we go out, it's only to the beach or a second-run movie. No more living from paycheck to paycheck. Each of us is saving for our own rainy day.

Steve refurbishes his backpack. Jeff shops for a new motorcycle. John buys a used truck and camper. Jo sells her model horse collection. I rent the house, store the furniture, give the cat away. I have been comfortable in my suburban home and its sunlit garden, but there is no way this well-defined plot can contain the chaotic jungle growth of two women's liberation.

It is decided that Jo will visit her father, my high school sweetheart whose blond curls and Aryan attitudes I can scarcely remember.

(Only when I see his fair face turned florid, a one-time athlete gone soft on beer and television, his mind unrecognizably distanced from its potential by provincialism and Southern bigotry, do I realize the distance I have already traveled.) I will send for Jo as soon as I have explored a bit of Mexico and set up a new home base. John will follow by camper, and Steve, in his vague way, promises to find us eventually.

I pack a few things and climb on the back of Jeff's motorcycle. Though our destination and much else is unshared, I am ready to go until I lose my nerve, if not to learn the limits of physical freedom, at least to road-test some of its ramifications.

MEXICO OF OUR IMAGINATION

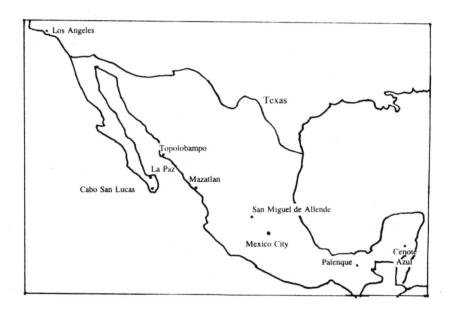

LA PAZ

On the 4th of July, Jeff aims the Honda south into Mexico. My exhilaration is as boundless as the desert sky, my confidence as sturdy as his body between my knees. Very soon I discover that Jeff speaks barely three words of Spanish, that choosing a hotel sends him into a dither of indecision, and he knows next to nothing about motorcycle maintenance. It doesn't really matter. Just as wearing a helmet allows me to feel that I will survive a motorcycle crash, traveling with this man allows me to feel that I will survive a year in foreign places. For the first time ever in the context of a man, I feel unrestrained.

We cycle through the desert for two days, coming down to the Sea of Cortez at Topolobampo. There we catch a ferry to La Paz, and within hours, are sailing into its palm-fringed bay, softened to photogenic perfection by the setting sun. We scan the shore for a spot where we can camp.

"There," I point to the most beautiful of the small crescent-shaped beaches lining the bay. "Just past that big white hotel."

The beach is further out of town than it had seemed. A few hundred yards past the big white building, we follow a sand track down to water's edge. We eat bread and cheese from our backpack, then roll out our bedding and sleep in sound and blissful ignorance of where we are.

When I open my eyes a single ray of golden light is slanting across the water from a half-risen sun. I sit up, dazzled. Two nights ago, a desert sky full of stars was the most beautiful thing I had ever seen. Now this is. Had Florida been so beautiful? Utah? California? Perhaps. But I am a woman who started work-for-wages at age eleven, married for the first time at fifteen, became a mother at seventeen, and by eighteen was supporting my child as well as myself. When had there ever been time to simply sit and absorb beauty?

Jeff sits up beside me. Silently we watch the colors change as the slanting rays angle upward with the rising sun. At the periphery of vision, a movement catches our attention. Three soldiers are walking along the beach toward us. They carry rifles, not on their backs but in their hands.

We are instantly on our feet, rolling the sleeping bags, securing them on the bike. The soldiers look us over, then turn their attention to the motorcycle. Despite a desert crossing that has put a thousand miles on the Honda's odometer, it still carries a show-room shine. The soldiers run their fingertips over the turquoise tank tenderly as one might stroke the muzzle of a high-strung thoroughbred. They smile. We smile.

I say, (smile) "We came last night. On the ferry."

Jeff says, (smile) "We're just leaving."

One of the soldiers says, (smile) "*Magnifico, tu motocycleta. Es nuevo?*"

We do not understand, or just barely. But we nod and keep smiling. Jeff climbs on the bike. I slide on behind him.

"*Gracias,*" Jeff says, utilizing one-third of his Spanish vocabulary.

I point to the building. "*Es hotel?*" I ask, calling on all of mine.

The men look at each other, and snicker. "*No, señorita. Es la casa del presidente de México. El Presidente Luis Echeverría Alvarez.*"

We ride away, our minds reeling with the contrast between that courteous exchange and what might have happened if some Mexican, (or we ourselves), had inadvertently wandered onto the beach of President Nixon's house in San Clemente.

Now that we know the name of Mexico's president, we understand the meaning of the letters "LEA" painted on cactus trees. We had seen the same three letters all across the desert of Northern Mexico, and consulting our Spanish dictionary, found that *lea* is the command form of the verb *leer*, to read. Graffiti on cactus might not be esthetic, but we admired the sentiment that had caused someone to cover these desolate areas with thousands of exhortations to READ. Only now does it register that LEA are the president's initials: a political slogan of sorts.

As we ride toward the tip of Baja Sur, I mull over what I do not yet know is a cardinal truth of travel: that if we haven't done our homework and don't speak the language, we are likely to come to a place and leave it with a seriously distorted view of where we've been and what we've seen.

Night falls and we find ourselves in the kind of glittering-black darkness that only seems to exist in a desert under a dome of stars. The evening turns chilly and I cling to Jeff for warmth, peering over his shoulder with growing anxiety at the nothingness up ahead.

Suddenly there is something — not the lights of an oncoming vehicle but our own headlights thrown back at us from the startled eyes of a cow and calf. I brace myself for the bike's swerve, not knowing which direction Jeff will chose but it doesn't matter because we're too close; there's no way we can miss them.

To my astonishment the bike sails smoothly ahead, passing between the animals in a space so narrow I feel the warmth of the cow on one leg, the brush of the calf on the other. Some yards beyond Jeff takes his foot off the gas and lets the bike slow down. He pulls to the side of the road and kills the engine. We sit there trembling in the black and sudden silence.

"I expected the cow and calf to huddle together," I stammer. "I'd never have tried to go between them!"

"Did I?" Jeff asked.

"What do you mean, did you?"

"I had my eyes closed."

CABO SAN LUCAS

Edges of the earth fascinate me. I love coastlines, islands, tips of peninsulas. I'm not sure if it's the way earth colors contrast with ocean blue on maps or the sculpted, free-form line that marks the meeting place of land and water, but I can be drawn to such places without having the vaguest idea of what they are like. Ignorant of everything except shape and location, we approach the tip of the Baja Peninsula.

This tip is the most satisfying land's end that a *finis terre* fanatic can hope to find. From north to south, the peninsula narrows, narrows, and narrows, until it is only a wall of jagged rocks. The rocks jut up like pointed scales along a dragon's back, ending with one final, sea-sculpted stone arch. On one side, great waves churn up from the depths of the Pacific to crash against the stone tail. On the other side, almost encircled by land, lies the smooth, sheltered water of Cape San Lucas.

The village is a short walk from the shore, irrationally (or so it seems to me) baking in the sun when it might have lined itself along the pristine beach and thus captured a share of the ocean's breeze and beauty. The one restaurant is palm-thatched and dirt-floored. It serves no seafood apart from a small bony fish flavored by the rancid oil in which it is cooked. We ask about hotels. There's one called Finis Terre under construction up among the rocks, and El Camino Real down on the beach.

The lush gardens which encircle El Camino Real inform us that these are not lodgings we can afford. We park our motorcycle in the hotel lot, ask the watchman to keep an eye on it, and take our sleeping bags down to the beach. In the morning we climb up through terraced gardens to the hotel dining room for breakfast, pausing at the pool rest room to wash up. As we are about to enter the open-air dining room, a gardener approaches and takes hold of my sleeping bag. I hang on. He tugs and wins, then reaches for Jeff's. The man, whose name we learn is Tico, motions to us to follow him. Down a couple levels of terraced gardens, he tosses the sleeping bags into a tool shed and locks it, showing us that he has the key, and pantomiming that he will give them back to us when the sun goes down. Smiles of understanding are exchanged all around.

After breakfast we go back to the beach and become acquainted with Bruce, a laid-back Californian who runs the local dive shop. This pattern is repeated for the week we remain at Cabo San Lucas. Mornings we turn our sleeping bags over to Tico, breakfast on the terrace, then go diving with Bruce. After several hours in the water, we return to the hotel pool to shower and change from swimsuit to shorts, then climb up to the dining terrace for a leisurely, many-coursed lunch. Afterwards we sit by the pool, Jeff socializing and I scribbling in my journal. At sunset Tico appears with our sleeping bags and we stroll down to the beach to sleep. Except for one night, we have the best of both worlds.

This is the evening that Tico does not appear. After many half-understood conversations with hotel employees, we gather that it is his afternoon off and only he has the key to the tool shed. This is bad news. By now he not only keeps our sleeping bags locked in the shed for safe-keeping but also our backpacks. We are dressed in shorts, sandals, and tank tops — perfect for Baja's hot days, but the nights, we already know, come on with a desert-like drop in temperature.

What to do? The hotel's several-hundred-dollar-a-night rooms are well beyond our budget. We decide to tough it out. We will keep walking all night to stay warm. After all, how much can you suffer in twelve hours?

It seems a workable plan, but toward midnight the wind picks up and the chill factor increases. Shivering uncontrollably, I wonder how long it takes to go into shock from exposure. Discomfort, if not desperation, gives birth to an idea. One wing of the hotel juts out from the main building. As this is off-season, almost all the rooms are vacant. Each room has a balcony. Perhaps we can find a bit of shelter there. With luck a door might be open. Are we unethical enough to "steal" a bed for the night?

Moments later we are shivering ourselves to warmth in a cozy double bed. Two hours into sleep there is a rattle of keys and the sound of a door opening. With the flashlight beam on our heels, we take a flying leap over the balcony railing, roll down through vindictively spiny desert plants, and are back on the beach somewhat warmer and slightly worse for the wear.

Eventually the sun rises on what will be another hot day at the Cape. Tico returns and apologizes for having forgotten to give us our sleeping bags. At breakfast, the waitress puts a bottle of hydrogen peroxide by my plate and points to my scratches. In the evening, as I sit by the pool trying to finish some writing before the light fades, the hotel manager sets a candle on my table. His knowing smile leaves me with lingering suspicion that details of our uncomfortable night have been told, and probably embroidered, for the amusement of everyone at the hotel.

During our days at Cabo San Lucas we pay little attention to its human history of poverty and piracy, but focus on a more timeless world which lays beneath the Cape. There are coves of crystal warm water where I float for hours as bright tropical fish dart among equally bright-colored plants, as well as a more athletic trip out to the point to explore an old shipwreck. But I had heard about something else from a diver who claimed to have seen it, although other divers had not, and thought it only a legend. Bruce is not immediately forthcoming, but finally he admits that what we have heard is true. One hundred feet and more below the Cape's serene surface, in a great reversal of elements, sand flows over a brink into a deep canyon. The first sandfall is slender, a bridal veil. Deeper, there is a larger one, and yet deeper, down where the water turns from blue to nearly black, a virtual Niagara of sand churns over a broad ledge into a chasm that disappears into something that looks like infinity.

Years later, I find myself sitting next to a man on a plane who has recently vacationed at Cabo San Lucas. When I tell him I once stayed there on the beach he looks at me as if I'm one of those people who brag about having been to places they've never seen.

"A person couldn't camp on the beach at Cabo," he snorts, throwing back a swallow of Scotch. "It's lined with big hotels. And patrolled. There are plenty of restaurants, and dozens of dive shops."

I do not dispute his description of Cabo, nor do I ask him whether there are now daily tours — perhaps a plastic bubble or some other technological wonder — to carry sightseers down to the marine trench to watch sand tumble into darkness accompanied by the sound of popular music and revolving colored lights.

If these changes have come to pass, I don't want to know. I choose to believe that no matter what the tourist dollar has wrought at Cabo San Lucas, silence and solitude still prevail those hundreds of feet beneath the surface; that nothing has changed in that mysterious world-within-our-world where *agua y tierra*, water and earth, he and she, have reversed roles and taken on each other's nature without losing an iota of power or beauty.

SAN MIGUEL DE ALLENDE

San Miguel de Allende's colonial architecture fits our image of "Mexican village" so perfectly that we have barely arrived at its main square before deciding that this is where we want to live. The decision has nothing to do with the town's history as the cradle of the Mexican revolution, nor our appreciation of the natives, some of them peasants-turned-service-providers to San Miguel's expatriate artist community, and many of them artists in their own right. What we see is what we have fantasized: a postcard-pretty Hispanic paradise, slow-tempoed yet stimulating, specially designed for wanderers like ourselves who have the money and inclination to spend a year in the sun.

Jeff and I had not planned to live together, but within the week we sign a year's lease on an apartment. Jo flies down to join us, and a month later John arrives. Jeff and I take the downstairs bedroom. Jo and John lay claim to the one upstairs which opens romantically onto a walled roof with a view of church steeples and hills beyond.

Steve eventually comes but doesn't stay, explaining that San Miguel doesn't match his fantasy, which has more to do with the sea. By then Jo is already enrolled in art school, and John at work on his version of a great American novel. Jeff is taking classes at the Spanish language academy, and I have begun a master's degree in creative writing. Overnight we have become part of San Miguel's North American community of artists, writers, and want-to-bes.

I have never been so happy. I am writing. I am having an adventure. And for once I'm sure of doing the right thing as a mother. Long before I become fluent in Spanish, Jo stops conjugating verbs and is conversing fluidly with Mexican boys in love with her translucent blonde complexion. At school she astonishes instructors by the quality of her work in batik, leatherwork, silversmithing, and sculpture. That blooming talent, vivid as the scarlet poinsettias lining our patio, vanquishes my divorce legacy of failure as wife and mother, and eases my mind regarding Jo's love affair with John. Not since she was a small child has she seemed so happy, so confident. For the first time I imagine I can see her future.

My relationship with Jeff is, in my mind, a solid friendship but a merely casual affair. I have no reason to suppose he sees it differently. From the beginning I have told him this is not to be an exclusive relationship; I've had enough of that particular illusion and all its restrictions. He accepts my pronouncements with a shrug and knowing smile; he thinks he knows me better than that.

In truth, neither of us understands the other's emotional landscape all that well. Of Jeff I know only that he has traveled far to escape the traditional expectations his Jewish parents so relentlessly demand of him. Despite a degree in education, two years as an English teacher in Africa and two more in a Cleveland ghetto school before joining Barbara's team in the jungle of inner-city L.A., he refuses to claim teaching as a career, just as he routinely dismisses marriage as a bourgeois concept. He fancies himself radical, a world traveler, and emotionally self-sufficient. It will take more than our year in San Miguel for me to see him for the conventional, comfort-loving family man he really is. Our relationship works during the year in Mexico largely because I don't see through it, believing him to be the adventurer I myself want to be.

None of us accept the definition of ourselves as family, and yet we are, so much so that other expatriates are drawn into our circle and bonds form that will last twenty years and more. We are, although we don't know it at the time, a modern extended family in the making. Meals are never just the four of us. The meals and the evenings that follow usually include Helen Epstein, the journalist daughter of Czech concentration camp survivors, David Fleisher, playwriting son of a Southern carpet manufacturer, and often one or more of our favorite neighbors, a Jewish family that had come to San Miguel from New York a couple years earlier. Only Jo makes friends with Mexicans, but as most of these are young males who fancy themselves in love with her, John tends to block their acceptance into our circle.

It is Helen's idea to celebrate the Jewish holiday of Passover. I have never been to a Seder, so Jeff takes charge of the event. Sue and Valerie, the mother and daughter next door, help prepare the traditional foods, and David, whose grandfather is a rabbi, handles the ceremonials. Nineteen are invited, all Americans. At the last minute, a wandering Jew from Australia, just arrived in town, is invited to take off his backpack and sit in the empty place reserved by tradition for Elijah. John is away, so Jo and I are the only WASPs present. There are no Mexicans at all until afterwards, when one of Jo's admirers drops by. Helen is playing her viola. The boy joins her on acoustic guitar and gives us what we all want — the illusion that we really belong here in his, the "real," Mexico.

That illusion shatters the night Sally is shot. Sally lives next door to Helen, not a year-in-the-sun person but an artist who speaks fluent Spanish and considers San Miguel her home. One night Helen is awakened by gunshots and hears Sally calling, *"Ayúdame, ayúdame!"* Helen runs out to find Sally lying in the courtyard, her warm blood streaming onto the cold tile floor.

Jeff, David, and other neighbors accompany Sally to the hospital forty miles away, but it is a holiday and there is no doctor on duty. It takes six hours to locate a surgeon, during which time Sally remains conscious and lucid. She explains that the intruder entered her apartment through a window thought to be too high to need bars. He held a knife to her throat and ordered her to undress, but she spoke reasonably to him and after several hours persuaded him to give her the knife and leave. At the door he seemed to change his mind. She rushed at him with the knife. He fled into the courtyard, then turned, and with a pistol she didn't know he had, fired six shots, five of which buried themselves in her slender body.

While Sally waits quietly at the hospital for a surgeon to come and dig out the bullets, Sue, Valerie, Jo and I try to calm a hysterically weeping Helen. After all, it was Helen who, after some moments of paralyzing fear, stepped out her door to find Sally lying in a pool of blood. The intruder is still at large. Her apartment and Sally's are similar; if he could enter one, he could as easily enter the other. She cannot go back to that apartment — not now, not ever.

The undercurrent of Helen's misery is that Mexico — picturesque, small-town Mexico with firewood delivered by burro to the door and flowers blooming year around — has betrayed her. To a certain extent it is something we all feel. How many nights have each of us, even Sue's thirteen-year-old daughter Valerie, walked home from a party or movie alone? On the darkest San Miguel street and at all hours, we felt safe. But by what logic? Hadn't I felt just this safe in Palm Beach the night I asked a policeman to take me home?

"It's not just Mexico," I tell Helen. "Rapists are like drunk drivers; they're everywhere. All you can do is take reasonable precautions, and hope that if you come face to face with one, you'll survive."

"I don't care," Helen howls. "It's this whole *machismo* culture. I'll never feel safe here again!"

"You think 'safe' is where the men speak English? Safe is when you're home before dark? Safe if you stay in bed? Sally wasn't."

"Neither was I." The husky voice is that of Valerie. We stare at her in surprise.

"When I was eleven. Back in New York. I was asleep, too. He came in through my window, and raped me."

"That's why we left New York," Sue says quietly. "We didn't feel safe there anymore."

"For awhile I got scared every time I saw a black man. I felt really bad about it." Valerie's dark intelligent eyes sparkle with humor. "But my father said it was okay. He said a person is allowed to be prejudiced for three months after they've been raped or mugged by a person of color."

Jo listens with close attention but does not share with us the fact that she too has been attacked, and very recently. It was mid-day in a field, the man a Mexican with whom she had gone to look at a horse. He failed to subdue her only because he was slightly built, and she a head taller with strength to match her size. He couldn't bring her down, nor free one hand to undress her because he needed both to hold her. They struggled for half an hour, until at last he gave up and allowed her to escape.

Helen is now raging not against Mexicans but men in general who make it impossible for women to be safe anywhere. I have felt such rage, as Sue must have, if not for herself then for her daughter. But we are silent. The rage has never comforted us, and we know it will not comfort Helen.

As we sit in Sue's living room, five females pulled up in a circle like a wagon train under attack, I remember friends asking, when they heard that Jo and I intended to live in Mexico, if I wasn't afraid of "trouble." After many trips abroad I would be able to answer with stories of getting caught in wars, riots, and police sweeps, but this is not the sort of "trouble" people have in mind when they ask that question. What they want to know is whether I have ever been raped. What I want to tell them is, "Only in America."

I never explained or even thought much about the fact that the first rape I ever heard of was that of a boy in my home town who was

58

assailed as he cut through an alley on his way home from school. From that time on I was never convinced that it was necessary for women to take more precautions than men, nor believed that absolute safety existed anywhere. In a way the two attitudes canceled each other, the one giving me a casual, almost-masculine assurance which would increase over the years, the other causing me to develop preventive techniques which in time would become more subtle and more effective.

The protective measure taken for this sojourn in Mexico is not subtle at all, but the commonplace one of traveling in male company. Later, when I learn other ways of keeping safe, I will begin to travel alone. But on this first trip abroad I appreciate the security of Jeff's presence. No doubt the same protective impulse contributes to my acceptance of John. In this foreign country, I'd rather have Jo tucked in with him at night than out socializing with friends neither of us know that well.

Nevertheless, the shots which struck Sally echo in our psyches. It seems urgent to talk the matter over with Jo, but in recent months she has rebuffed my efforts at intimacy. No matter what subject I broach, she responds with a curt non-answer and if I persist, an exasperated sigh. Usually that's enough to deflect me, but this time I need an answer.

"Are you afraid of living here now?" I ask.

"No."

"Are you sure?"

"I can take care of myself."

She picks up a pencil and begins to sketch a skyline punctuated with church spires. I wait for more. She is silent.

I am about to give up when she adds, "Just the same, I am getting tired of living where even the bushes whisper *'Mamacita, mamacita'* when I walk by."

I reach for a pencil and begin to doodle our names on a note pad. For a few minutes, there is only the sound of church bells ringing in the distance and pencil lead whispering on paper.

"It's been a pretty good year," I say finally. "But maybe it's time to go back home."

She continues to sketch as if she hasn't heard. At last she lifts her pencil from the page and shoves it into the tangled curls massed over her ear. "Yes, it's time. But I don't think there's any going back."

"What about the guys? Shall we take them with us?"

"If they want to come."

I watch her carefully, looking for clues regarding how she feels about John. "You think it's forever?"

"Is anything?"

"Not so far as I know."

"That's what I thought."

She tilts the sketch so I can see it. She has added a horse, wings outstretched, sailing over the church spires.

WILDCAT CROSSING

We have had the margay kitten only two months. It is still very small, though the Mayan hunter said its mother was large. His hands had measured three feet, suggesting an ocelot, perhaps even a jaguar, but I was skeptical. He was obviously trying to impress the *mestizo* campsite owner who had just bought the kitten that this handful of gold and black fluff would grow large enough to produce a valuable pelt.

As the men stood discussing its chances of survival to an age where it could be profitably skinned, the kitten crouched on its hind quarters and swung tiny claws at their ankles. Its fierceness in the face of such odds fascinated me. Against all common sense, I found myself saying to the new owner, "Don't kill it. Sell it to me instead."

He refused. For two days I sat on the shore of Cenote Azul, a small blue lake sacred to the Mayans, so deep that even yet some still believed it to be bottomless. Every day I pleaded with the owner. He just laughed and shook his head. I thought of the margay kitten choking on the end of the string, the months of misery it would endure before being killed, and cried, and cried.

Finally the *mestizo* relented. I handed over the money that was to have paid for my bus ticket back to Mexico City. He untied the dirty string around the kitten's neck and placed her in my arms. Tucked in the crook of my elbow, the margay looked back at him with fierce, unrelenting eyes. A Mayan employee who had shared in the conversation about the potential value of her fur looked deep into the kitten's eyes and said, "Cenote would be a good name for this *tigrio*, because its eyes are blue, and they too are bottomless."

Later I would become accustomed to the everyday poetry of the Mayans, but this was the first time I had been spoken to by one of them, and it took me by surprise.

"Cenote," I said, trying on the name. "Cenote Azul."

An old woman weaving a hammock nearby unfolded her arthritic legs and hobbled over to us. With the quiet authority one sometimes hears in the voices of old people in cultures where they are respected, she announced, "You will call the little tiger Hopichen, so the name of my village can go with you to far places."

On the way home we stopped in Mexico City to see a veterinarian at the university. He told us Hopichen might be a margay or even an ocelot, both species of spotted jungle cats much smaller than the jaguar. If she were a jaguar he was certain the hunter would have called her that instead of using the generic term *tigrio*. He gave me instructions on care and feeding, and asked, "What are you going to do with her?"

"Look after her until she's a bit older, then release her back into the jungle."

"She'd never survive. She was taken from her mother too young. Her eyes are barely open. She couldn't have been taught to hunt yet."

"Then I'll take her back to the States when we go."

"That's illegal. This is an endangered species."

I had no answer for that. The vet stroked the kitten's soft fur, and I could see that he, like me, just wanted her to live. Finally he handed me a pill.

"A tranquilizer," he said. "For traveling."

This is our last hour in Mexico. I push the tranquilizer down Hopichen's throat and wish I had one for myself.

"I hope the border guards are mellow," Jo says in the slightly humorous tone she uses to conceal annoyance and anxiety.

"Don't worry. I won't get caught."

When the tranquilizer takes effect I press the relaxed kitten against bare skin just under my breast. Jo wraps surgical tape around us, taping the kitten tight to my ribs. The plan is for Jo and John to cross the border in his camper, loaded with the paraphernalia of our year in Mexico. Jeff and I will cross ahead of them on the motorcycle, posing as tourists who have just gone over to the Mexican side for the evening. We figure the last place anyone will look for a smuggled animal is on a motorcycle.

We had not counted on Jeff having to turn off the engine while we were being questioned. I can feel Hopi chewing on the tape. At last we are waved through, but the bike is slow to restart. As Jeff grinds the starter, the corset-tight tape is snapping strand by strand under the kitten's razor-sharp teeth. The engine catches. Just as we pull away, the margay breaks free, struggles to the throat of my shirt, and lets out a growl that would have done justice to a jaguar.

We stop at a park on the U.S. side of the border where we are to rendezvous with Jo and John. When they have not appeared in an hour, Jeff leaves me there and circles back to see what's wrong. What he sees at the border checkpoint is all our possessions spread out on the pavement. One inspector is running wires up inside Jo's precious, hand-tooled saddle, while another searches the camper. When Jeff reappears, the inspectors are sure that their intuition is right. They order him to disassemble the motorcycle from headlight to exhaust pipe. When no contraband can be found, they decide that an ornamental bird cage Jo brought from San Miguel must be a clue.

"Where is the bird?" they keep demanding.

It is dawn when Jeff, John, and Jo finally extract themselves from the Texas border guards and come to the park to collect me and my hyperactive bundle of contraband. A thrill surges through me. I have saved the little margay. She is mine.

Actually, I had given Hopi to Jo for her fifteenth birthday. "By Mexican tradition, the *quienientos* is a special birthday," I had explained to Jo with fake solemnity when Jeff and I returned from the Yucatán. "So I've brought you a fur coat."

Fur in San Miguel's mild climate for a daughter whose interest in clothing never extended beyond jeans and oversized shirts? Jo looked at me as if I had lost my mind.

"Close your eyes and hold out your hands," I commanded.

Her expression accused me of childishness, but from force of habit, she obeyed. I lifted Hopi from my jacket pocket into her cupped hands. For an instant Jo's fingers trembled around the warm ball of fur, then her blue eyes opened, shining, as if to a miracle. Her lips formed a silent "Ooooo" and Hopi, who had her own way of expressing surprise, let out a roar that vibrated off the walls.

It hadn't occurred to me when I gave the margay to Jo that I was giving it away. After all, Jo was my daughter, the kitten was hers, we were one family. Or so it had seemed that year in the Mexico of our imagination.

LEAVING HOME

Colorado 1973

As none of us had wanted to return to L.A. Jeff proposed we look for a small town in the mountains. John and I agreed, providing we could find one where the cost of living was low. John, like me, was in the midst of writing a novel and did not want to work more than part time.

"What about you?" I asked Jo.

"I'm not going to high school," she asserted.

We discussed her academic qualifications and agreed. A year of private tutoring, followed by a year of art classes and Spanish in San Miguel, had moved her well beyond what I knew to be required for high school graduation.

"We'll look for a small college," I promised her.

The four of us had sat in our San Miguel apartment with atlas and almanac, identifying small mountain towns whose amenities included ski area and college. The route we plotted took us through the Sangre de Cristo mountains of New Mexico and north into the Rockies. By the time the aspen leaves turned autumn gold, Jeff and his motorcycle, John and his camper, and Jo and Hopi and I were parked in Durango, Colorado.

Jo, at fifteen, can easily pass for eighteen. By pretending that she has been tutored abroad for four years instead of one, I manage to enroll her in the local college. John gets a job as teacher at an alternative school. Jeff says he is tired of teaching and opts to work as night cook in a café so he can ski during the day. I start another novel although the first one, completed in Mexico, has not yet found a publisher. I intend to go on writing through the winter, and not look for work till spring.

The only difficulty in establishing ourselves is finding a place to live. In desperation, I use most of my savings to buy an old house. This lends a twist to our fortune which none of us had anticipated. While I play the starving writer and Jeff the ski-bum cook, a precipitous jump in property values boot-straps us into near-affluence.

Real estate opportunities are plentiful, but don't engage me like writing. I send out articles and work on the novel. Rejection follows rejection. The more I write the more I'm tormented by a question I haven't yet learned not to ask: do I have a right to consider myself a writer if no one will acknowledge that I am?

At first there is some consolation in the fact that Helen, back in New York with a first-rate agent, has not found a publisher for her first novel either. ("The only thing more boring than a novel about the Holocaust," one editor tells her, "is a novel in which five healthy young people sit around talking about the Holocaust for 350 pages.") However, Helen is a consummate professional and eventually transforms the material into a powerful nonfiction book called *Children of the Holocaust*, which wins international acclaim. We stay in touch, but when I send her a draft of my second novel she finds it too tedious to finish, let alone critique.

John also makes slighting remarks, not just about my writing, which he considers inferior to his, but about my "bourgeois tendencies" — this in reference to the property I've bought. I take him seriously on both counts and struggle to understand what I am or am becoming. Is writing my escape or my life?

All I know is that day after day I am drawn in on myself and spend hours in what we of the counterculture would call the "head space" of a writer. Sometimes entering it as a time warp, sometimes as a pressure chamber, I emerge only when the sheets of paper that have rolled out of my typewriter reveal to me, in black and white, some fragment of self or other that I hadn't previously understood. The novel continues to flounder, but little by little my journalism begins to sell — a hopeful trickle.

If there is one understanding that eludes me, it is Jo. Close as her life is to mine, it is rendered nearly invisible by something I cannot name, something which, although intangible, lays across our domestic landscape like heavy fog. She wears a cloak of self-possession under which walks a woman-child I can scarcely call "mine" anymore.

There are chilly nights when, in those middle moments between sleep and awake, I feel something warm against my body, digging its claws into my skin as it pushes to be free. When morning comes, Hopi's jungle growl wakes me, demanding breakfast. Jo is off to school, and will return not to me but to John. I carry coffee to my desk and move quickly into the day's writing. Otherwise my emotions will behave like a delinquent's jackknife, defacing thought with graffiti of doubts. Convention insists I am too permissive, yet I am unable to escape a sensation, almost physical, of myself as captor.

Hopi, always voracious for food, begins to lose weight. The lush spotted fur now sags over her ribs like an oversized coat. Is it is my fault for having brought her from her native jungle here to the mountains of Colorado? A veterinarian examines her. No, it isn't the climate, he explains; it's hookworm. "Something she picked up in the tropics. Lucky she's living in captivity. Otherwise she'd be dead by now."

By Thanksgiving Hopi is back to normal. While Jo makes pies and I stuff the turkey, Hopi moves overhead in the jungle canopy of our kitchen, from the top of the refrigerator to the top of an open door to the top of the highest cupboard, vibrating the air with jaguar-sized roars to remind us of her divine right to birds as food.

"Give her this," I say to Jo, but before the turkey neck passes from my hand to Jo's, Hopi sails through the air and snatches it clean away. Off she is and running, dragging it across the living room carpet like a lioness with a fresh kill crossing the veldt.

"Gratitude!" Jo grumbles as she tries to extract Hopi from under my desk and gets for her trouble a rake of claws across the hand.

"Leave her alone," I advise. "She'll come out when she's ready."

Hopi becomes social after dinner, entertaining us with fantastic leaps across the room from Jo's arms to mine and back. We take the tape from Jo's sewing kit and measure the longest leap at eight feet; we laugh, we play at being a family. It is a familiar game but something about Jo is not familiar, is more obscure, even, than the foggy half-presence I have grown accustomed to in recent months. I ache to push back the bangs that shadow her eyes, but she has taken to reacting to my touch as an imposition, so I keep my distance, and wait.

Then it comes, swift and unexpected.

"My IUD failed. I need an abortion."

I want to take everything hurtful from her, including the decision, and replace it with all she needs for comfort. But her feelings lay camouflaged behind the sharp edges of her now-absolute (or so it seems) separation from me. There is no taking anything, even the pain, she deems her own. She has already discussed it with her doctor, made the decision, made the arrangements. She and John will drive to California over Christmas break.

"I'll have it taken care of at the USC hospital. After all, it's their stupid zero-failure design that's failed. We'll stay with the Hamptons."

No, she says when I ask for the third time, no, she doesn't want me to come along. At last I retreat, unable to tell which fears are hers and which are mine. All she accepts is money and I am thankful, that Thanksgiving Day, to have that much of her need of me left to hold onto.

I hope that Jo will confide in the Hamptons, whom I know she likes, as she teasingly (but truthfully) refers to them as "the best thing you got out of your marriage to Frank." I talk to Grace on the phone before and after the operation. She tells me that Jo, while outwardly cheerful, has not revealed very much. Whatever is going on with my daughter, she shares only with John.

"Are things okay with you and Jo?" I question John afterwards, on one of the rare occasions we find ourselves alone together.

He laughs in a way that is not reassuring. "Madam, don't ask."

"I am asking." I set a cup of coffee down in front of him so hard it sloshes on the grey formica table top.

He dabs despondently at the spilled coffee. "The subject of intimacy lies heavy on me at present, oppressed as I am by the cross-currents and shoals of intercourse, small lies and deceptions which seem to make up whatever bridge exists between two separate souls."

I am accustomed to John's way of retreating into writerly lingo when he feels uncertain, writing being where his head is most of the time anyway. I mentally translate what he has just said into plain English, and am not reassured.

"Look, I'm not trying to pry. I'm just concerned about her. And you, of course. Are you okay?"

"All I can tell you, Rosa, is that we give each other the most we can. But we're both, in diametrically different ways, so un-bourgeois."

I cut him a bourgeois-sized slice of pie. He has an adolescent's appetite, and a body that remains boy-thin no matter what he eats. Before digging into the pie, he makes one more attempt to articulate an ache that comes from the knowledge that something he thought would last forever just isn't going to make it.

"The trouble is that our best points constantly conflict, and our worst brutally agree. So while we remain close sympathetically, we're often on two not-very-parallel tracks spiritually."

Once I get the gist of what he's trying to say I leave him alone, poorly concealed behind his empty pie plate and that mound of abstractions. Nobody wants other people watching while they fall out of love.

The truth is I'm less concerned about John's eventual separation from Jo than my own. Fear brings an ache to my chest and the ache reminds me of my fear. I don't need John to tell me that my child, no longer a child, is moving further and further away.

Soon after the abortion and Jo's sixteenth birthday, what I feared becomes reality. John accepts a teaching position in Los Angeles. Jo tells me she is going with him, and plans to take Hopi. I counter with a multitude of objections. The end of the school term and date of their departure approaches swiftly. Neither she nor I have agreed to give up the margay.

Our quarrel ends on a spring morning when the sun is warm and the sky so blue it seems almost purple. On this morning I find Hopi where she has been crushed by the wheels of a speeding car as she dashed for the wooded hillside behind our house where she was accustomed to roam.

Jo packs in silence, anger lidded over by anguish. She leaves for L.A. carrying with her the bitter conviction that had she left sooner, and had the kitten properly confined in a city apartment, it would still be alive.

How many times we had argued about it and I, impatient with what seemed to me her refusal to understand, had shouted that for a wild-born animal, confinement *is* a kind of death. So absolute, those words. So unrelated to the grief that engulfs us now. I only wanted us to be free — my daughter, our margay, and me. I never imagined it could hurt so much.

After Jo and John are gone, Jeff and I sit on the steps in the May sunshine sipping our morning coffee. Each day a little more of the motorcycle emerges from the snow bank where it has been buried all winter: black windscreen, silver handlebars, turquoise gas tank, and finally the tires that carried us through one year and ten thousand miles of Mexico.

Beautiful morning after beautiful morning I drop *It's A Beautiful Day* on the turntable and listen to the lyrics of "White Bird:"
"...sits in her cage, growing old
White bird must fly, or she will die."

The irony of this is that if we had stayed there I might have, and sooner rather than later. But by the time it is discovered that our funky house in this idyllic Rocky Mountain town has beneath its foundations a pile of radioactive uranium tailings, it will no longer belong to us or to the people to whom we had sold it. However, my thoughts at the time are of a subtler, psychological kind of death, and I'm not ready for that either.

"Do you think the bike will make it to Florida?" I ask.
Jeff walks over and kicks the tires. "Maybe," he says dubiously.
"We could leave it there with my brother."
"And?"
"Fly to South America."

Despite the rising value of our irradiated property, Jeff's cooking job and the few articles I am beginning to sell provide us with very little cash. We do some brain-storming and hit upon the idea of leasing a motel coffee shop for the summer tourist season. Our plan is to work as many shifts as we can, Jeff cooking/managing, I waitress/cashiering, to put together a travel fund. It will mean opening at six in the morning and closing at eleven at night, seven days a week, but only for three months. We can do it.

In truth, I welcome the physical demands of those eighteen-hour days which do not leave me, at bedtime, wakeful and fretting about how my daughter is faring in L.A., or what I might do to salvage my novels. Walking half a mile to the restaurant on a Colorado pre-sunrise summer morning is as calming as meditation, and returning home near midnight under a Van Gogh sky of swirling stars isn't bad either.

Even so, it's a more difficult summer than I had expected. It isn't serving unhealthy meals of hamburgers, french fries, and brand-name carbonated sugar water to bickering kids and resentful parents who've been cooped up too long on their too-short family vacation that wears me down. What's burning me out is the three-hour break I take each afternoon.

I peel off my restaurant-sweaty clothes as I come through the door, flip on the television, and collapse on the bed intending to let its babble lull me to sleep. But the TV is tuned to the Watergate hearings. Along with the rest of America, I watch as the lid is pried off Nixon's White House to reveal the crimes and corruption of his administration. I grind my teeth at the posturing of Montoya, Inoye, Talmadge, and a forgettable, brown-mouthed politician from Florida, but can't resist the entertaining folksiness of old Sam Ervin, Lowell Weiker's probing intelligence, and Howard Baker drawling the key question over and over, "What did the president know, and when did he know it?" I cannot sleep.

I am, however, less than fully attentive on the sweltering afternoon that Haldeman's deputy, Alexander Butterfield, takes his seat before the Committee. The question asked of him lulls me like the white noise of a fly circling overhead. But when his crisp, matter-of-fact answer covers the distance from TV screen to my barely-listening ear, I think I must have dreamt it. I sit up, lean forward. Is the man in the blue suit telling us that every conversation in the Oval Office before, during, and after the burglary was recorded? I can't take my eyes off the screen; I must see and remember the face of the one honest man they've finally found. For a single crystal moment I really believe that this is the end of the road for the liars, that things will change and no one in high places will ever scam us again.

I need sleep more than I need the weeks of testimony, court battles, tape erasures, and lies that follow, but the TV stays on. Long before the hearings end it's obvious that the four who broke into the Democratic National Headquarters will go to jail, along with Nixon's top aides, who will use their brief time behind bars to draft best-selling "I-was-there" books. It isn't necessary to watch the last episode to know that Nixon will walk away from it all, supported by a citizenry's nervous insistence that "the system works" and United States government is still the best of all possible.

I fling on my clothes and head back to the restaurant. Jeff has not yet had a break and is looking harassed. Just as I walk in, a child spills Coke all over himself, his parents, and the floor. After wiping it up I check the calendar behind the cash register. Less than a month hangs between our all-American coffee shop and the ski slopes of Chile.

TRAVELING WITH A MAN

ARGENTINA MORNINGS

"*Café, té, o whiskee?*"

I open my eyes to see a red ball of sun just rising over endless plains. Along the highway, pink flamingos stand in a field converted to a shallow lake by last night's rain. I have lost track of time. Is it one day or two that we have been rolling across the Argentine pampas in this big Mercedes bus? Beside me, Jeff is accepting cups of coffee from the stewardess.

"Awake?" he asks, and seeing that I am, passes me a cup of espresso-strong coffee, along with a pot of steaming milk.

I take it gratefully, wondering how I could have fallen asleep when a smiling stewardess seems to have been at our elbow all night long, offering pillows, blankets, sandwiches, sweets, or a choice of *café, té o whiskee.*

I sip coffee and stare out the window. Now that the flamingos have been left behind, there is no scenery to hold my attention. I cannot envision the ski area where we are headed rising out of such a vast plain.

There is a cleanness to the pampas like the wide-open spaces of west Texas that makes me think of strong, decent men — an image probably dredged up from the cowboy movies I used to watch at Saturday matinees. But Argentina has its own images. The big Mercedes bus passes under an arch that marks entry to the state of San Luis. The arch is decorated with a bas relief of a gaucho on horseback trampling an Indian underfoot.

I know nothing of Argentina history, do not know that well into the twentieth century bounties were still being paid for the delivery of a pair of Indian ears (less if they were small and likely from a child). Nor do I know that in Argentine military barracks seeds of a dirty war are being planted even as our bus rolls along. I assume the appalling emblem reflects attitudes from the past.

Jeff reads aloud from a guide book. "It took centuries for Europeans to subdue the natives of this region. When the conquistadors first came to claim the pampas, the Indians ate them."

"Good," I mutter, and add, as an afterthought, "I wish we had stayed in Chile."

"No you don't, not with a coup coming."

"I've never seen a coup. I might've enjoyed it."

"I've seen three. I promise you, they're not fun."

Of course he's right. Even I had realized, when we arrived in Santiago, that fun would be difficult to find in a country where gasoline stations were guarded by men with machine guns and the streets filled with crowds verging on riot. A taxi driver told us that with U.S. dollars he could get enough black market gasoline to take us to the ski area at Portillo, but warned that we should not remain in Chile. From the ski area, he said, we should take the train over the Andes to Argentina.

Outside Santiago we had passed caravans of trucks parked in fields. The striking truck drivers were barbecuing steaks and passing wine bottles. "They used to work for Chile," remarked the cabbie. "Now they work for the CIA."

We were not prepared for this. Insofar as we concerned ourselves with political issues, we had focused on the criminality of Agnew and Nixon, Watergate, and the Vietnam war. All we knew of Chilean politics was that a Marxist president had been elected. We were vaguely interested in seeing how Salvador Allende's brand of socialism would work in the context of Chile's democracy, but for the most part our attention was elsewhere.

Portillo's snow-covered slopes formed the most dramatic mountainscape I had ever seen, and the skiing was beyond our wildest dreams. But the once-a-day train was no longer bringing in food. The coup, they said over fruit juice (the only thing left in the bar), was imminent. So at Jeff's insistence we had taken the train to Argentina. We spent a few days with friends on a ranch outside Buenos Aires, then headed for San Carlos de Bariloche to ski the Argentine side of the Andes.

The bus driver makes an announcement we don't quite understand. We are discussing it when an Argentine woman leans across the aisle and says in English, "He said dinner will be served at the next stop. It's included in your fare."

I fall into conversation with the woman, whose name is Maria Elena. She is an atomic physicist, also headed for San Carlos de Bariloche, but not to ski. There is a research center there, she says, where she and her husband work. She understands from our conversation that we have just come from Chile; how are things there?

We tell her about the truckers strike which has shut down commerce all over the country, and how everyone seems to think a coup is in the offing. She flings her words across the aisle at us, angrily.

"If only Allende could have succeeded! It was so important to us to have a model of social justice without revolution."

"Allende's still the president," I counter lightly. "Maybe all this coup talk is just an attempt to get him to step down. If he hangs in there, maybe he'll even get re-elected."

She looks at me as if I've lost my mind. "But you were there! You saw how the CIA has undermined him." Her voice, low-pitched, is shaking. "Salvador Allende will be dead within a week."

I am swept by a sudden sense of shame. Back in the U.S. I counted myself part of an educated, politically savvy elite. Yet here is a woman on a bus in the middle of nowhere looking at me as if I'm hopelessly ignorant. Why else would we choose to go skiing in a country where our government is engaged in the overthrow of a 187-year-old democracy?

But is that really what's going on? Maybe it's all just spy-talk and gringo-bashing. I close my eyes and let the big Mercedes lull me to sleep.

The following morning we reach the edge of the pampas. Gently at first, then steeply, the road climbs into the mountains. At last we reach San Carlos de Bariloche, an alpine village perched on the edge of a lake. We climb out, stiff-jointed from two days on the bus. Maria Elena's husband is there to meet her. She writes down their address and invites us to visit, but her husband's eyes are cold.

"Americans?" he asks, in a way that makes me feel he sees me as I have been trying to avoid seeing myself: a tourist from a bullying nation, either callously indifferent or incredibly ignorant.

"Thank you," I say to Maria Elena, too embarrassed to accept the hospitality she offers.

Jeff and I ski in the warm September spring sunshine. Below us lies dazzling Lake Nahuel Huapi. In the center is a forested island where, local history has it, the book *Bambi* was written. Evenings we walk the streets of Bariloche, all wooden chalets and shops selling chocolates and hand-knitted sweaters. Its ambience is as Swiss as the

Swiss who settled it. There is only the flow of Spanish to remind us that this is South America.

We stay until the morning we wake to the sound of rain dripping from the eves of our chalet. This marks the end of the ski season in San Carlos de Bariloche. That evening we catch a Mercedes bus north through another long night of broken sleep and pampering stewardesses offering, *"Café, té o whiskee."*

Morning sunshine pries open my eyes. The bus is grinding to a stop in a small town which, judging by the faces and the poverty, is an Indian reservation. In the town square there is, incongruously, a larger-than-life statue of John F. Kennedy.

Jeff gets off the bus to stretch his legs. A boy gets on, selling newspapers. He looks at a round-faced man across the aisle, then at me, and says, *"Salvador está muerto."*

Because I am sleepy, and because *Salvador* translates as savior, I don't quite get his meaning.

"The Savior is dead?" I repeat in halting Spanish.

The round-faced man, whose features I have come to associate with Chileans more than Argentines, looks directly at me, dark eyes wide, not blinking once as a wash of tears spill over.

"Yes," the boy replies in Spanish. "The soldiers or the Americans — they have killed him."

DEATH IN BOLIVIA

It is not easy for us to be cheerful here in this windswept town on the border between Argentina and Bolivia. The Indians whose crafts stalls line the roadway tug at the earflaps of their knitted caps and wrap the lower half of their faces with woolen scarves against the biting wind. Hostile eyes follow us as we wander past, eyes which are no less hostile when we stop to buy something.

We do not linger here by choice. Each day we go to the railway station and read a posted schedule which indicates that a train is due to arrive from the Bolivian capital of La Paz in the morning and return in the afternoon. We wait on the platform in a cutting wind along with a hundred or so Bolivians, but no train arrives or departs. By noon the crowd loses hope and drifts away. We go back to our hotel, which is the best in town. It is marginally less bleak than the railway platform, and warmer only because its cement block walls shut out the wind.

There is just one other guest in the huge hotel. An aging man with pale eyes and frayed suit, he sits in a spot of sunshine in the dusty courtyard, sometimes reading a book with a German title, sometimes staring at the stone wall, or to memories beyond. In the evening he comes down to dinner and without a glance in our direction, makes his way to the other end of the cavernous dining room. Jeff says he looks like a Nazi war criminal. I tell Jeff he has seen too many Holocaust documentaries, but privately I think he's right. Everything about the man says he is a person with a past, and nothing in those flat blue eyes encourages us to ask him the usual questions of "Where are you from?" and "How did you end up here?"

The dining room decor is memorable. Pin-ups torn from outdated calendars and cheap skin magazines are tacked up on one side of the room and down the other at two-foot intervals. Apart from this exhibit of semi-nude women, the only distraction is a large poster. During the interminable wait that precedes each meal, I study the poster. It is five or six feet square, and bears the caption "WANTED," beneath which are one hundred faces. They do not have the same beaten look of criminals shown in Wanted bulletins in U.S. post offices. These faces are mostly young and somehow hopeful; photos that might have been taken from high school albums or college yearbooks. Many have large black Xs drawn across the picture. I ask the waiter what this means.

"*Muerto.* Dead." He sets our food down on the stained tablecloth.

I continue to stare at the poster. There are thirty-nine Xs, ten of them across the faces of young women.

"*Señora,* your dinner is getting cold," the waiter says accusingly.

"Who killed them?"

"Who cares? They are Communists."

"Are they really? They look so young."

"Who knows?" His eyes are inexpressive. "It is an official poster. It says they are Communists. So they are Communists."

Each day we go back and forth between the chill of our bleak hotel and the biting cold of the street, each seeming, after an hour, more intolerable than the other. We do not take pictures here. The buildings are too ugly, the people too hostile. Even the children, with their raw, wind-burned cheeks and unwiped noses, seem sad and unappealing. Jeff and I handle road weariness well enough, but this feeling of being trapped in a place of unbearable ugliness is something else. We grow increasingly irritable, and walk the streets looking for escape.

At last we find one. The movie is *Women in Love*. I am cheered by the knowledge that the filmed backdrop against which D.H. Lawrence's story unfolds is not imaginary; such green, flower-brightened places do exist. From the sides of my eyes I watch *indio* residents of the altoplanao gaze at a world, physical and social, that they have never seen. Even with the aid of moving pictures, can they imagine it? Maybe, maybe not. Even though I am here in the flesh, can I imagine theirs? No, not really.

Traveling with Jeff is a pleasant experience when we are tucked into a comfortable hotel, lingering over a good meal, or cruising across the pampas in a big Mercedes bus. He is also a good companion in serious times, being the one to convince me that I must see a doctor when I am really sick, or should not stay for the Chilean coup just because I've never seen a coup before. But when travel is mildly uncomfortable as it is now, he has a tendency to complain in ways that make me feel blamed.

"I knew we should have taken the bus to La Paz," he grumbles.

"Why didn't you say so?"

"I did."

"You said the Pan American highway isn't paved in Bolivia; it would be dusty."

"It would have been better than hanging around this dump waiting for a train that never comes."

"It's not my fault."

"I never said it was."

This is true. Nevertheless I am snappish with him and remain so until he buys a Bolivian newspaper with a headline announcing that Allende has committed suicide. Despite the article's praise for the military's efficient "restoration of order," I glean enough about the coup's attendant atrocities to feel a fresh appreciation for Jeff as a travel companion.

When the train finally arrives it is visible on the plain far off, moving toward us so slowly that seems to be not moving at all. When it reaches the station I am incredulous. Back in Colorado we had seen the movie, *Butch Cassidy and the Sundance Kid*. According to the story, their end came with a train robbery here in Bolivia. I ask the elderly station master if this is the train that was used in *Butch Cassidy and the Sundance Kid*.

"It is the same train," he tells me.

"They filmed the movie here in Bolivia?"

"I do not know about the movie," he shrugs. "This is the same train that Cassidy and Sundance Kid robbed, for which the army pursued them, and they were brought to justice." He slashes a hand across his throat.

Our interest in riding the same train across the same plain where two American outlaws robbed and rode their last fades rapidly. The miserable hotel we've just left was luxury compared to this train. It struggles across the altoplano at ten miles an hour, at which rate, we calculate, will take thirty hours to reach La Paz. It would seem less interminable if the train boasted such simple amenities as food service and toilets.

When I ask where the toilet is, I am directed to a jagged hole cut in the metal floor at the back of the coach. Within a few hours the floor around the hole is so slimed with human waste that only the most desperate will go near it. Each time the train stops people rush out onto the barren plain and do their business in full sight of anyone who cares to watch. I envy the Indian women who are able to crouch under full skirts and do not have to bare their bottoms to the biting wind.

It was naive of us to assume the train would have a dining car and there would be food vendors along the way. We are passing through a region so short of food that local residents rush to the train to trade for edibles, not to sell them. The most common item of barter is salt. Where this comes from I do not know, but in village after village the train is stampeded by women and children pleading with us to buy large or small bags of salt.

Naturally we aren't going to starve in thirty hours. Nevertheless, sixteen hours into the trip we are more than a little hungry, so hungry that when the smell of roasting meat fills the car we think we must be imagining it. A conductor appears to take orders. When Jeff asks what is being served, he is told only that it is *la comida* — lunch. We are tantalized by two further hours of mouth-watering aromas, but finally meal service reaches our car. We sit near the front, and receive the first two plates. I look down at what has just been shoved into my hand. On a bed of rice nestles half a goat head, sliced lengthwise. I do not know where to look — at my goat with its one eye staring up at me, or Jeff's, where the eyeball has fallen out and lays in the rice like a brown marble.

Jeff, who claims to have eaten monkey in Africa, pretends to enjoy what is undoubtedly a nutritious meal. I pass my untouched plate to a woman with children, some of whom I think must be hungry, although they have not ordered any food. I do not watch to see which one eats the eyeball.

Daylight hours on the train are uncomfortable, but the night is worse. At one jarring stop soldiers burst into the car like pirates. They snatch bundles from poverty-stricken Indians and fling them in a great pile at the end of the car, sometimes with such force that the packages, mostly food, break and scatter on the floor. A woman seated across the aisle from me gives one of her bundles a swift kick which sends it directly under my seat. I bend over, pretending to tie my shoe. If I am to be charged with smuggling, I want to see what sort of contraband it is. The top of the burlap bag has fallen open. It contains macaroni. Even so, I am a little worried, as I do not know what happens to people discovered with "illegal substances," which seem to include anything manufactured in Argentina. The soldiers do not notice the macaroni. They have discovered our ski bag on the luggage rack above, and are going crazy.

"*Armas, armas!*" they shout out the window to a superior.

More soldiers push into the crowded car, guns at the ready. Passengers cower, anticipating bloodshed. Jeff is already on his feet, trying to explain that the bag contains skis, not guns. We are on our way to the world's highest ski area which as they must know, is here in Bolivia.

Neither the English nor the Spanish word for ski seems to be in their vocabulary. Only after each piece of ski equipment has been removed from the bag and minutely examined do the soldiers concede, with obvious disappointment, that they are not weapons. They go back to demanding bribes from Bolivians, or if they cannot pay, confiscating their pathetic parcels of food.

Early next morning, as the train becomes less crowded, Jeff moves to an empty seat where he can stretch out. A stranger sits down next to me. My contact with Bolivians having been limited largely to bullying soldiers and sullen Indians, I am delighted to discover that my seatmate, a shoe salesman from La Paz, is an excellent conversationalist. We discuss the recent *coup d'etat* in Chile, the return of Peron to power in Argentina, the Vietnam war, and Watergate. He has some idea of how the U.S. political system deals with leaders who run amok, but finds it all rather confusing. Do I think Nixon will actually go to jail for his crimes? His information goes well beyond what one might pick up even from American newspapers, let alone the Bolivian press. I ask where he has learned so much about foreign affairs. He smiles, appreciating the fact that I have noticed.

"I live in the capital, very near the central library. Traveling as I do, I have lots of time to read."

What about Bolivian politics, I ask him. Are Bolivians satisfied with their government?

A stricken look crosses his face. "I don't know. I have no interest in politics." Without another word, he turns away and stares out the window. I wonder what I have said to offend him.

The train stops in a small town, and the aisles are suddenly crowded. My seatmate prepares to leave the train. He leans over to retrieve a parcel from under the seat and, with his head near my knee, whispers, "The man behind you is a colonel. One must not speak of Bolivian politics."

When the train resumes its journey, the colonel moves up to sit beside me. Despite the salesman's warning, I lure him into conversation. He speaks openly and warmly of his many years in the Bolivian army. At the next stop we both get off to stretch our legs.

"See there," the colonel indicates a sturdy concrete block building next to the train station. "That is a gift from your government." He points to a bronze plaque on the side of the building. I read the inscription, from which I gather that it is some sort of military mission, donated to Bolivia by the United States government.

"What is its purpose?" I inquire.

"To fight Communism, that is the purpose. President John Kennedy established missions such as this all over Latin America. A very great man, your President Kennedy. American advisors come here to train Bolivian soldiers. Officers like myself are trained in America. You know Fort Brag? I spent four months there."

"That must be where you learned your excellent English."

"My English is not so good as your Spanish," he replies modestly. "Fortunately, one does not have to speak English well to fight Communists. I myself have killed many."

"Young communists or old ones?" I ask innocently.

"Mostly young," he admits. "Older people, they understand that life is hard, that it is meant to be so. Young people become corrupted when they go to university. Many of the professors are Communists."

"And do you kill them, too?"

"When they are known to be Communists, yes. It must be done."

In the courtly Latin way, he takes my hand and assists me back onto the train. On the top step I pause and ask, "Will your own children go to university?"

"All of my sons have gone to the military academy," he says proudly. "And my daughters to convent schools. There are no Catholic Communists."

I want to say that Che Guevara was a Catholic, but I'm not certain he was. Anyway, Che is dead, betrayed by a Bolivian peasant who informed on the revolutionary because, the peasant explained, all the shooting was causing his goats to give less milk.

I wonder whether it was this colonel who killed Che. Probably not, or he would have said so. Likely Che was killed by a soldier of lesser rank — with a little help, of course, from the great President Kennedy.

UNBEATEN PATHS IN PERU

We pole across Lake Titicaca on a lazy warm day, put in at several floating islands, and distribute oranges to runny-nosed children.

"Oranges, hell," mutters Klaus, an Austrian physician who has been traveling with us since Bolivia. "These kids need megadoses of Vitamin C."

An English girl is handing out candy to the malnourished children. I give her a disapproving look. Klaus' guidebook had explained that people who live on the floating islands are short of fruits and vegetables. I conveniently ignore the fact that, until he pointed this out to us, I too had dispersed candy to children who never had, and probably never would, see a toothbrush.

We had met Klaus at Chacaltaya. None of us had actually skied the world's highest ski run, as the lift wasn't operating and we were at 14,200 feet. Along with a dozen others who had come up from La Paz, we sat in an unheated lodge perched on the edge of a spectacular cliff. For two hours we tried to gather, and ultimately lost, our courage to ski a steep slope of cement-heavy snow that disappeared both upward and downward in thick fog.

One of the group in the ski lodge was a Texan whom we had encountered a few weeks earlier at Portillo, the loudest in a bunch that had bulled its way around the gift shop asking a clerk who spoke perfect English, "How much is this in *human* money?"

At Chacaltaya he had passed around a bottle of whiskey and brayed unflattering comparisons between South America and his home state until I lost my patience. The pointless argument that followed was a fitting finale to our sojourn in Bolivia, a country's whose desolation, I pointed out to the Texan, had only been worsened by U.S. contributions.

Jeff had tried to shut me up. The sense that he wasn't on my side (though I knew he was) only made me shriller. Finally, Klaus stepped in and diverted my attention with intelligent conversation. We learned that he was also leaving for Peru next morning, and we'd be traveling the same route as far as the ancient Inca capital of Cuzco.

Like most European travelers, Klaus speaks several languages and has done extensive research on each area in his itinerary — research from which we benefit daily during the week our journeys run parallel. Bolivia and Peru both have large populations of indigenous people that were once ruled by the Incas, thus they are said to be cousins if not sisters. But Peruvian poverty has a decidedly more appealing face. Quechua Indians who come to the window selling soft alpaca clothing, delicately carved gourds, and delicious food are warm and shy. The train is comfortable and the scenery pleasant. By some marvel of ancient engineering, terraced green fields are still being tilled on near-vertical mountainsides. Klaus, history, or anthropology, or guidebook open on his knees, provides us with more information than we have had about any other area on our route.

Once we have done the obligatory trip to Machu Pichu, Klaus heads overland to Lima. Jeff and I go to explore lesser-known ruins in the vicinity of Pisac. After the crowds at Machu Pichu, we are surprised to find ourselves alone at the foot of a small mountain said to conceal the remains of Inca terraces, tombs, temple, and a major fortress. Several paths lead up the mountain. As we stand there trying to decide which way to go, a barefoot boy of about ten appears.

"You want to see tombs I am guide," he says in one breath, and trots off up the path. We scramble after him. The upward climb takes less than half an hour. The path starts to wind downward on the back side, becoming suddenly precipitous. We see the child some distance below, standing on a wide smooth ledge. That must be the main trail, I think, sliding toward him. When we reach the ledge he has disappeared.

The ledge is only twenty feet long. There is no path leading from it in any direction, unless one counts the rubbly mountainside we have just slid down. I peer over the edge. The boy stands on another ledge, six feet below. He smiles and waves. "Come. Now very easy."

What I see, just inches behind the boy, is the empty space of a canyon thousands of feet deep. On the opposite side of the canyon are rows of black holes in an equally sheer cliff face. One cannot see how they could have been reached from either above or below.

The boy points to the black holes. "Tombs," he says proudly.

"Yes," I quaver. "But where is the path?"

"Here." He stomps a dusty foot on the narrow ledge.

Logic tells me that if the boy has dropped safely from one ledge to the next, so can I. But terror informs me that there is only one way to go safely over the edge of this broad ledge onto the narrow one below, and that is with perfect balance. There is nothing to hold onto.

Jeff takes a quick breath and drops down to the next ledge. I think, I cannot do this. This is not how I want to die. My ideal death is instantaneous, not one with a long preamble of terror as I plunge toward eternity.

Face pale, Jeff holds up a hand to steady me. But he, standing on a two-foot-wide ledge without a shred of vegetation or any kind of outcropping, has no more to hold to than I. If he tries to save me when I lose my balance, we will both fall.

As these thoughts race through my head I realize that my only chance is to act before I am completely frozen by panic. That must have been why Jeff moved so quickly. With terror in my gut and a conviction that I am about to die, I slip off the wider ledge. For an instant my feet are in the air, then thud solidly on the narrow ledge below.

Jeff's arm comes behind me, pressing me against the stone wall. "Don't look down," he whispers.

At each end of the ledge there is a sheer stone face, but no path and no boy. Then the child materializes out of a crevice. "Come," he says impatiently.

We inch our way along the ledge until we can see that the crevice is actually a tunnel. We squeeze through the tunnel and find ourselves back on ordinary mountain terrain. A short walk takes us back to the same side we started from. The path to the bottom is clearly visible.

"I take you more places now?" the boy asks.

"No," Jeff says decidedly. "That's enough for today."

The boy looks at us reproachfully, and holds out his hand for the guide's fee.

I wave toward the ledges. "Is that the way other tourists go?"

"No," he says, biting on each of the coins Jeff has poured into his hand. "My brother, he has a better way. I got a little bit lost."

"You shouldn't take people up alone," I admonish. "It's better to go with your brother."

"Today is Sunday. He visits his girlfriend. Besides, when he is here he takes all the money. You want me to guide you to the bottom?"

"No thanks. We can make it down by ourselves."

"Okay." With a grin and a wave, he skitters off the path and, picking a straight line down the mountain, instantly vanishes from sight among bushes and boulders — not a boy at all but a small brown Pan.

Cuzco is a city of both pre-Columbian and colonial splendor, the violence and ruins of one layered upon those of the other. Both the Inca ruler and the Spanish conqueror died there in ways outstandingly brutal even in that brutal era, and what the common people suffered, had it been recorded, would probably make even bloodier reading. The past clings to the present in a way that makes Cuzco the most fascinating city we have yet visited. We hang around for awhile, toying with the idea of spending a year here, as we did in Mexico.

In the end we decide against it. Despite the fact that Jo made it clear the last time I saw her she is no longer mother-dependant, I am still uneasy at being so far from her. Also, here in Cuzco we are in a cross-current of travelers. Descriptions of where they have come from and where they are headed entice and excite us.

While deciding where to go next and by what means, we meet Marty Kramer, a twenty-four-year-old red-head engaged in buying Andean sweaters for a New England mail-order company. He is the first knowledgeable American we have met, and has a warmth that makes us feel as if he has always been our friend. We tag along behind him in the Cuzco market, picking up tips on how to distinguish quality merchandise from flawed items. He urges us to think in terms of what would be a reasonable price, not merely a bargain. He examines an alpaca sweater offered by a Quechua woman with two toddlers sleeping on the pavement at her feet.

"The cost of her materials are fixed. If you figure out how much time she put into this, you'll see she's only asking ten cents an hour for her labor. So when you bargain her down, what you're doing is forcing her to work for less than ten cents an hour."

It sounds like a lecture he has given more than once, but we don't mind. Nothing like this was suggested in our guide book.

Marty stuffs the sweater into his shopping bag and counts out some bills. "If tourists aren't willing to pay a reasonable price for quality products, the first thing to happen — and it's happening already — is that the locals stop producing quality products. If we push prices down still further, which of course we can because they're so desperate, they'll stop making the stuff altogether."

The woman looks at the amount he has handed her with surprise. "You do very fine work," Marty says in Spanish, and is rewarded with a fleeting smile in her otherwise expressionless face.

Marty recommends that we fly rather than bus to Lima. He will travel that far with us, then catch a plane on to Ecuador, where he lives in a village not far from the capital.

"Come visit us when you get to Quito," he urges. "My wife doesn't speak much Spanish; she'll be glad for the company."

He insists we take the last of his Peruvian money, as it is the weekend and we will find it difficult to change our travelers checks before banks open on Monday. It amounts to $40, and seems a lot to hand over to a couple he hardly knows, but Marty waves away our protests.

"No problem. You can pay me back when you get to Ecuador."

We linger in Lima only long enough to see its spectacular museums, then decide, for adventure's sake, to hitchhike to Ecuador. After several frustrating hours on the side of Peru's main north-south highway, we agree that this was not a good idea. There are too few private cars.

Just as we are about to give up, a Land Rover stops. The driver is a British aid worker involved in dairy development. He says there is little to see in the one thousand kilometers of desert between here and the Ecuadorian border, and invites us into the highlands with him to see his project.

We follow a road up to the Continental Divide through mountains that peak at twenty thousand feet or more. The rubble-strewn road hairpins its way along drop-to-nowhere canyons, a constant reminder that we are no longer on the main tourist route.

The Englishman's dairy project, cooperatively owned by the people who work it, is worth seeing. We hang on the fence watching colorfully-dressed milkmaids come to the corral gate and, one by one, call the cows by name. "Rosita!" "Maria!" "Coco!"

At each shout, a placid animal breaks from the herd and gallops to the gate. She is let into the milking barn where, shortly, her contented munching mingles with the sound of milk streams hitting the bottom of a bucket. The roll call continues until all three hundred cows have been fed and milked — a process repeated morning and night, seven days a week.

The British aid worker is going on to the next town, and suggests we spend the night there. It's well after dark when we arrive. Streets are piled with the rubble of buildings destroyed by an earthquake which appears to have happened yesterday, but in fact occurred two years ago. Our driver winds his way through the debris to a long narrow bridge. We are halfway across the bridge when we see a crowd surging toward us. What are the people are shouting? *Piedras?* Stones?

Well, yes, there are stones everywhere. Can that account for the anger in their voices? The crowd is coming closer, the word more distinct. Something bounces off the hood. Simultaneously we realize that the word they are shouting does not mean "Stones," but "Stone them!"

Suddenly an old man is at our window. In clear English he asks, "Are you Americans?"

"No," replies our driver. "British."

"Back up," the man tells us. "You are in great danger." He jerks open the car door and jumps in beside Jeff. It is no simple matter to back up along the narrow bridge, but our English friend does a remarkably smooth job of it. Several rocks are tossed in our direction, but fall short.

"So sorry about this," the old man says. "But the people are very angry. The government has received a great deal of money from abroad to repair earthquake damage, but two years have passed and as you can see, nothing has been done except that the aid officials from all nations have built themselves fine homes up on the hillside near the hotel. Last night some of the townspeople met to organize a protest. The police arrested them — many of them women, our schoolteachers. All day the people have rioted outside the jail. And tonight, well, you see, the police drive Land Rovers, like you. They think you are with the police."

The old man directs us several miles downstream where he says the river is shallow enough to be forded. It is too dark to see the other side. We sit there a moment studying the swirling water.

"Go!" the old man urges. "The hotel is quite near now, quite near."

The Englishman puts the Land Rover into four-wheel drive, and moves forward. Moments later we are churning safely up the other bank. Our tension keys down to a pleasant tingle. Jeff and I grin at each other, pleased to think that wherever we are, it's definitely not on the beaten path.

PRISONERS IN ECUADOR

We are in Ecuador's beautiful colonial capital, Quito, and it is Jeff's birthday. To celebrate and recover from some days of hard overland travel, we have just spent a luxurious night at the Hotel Inca Imperial. For twenty-four hours we have enjoyed decor inspired by the golden era of the Inca empire, a beautifully-tiled sunken tub large enough to hold us both, and a bed that alternately entices erotica and invites sleep. But already we are bored with its adventureless luxury, and arguing. Jeff wants to catch a bus out to the village where Marty Kramer lives, to repay him the $40 he loaned us in Peru. I want to find a restaurant and have a good meal.

I win. We eat at a place called "The Texas Barbecue." Its authenticity is enhanced by bullet holes in the wall, put there, we are told, by Texans involved in oil exploration in the jungle. Bullet holes or no, the barbecue is excellent. Now I'm ready for a bus ride out to Marty's village.

We get off the bus at a dusty square enlivened with equally dusty children, and follow the map Marty has drawn for us. It's a half-mile walk past pastel houses to the outskirts of the village. There we identify Marty's place, as shown on the map, set in a cool green grove of avocado trees. We step onto the shaded veranda with relief. The sun is hot and our backpacks heavy. Jeff knocks. The door opens a crack.

"Does Marty Kramer live here?" Jeff asks.

The door opens wider. A dark-faced stranger motions us in. My smile collapses. He is not motioning with his hand. He is motioning with a pistol. We hesitate. He points the gun directly at us. We step into what must recently have been a comfortable living room. Drawers are upended, lamps overturned, sofa cushions slashed. The man motions to us to drop our backpacks. Have we interrupted a burglary at high noon?

A second man, smaller and lighter-skinned than the first, comes from the kitchen, pistol in hand. I notice he is wearing a badge.

"*Policia?*" I venture hopefully.

He jerks a wallet from his pocket and with one hand, flips it open to reveal an ID card. "Interpol," he says tersely.

Interpol? Isn't that the acronym for International Police? Isn't it funded (by whom I don't know) to track down cold war spies and diamond smugglers? What the hell are they doing here?

"Where is Marty Kramer?" Jeff asks.

"Where *is* Marty Kramer? You must know, *gringo*."

"No!" Jeff replies earnestly. "We met him in Peru two weeks ago. He said his wife would enjoy having company."

"She has company now," remarks the dark man, who has dumped our backpacks on the floor and is helping himself to everything that appeals to him. I watch him take the camera, a dozen rolls of film, a new toothbrush, and my "Ski Colorado" t-shirt.

The light-skinned one snatches my purse and motions to Jeff to hand over his wallet. He empties both of cash and travelers checks, which he stuffs into his pocket.

"I see you expected to buy a lot of drugs from Mr. Kramer."

"No!" we exclaim in unison. "We don't use drugs."

"But you traffic in them, don't you?" From a table he picks up a plastic bag of what appears to be marijuana. "This was in your backpack."

"That's not ours!" Jeff says firmly. "We do not traffic in drugs!"

The man pawing through our possessions smiles a polite rebuke. "All North Americans traffic in drugs," he says calmly.

We are told to sit down at the kitchen table. A half-cooked egg lays in a skillet on the stove. We are interrogated after a fashion, and deduce from their questions that Mrs. Kramer has been arrested but Marty, who wasn't at home when they arrived, is still at large. I ask questions which they do not answer, but as the hours drag by boredom relaxes their tongues.

We learn that an American narcotics agent is in Quito training local Interpol agents in the tactic of "surprise search and seizure." I think of our possessions, a costly portion of which have been seized. They certainly seem to have grasped the tactic, if not its purpose.

The light-skinned agent brags that he is part of an elite corp trained in Texas; that's where he learned to speak English. I wonder if his language class focused on lip-curling, which he uses with far more fluency than words.

In mid-afternoon a third Interpol officer arrives. The two guarding us tell him that Kramer's wife has been taken to headquarters along with another American woman. While waiting for Marty to come home, they've captured these *hippies norteamericanos*. Jeff and I look at each other, marveling at the description. We left the hotel neatly dressed, and Jeff's hair is very short.

"Must be the backpacks," Jeff mutters. "You don't think they'd call us hippies if we were carrying matching leathers from American Express?"

"I don't think they think," I answer tersely. "At headquarters, at least we should be able to talk to somebody who isn't brain-dead."

They prod us into the back seat of a jeep and bounce off in the direction of the city. When I ask where we are going, the driver yells back, "To the Rat Sewer, *gringa*."

The name has no meaning for us but sounds ominous enough. I am not reassured when, at a bus stop on the outskirts of the village, they demand of an attractive young woman waiting there that she allow them to give her a lift to town. They squeeze her in between them with the gearshift protruding between her knees and for the next twenty minutes proceed to fondle her.

While they are preoccupied I take a pen and paper from my purse, which had been returned to me once it was emptied of money. Quickly I write, "Help! American tourists, Jeff Swartz and Rosa Jordan, kidnapped by men claiming to be Interpol. Please contact U.S. embassy!"

We pass through an affluent suburb on the outskirts of Quito. I see a blonde woman walking down the sidewalk and fling the note in front of her. She bends over and picks it up.

The driver brakes so sharply that we crash against the back of his seat. Both agents leap from the jeep and grab the woman. One jams a gun in her ribs and orders her into the jeep. My stomach turns. She is not a woman at all, merely a big girl, maybe fourteen, sixteen at the most. She hands them the note, says she has never seen us before, and flatly refuses to get into the jeep. When one grabs her by the arm, she jerks it away. I stand up, preparing to make a break for it, anything to turn their attentions away from the girl.

"Sit down," Jeff hisses.

"No way," I retort. "This is how the Jews ended up in concentration camps."

I leap to the ground, Jeff behind me. But the ground is as far as we get. Both agents turn on us. One hits Jeff in the face with his pistol.

The other jams a gun into my belly so hard I gasp. He waves the note in my face. "What does it say?" he shouts. "Who is that woman?"

From the corner of my eye I see that the girl is now half a block away, just disappearing through a doorway. "I don't know who she is! The note wasn't for her. It was for the U.S. Embassy. We are NOT criminals!"

He shoves the note against my nose. "Read it!" he shouts.

I read it.

"You"re lying. That's not what it says."

I push it back at him. "Read it yourself. You speak English."

"*Puta!*" He manhandles me back into the jeep.

They careen down the quiet street and through downtown Quito with life-threatening disregard for human and vehicular traffic. Absurdly, I find myself wishing I had a seat belt.

Interpol headquarters is a dim high-vaulted room. At one end is a ten-foot-high Interpol emblem and a long list of countries in which Interpol operates. Beneath the emblem, at a massive desk totally bare except for a telephone, sits a Mafia-looking official: the Ecuadorian Chief of Interpol.

The Chief nods to his agents when they bring us in, but asks no questions. We are told to sit down. There are two other women in the room, both Americans who look to be in their early twenties. The younger of the two mouths "Marty?"

"We didn't see him. Are you his wife?"

An agent yells, "*Silencio!*" and waves his gun at us.

The anguish in her eyes tells me that she is Marty's wife, and more frightened for him than for herself.

I look around, trying to dispel my anxiety by pretending that this is not a real place but a movie set. Eventually, though, I am forced to acknowledge an essential difference between real life and the movies. A film, no matter how bad, ends within a couple of hours. We sit in the hot dim room, forbidden to speak or move from our hard chairs, for six interminable hours. Outside the light is fading. The phone rings.

The Chief picks it up. "*Sí, Señor* Kramer." His eyes rest on the young woman across from me, who begins to cry. "I understand, *Señor* Kramer. If you turn yourself in, we will release her."

An hour later, a pale Marty Kramer walks into the room and up to the Chief's desk. Agents move in on either side, and with an almost-comic amount of fumbling, handcuff him. Marty looks past them to the Chief and says in a strained voice, "You'll release Karen now?"

The Chief tilts back in his chair in a self-satisfied way and shouts the now-familiar command: *"Silencio!"*

Near midnight we are fingerprinted, and what remains of our personal belongings are painstakingly recorded. We are taken in a jeep to another part of the city. A guard unlocks a heavy iron gate. He smiles and says in Spanish, "Welcome to the Rat Sewer, *gringos.*"

We are marched through a courtyard lined with large crowded cells. Marty is shoved into one, Karen into another, Jeff into another, myself and the other American woman into another. The barred door clangs shut.

Dark faces encircle me, then fall back to let a big black woman through. She moves in very close and looks down at me from what must be a height of six feet. I am terrified and do the only thing I can think to do. I smile. She studies me carefully for a moment, taking note of what I am wearing and whether there is anything in my pockets. She must see that I am shaking, because she asks, in Spanish, "You got a blanket?"

I glance at the bare wood bunks and shake my head.

She pulls a woolen serape from around her shoulders, hands it to me, and points to a top bunk. "Sleep there. The rats, they don't climb."

Beyond the circle of women I see cat-sized shadows skulking along the walls.

"*Gracias,*" I murmur, and climb swiftly onto the top bunk. The other American woman climbs into the next one over.

The big black woman, whom the others call Luz, follows me and peers into my face. "You got money?"

"No. The police took it."

Luz walks to the corner of the cell and hunkers down over a smoldering fire.

From the next bunk, the American woman says, "My name's Lynn. What's yours?"

"Rosa."

"You're a friend of the Kramers?"

"Not really. We just met Marty a couple weeks ago in Peru."

"I'm a neighbor. I stopped by this morning to see their new kittens."

"You live in the village?"

"For the past seven years. Marty and Karen have only been there a few months. Nice couple. Their first time abroad."

Luz returns and hands us each a tin cup of hot tea.

"Drink it," advises Lynn. "They don't provide food here. Unless you've got money to buy from the vendor who comes once a day, or friends to send something in, it can be a long time between meals."

"You seem to know this place pretty well."

"Too damn well. The guy I was living with got busted five years ago. I had to drag food in to him every damn day for a month."

"That's how long he was in jail?"

She gives me a look. "Not hardly. But they only keep prisoners here in the Rat Sewer for thirty days. Then they're sent to the main prison."

"That's if you're guilty, like after the trial?"

"You're speaking American, honey. This is Ecuador. My old man didn't go to trial for two years. Then got sentenced to five."

"So he's still locked up?"

"Just got out. But we didn't get back together. He joined a Jesus group. We're still friends, though."

"What did they catch him with?"

"Only what they planted on him. I mean, he was a real pot-head, but he wasn't stupid. He kept his stuff buried in the back yard."

"I don't understand. I mean, what's the point?"

Lynn shrugs. "The point is that where drugs are concerned, this backwater country is under the thumb of the U.S. Unless Ecuador is very what they call 'cooperative' about busting people, its foreign aid gets cut. And of course, these asshole Interpol agents love being 'cooperative.' Arresting gringos gives them a chance to work out their anti-American prejudices."

"The ones who arrested us said there's an American agent here directing operations. You think he might help us?"

"You kidding? Those guys want notches on their gun just as much as the Ecuadorians. You ever meet one, you'll see what I mean. They're evil bastards. Meaner than the locals, who're mostly just lazy."

"They must've had a reason to suspect us," I insist.

Lynn finishes her tea and stretches out on the narrow bunk. "There is a drug dealer in the area. Not in the village, but somewhere up in the mountains. I've heard he lives in a big hacienda with a swimming pool, the whole bit. I don't really know anything about him, except you know, word gets around."

"So it's him they're after?"

"More or less."

"What do you mean, more or less?"

"It's a sweep, that's all. They hear there's an American in the area running drugs, so they arrest all the Americans they can find and figure the one they're after will be among them. They don't need material evidence, and the idea of a person being presumed innocent is not even on their mental map. That's why U.S. narcs love working down here. They don't have to worry about civil rights. They bust whoever they please, and you can rot in jail five fucking years before you're ever brought to trial."

Lynn stops talking. I look across the narrow space between our bunks and see that she is crying.

I don't feel like talking to the other women tonight. I'm scared and hungry and disoriented. Anyway, it's after midnight and most of them are asleep. As the cell grows quiet, I can hear men's voices from the next cell, coming through a high transom. One I identify as Jeff's, speaking sometimes in Spanish, sometimes in English. There must be another American in there. Maybe it's the drug dealer. I can't make out what they're saying.

I roll over to get the light out of my eyes. Dozens of rats are out in the open now, with more emerging from the shadows every second. They slink from beneath the lower bunks and leap through the iron bars of the door that separates our cell from the courtyard. They scurry about the floor, snatching at crumbs of food. Sometimes two or more claim a morsel, and a fight breaks out. Amid piercing squeals, sharp teeth are bared, and if neither backs off, the competitors lunge at each other until one or both are bloody. I have never had a nightmare this terrifying.

I try to convince myself that no aggressive members of the seething mass will climb the metal poles of the bunk and fight over my flesh the way they are fighting over scraps on the floor. Luz said the rats don't climb. Or did she say that they *can*'t climb? Over and over I whisper like a mantra, "Rats can't climb, rats can't climb, rats can't...."

It doesn't work. The more I say it, the more I recall mouse droppings on high shelves in summer cottages, my cat chasing a field mouse up a tree, the rat I once saw running along a rafter in our barn.

Rats are but one in a triad of fears that threatens to skid me into hysteria. Another comes simply from being here. I have always been uncomfortable in walled-in places like elevators and narrow canyons, and find any form of physical restraint intolerable. I look up at moths swarming around the bare bulb, and across to the locked door. How many years did Lynn say we could be held awaiting trial?

Near dawn I glimpse my third and deepest fear. It is that the combination of rats and claustrophobia will drive me crazy. I think about that awhile, about what has been taken away from me, and what I have left. What I still have is my mind. That's where I'll take my stand. I will not, repeat, will not, let go of my mind.

I sit up and look down at the scurrying rats. "Don't you mess with me," I say aloud. I pull off one shoe and grip it like a club. "Try to climb up here and I'll bash your brains out."

With first light prisoners wake and begin to move about the cell, reclaiming it from the rats. There is a single toilet in the corner, and a water tap. Lynn is still sleeping on the bunk to my left. On the right is a woman wearing the traditional clothing of Otavala Indians: white dress with a blue apron, delicately embroidered blue slippers, and a blue *reboza*, that long scarf women here use for wrapping themselves against evening chill, padding the skull when balancing heavy loads on their head, or tied to form a cradle for a baby on their back. There is another Otavala woman on the bunk below. She is nursing a six-month-old baby. I ask why they are here. They explain that a street riot broke out near where they were selling weavings. Many people, themselves included, were herded into police vans. No one has talked to them, or said how long they might be held.

Besides the Otavala baby there is another child in the cell, a four-year-old girl. The mother tells me she was arrested for coming back to beg in a restaurant after she had been thrown out. She had the child with her, so naturally they were jailed together.

There are about thirty of us in a room thirty feet square. Throughout the day I wander around the cell getting everyone's story. Most of them are here either for petty thievery or prostitution without a permit. Each person has a tiny bundle of belongings, a few coins, a comb, one or two hard rolls. The owner may go to the toilet, wander off to talk to other women, or go to the barred door and stare out, but no one touches her pitiful possessions.

Although Ecuador has only a small black population, most of the prisoners in the cell are black and come from the coastal region of Esmeralda. Luz tells me that she and they are descended from shipwrecked and runaway slaves. Luz says she was arrested for backtalking a policeman who demanded protection money for the privilege of selling herb teas on a particular street corner. I can believe it. She is not the sort of woman to take guff, and no one in their right mind would give her any.

Initially I think it is size that makes Luz the person of authority in our cell, but soon realize that it has more to do with her skills. She is a born manager, and plays no favorites. I watch her make territorial decisions in the overcrowded space, head off conflicts before they start, and distribute food to those like myself who have no money to buy from the vendor. Occasionally Luz pauses at the bunk of a person who seems to have more than the others, and asks for a hunk of bread or piece of fruit. It is handed over. She carries it immediately to someone in the room who has nothing. I remember the hard roll she gave me at breakfast.

In the adjacent cell, Jeff is doing the same thing I am — talking to other prisoners, trying to comprehend our situation and get a feel for the system. There is an eleven-year-old boy arrested for sleeping in a telephone booth, and a fourteen-year-old who lost a set of car keys at the parking lot where he worked. Later in the day the older boy is taken out into the courtyard and in view of all the cells, beaten with a strap in an attempt to make him confess that he stole the keys.

There is also an American in Jeff's cell, a businessman from San Francisco who casually identifies himself as "the cocaine dealer they were after." He says the narcs ransacked his ranchhouse and found enough "stuff" to put him away, as well as a quantity of emeralds. He figures that if he can get deported to stand trial back in the States he'll be okay; if not ... well, Ecuadorian prisons are pretty hairy.

On our second day in the Rat Sewer, Luz buys a newspaper from the vendor. The women gather around her, some reading over her shoulder while the majority, illiterate, wait for her to read aloud. Luz motions me over and points to a headline halfway down the front page. *Seis norteamericanos que cultivaban, traficaban y consumian drogas, detenidos.* The article informs its readers that an Interpol investigation has resulted in the arrests of "two North American hippies, Jeffrey Swartz and Rosa Jordan, when they came to buy drugs at the house of Marty and Karen Kramer. The Kramers were also arrested, along with cocaine trafficker William Hart, and Lynn Seyferth who smoked drugs."

A guard comes at noon with food packets sent to prisoners by family and friends. I am astonished to hear my name called, then Lynn's. Each of our packets contains a soyburger, fresh fruit, an avocado, oatmeal cookies, a bottle of purified water, comb, toothbrush, and sanitary napkin. I have no idea where these things have come from.

"Probably from the Christians," Lynn says. "The bunch my ex belongs to. They do things like this — visiting the sick, helping the imprisoned, just like Jesus said. These are the only Christians I ever heard of who actually do it. They probably got our names from the newspaper."

Earlier I had been hungry but simply receiving the food, knowing somebody out there knows I am here, gives me all the nourishment I need. I eat an orange and divide the rest of the food between the mother with the four-year-old and the Indian woman with the nursing infant. Luz asks for the sanitary napkin. I give it to her. She carries it across the room to a girl whose need is immediate and obvious.

In the afternoon Jeff and Hart are taken out of their cell to be interrogated by the Ecuadorian Chief of Interpol under the watchful eye of the American narcotics official. Waiting his turn in an outer office, Jeff listens as the Ecuadorian head of Interpol offers Hart a deal. If Hart will sign over a restaurant he owns in Quito to the Chief, he will be deported to stand trial in the U.S. Otherwise he will remain imprisoned in Ecuador. Hart needs no urging to accept the offer.

When Jeff's turn comes, he is handed a "confession" and told to sign it. He refuses. Over and over he repeats that we did not come to Kramer's house to buy drugs, do not use them, and had none in our luggage. He is told that it is pointless to stonewall, as "your girlfriend has already admitted that you both use drugs, and the Kramers have confessed that you were one of their customers. They will be deported to the U.S. on tomorrow's flight, but unless you sign this, you may well be imprisoned here in Ecuador for up to seven years."

Jeff sticks to the truth and refuses to sign anything.

The following morning Lynn is taken out for interrogation. She returns with a welt on one cheek and an eye that is beginning to purple. "The bastard tried to make me sign some bullshit confession. I told him, 'You wrote it; you sign it.' He swore I'd get seven years in the slammer, and belted me in the face for good measure."

As we stand there we see Marty and Karen being marched across the courtyard. Marty has his arm around Karen. She is weeping inconsolably.

"Karen!" Lynn shouts. "What happened?"

"I signed it," Karen sobs.

"They lied!" Marty voice is hoarse; he is also crying. "They told her I signed a confession admitting we smoke marijuana. They said we'd been sent back to the States; that she was the only one left, and could go if—"

Marty's sentence ends in a gasp as the guard jabs him in the kidney. They are prodded through the gate to the street, and out of sight.

"Where are they taking them?" I ask.

"To the big prison."

Lynn climbs up on her bunk and lies there in fetal position, tears sliding sideways off the edge of her face.

Across the courtyard an Interpol agent pauses to speak to a guard. I stand at the bars, waiting. I am the only North American who has not yet been interrogated. They stop laughing and begin to walk across the courtyard toward our cell. I know they are coming for me.

I seem to be gazing into one of those mirrors that turns things upside down. Less than a week ago I might have looked to men such as these, strutting confidence behind their black guns and silver badges, for protection. My cellmates — jailbirds, thieves, prostitutes — would have frightened me. Now these women, criminals by definition, are the ones I trust, while the police I fear as dangerous men, more dangerous than other men because they draw from their guns and badges a terrifying power. I do not know how much of it they will use against me. But this I know absolutely: they are against me.

The guard slides his key into the lock. The gate of iron bars swings open. The gun points, motioning me out. Behind me whispers cross the room, scarcely more audible than a sigh. *"Suerte."* Luck.

We climb a stone stairway and enter an unlit corridor. Far ahead I see an open doorway into a room lighted by a single bare bulb. Below the dangling light bulb is an empty straight-backed chair. There are people sitting in the room but I cannot see their bodies. Only their legs, protruding toward the chair, are visible through the open door. Long legs, short legs, trouser legs. Men's legs.

I stand at the edge of hysteria, unable to walk toward something I fear more than death. *They're going to destroy my mind,* I think. *They're going to torture me till I'm crazy.* The guard's gun jabs hard against my vertebrae, sending a flash of pain in all directions. Involuntarily, I move forward one step. Another jab. Another step. Jab. Step. Time, not I, moves us slowly down the corridor toward the bare bulb, the empty chair, the men's legs.

A last step carries me into the room. The two men on my right jump to their feet. One is a tall stranger. The other is Jeff.

"Rosa!" Jeff's voice rings with relief. "This is John Hope. Our vice-counsel, from the embassy."

Vice-Counsel Hope extends his hand. I walk past the hand, put my arms around his thin body, and drench the front of his fresh white shirt with tears.

John Hope is the perfect embassy official: friendly, efficient, honest, and careful. He asks the guards to give us a few minutes alone, then quickly explains our situation and his.

"We got an anonymous call from some woman on the weekend telling us you were here, but Monday being a holiday, I didn't get the message till today. Luckily, no charges have been filed yet. They probably wanted to see what you'd confess to before deciding what to charge you with."

"We haven't signed anything," Jeff says quickly.

"I know. If you had I couldn't help. I may not be able to help anyway. The Embassy is under strict orders not to interfere with narcotics operations. As long as you're in Interpol custody, my hands are tied."

"What if they won't release us?"

"They definitely won't release you. But maybe I can get them to transfer you to Immigration. If they'll agree to that, I can probably get you out of here."

"How?"

Hope smiles. "Oh, let's say the folks in Immigration owe me a few. If I ask them, as a favor, to deport you, they will."

"Deport us?" The phrase has an unpleasant ring. "To where? For what?"

"Back to Miami. For something vague, say, being undesirable persons."

"But we haven't done anything," I protest. "They've got no right—"

"Do you want out of here or not?"

"Of course, but—"

"This is the only way it can be done. If it can be done." Hope makes some notes on a pad, giving us a few seconds to assimilate what he has told us. "There's just one more thing. If I can get you transferred from Interpol custody to Immigration, and they agree to deport you, you'll need plane tickets."

"They've taken all our money. Cash, travelers checks, everything."

Hope shrugs. "The police here get paid the same way armies were paid in ancient times, mainly by what they can loot. The embassy has no funds for this sort of thing, and we're not allowed to make personal loans. The only way to get you out of here is if you can come up with money for the tickets."

I slip off my left shoe, and from under the insole, take a blank check. I unfold it and pass it to Hope. "Will this do?"

Jeff looks at me in surprise. "Where did you get that?"

"I didn't see any point in carrying a checkbook all over South America, but thought, well, you never know. I decided to bring along one blank check, just in case." I look at Hope anxiously. "Is it okay?"

Hope studies the check. "Well, the name's legible. "Is it any good?"

"Oh, definitely!"

"I'll run it through my own account. I'm not supposed to, but—" He shrugs. "Just remember, if it bounces, I'll be the one out of pocket."

The guard signals that our time is up. Jeff fills in the check for the amount of two plane tickets. Hope slips it into his briefcase.

"What about Lynn and the Kramers? I think they're innocent, too."

"I might be able to help Lynn, but the Kramers, no chance. Mrs. Kramer signed a confession."

I want to protest, but Hope's expression tells me that he already knows how the confession was obtained. Questions hang on my tongue, but there is no time to ask. The guard's gun barrel finds the bruised spot on my spine again, and I am marched back to the cell.

Another fat food packet arrives from the Christians. I divide some of it between the women with children, and give the rest to Luz for distribution. I hear my name floating down from the high ceiling. It is Jeff, calling through the transom.

"Rosa, can you hear me?"

"Yes!" I shout.

"Agnew resigned!"

It's always cold in the cell at night, and still cold when I wake at dawn. The Otavala women are the first to rise, scattering rats as they cross the cement floor to the water tap. In pre-dawn chill they wash themselves and the baby, along with its clothing and some of their own. The clothes now hang drying on the end of the bunk. The baby lies naked between them, cooing and kicking its legs, tiny penis bouncing. I want to pick him up, but am conscious of how clean he is and how grubby I am. It has been days since I bathed; my hair is dirty, my clothes filthy. Most of the women in the cell look the same. Only the dresses of the Otavala women are still white, their blue aprons freshly washed. Each day, with infinite patience, they have untangled each other's long black hair and rewoven it into smooth braids. Like all of the women here, there are some moments in every day when they turn their faces to the wall and weep. The rest of the time they speak quietly in their own language, and play with the baby. I have never heard him cry.

An hour drags by, another, and another. Then I hear Jeff shouting through the transom, his voice pitched high with relief. "Rosa! Braniff leaves at eleven a.m.!"

The cell door swings open. A guard motions Lynn and me out. A moment later we are in an outer office with Jeff and John Hope. There is another American in the room, a tall unsmiling man who bears a strong physical resemblance to Nixon's aide, H.R. Haldeman. The man is not introduced to us, nor we to him. I know without being told that he is the American narcotics official.

A clerk slides documents across the counter for us to sign, testifying that the personal possessions taken from us upon arrest have all been returned. I look up at John Hope, indignant. He makes a "shut-up-and-sign" motion. Jeff and I each sign a document, and are handed our near-empty bags. We start for the door.

Without looking up, the American narc says to no one in particular, "Being deported, are they? Guess I'll have my men in Miami put them under surveillance."

Something in me snaps. "Haven't you ever read the constitution of the country you work for?" I shout. "We're American citizens; we pay your fucking salary —"

The narc does not hear most of this. Before the first sentence is out of my mouth, Hope has jerked me out the door and pushed me into his car. He slides under the wheel, grim and shaken, but with diplomatic control, says nothing. Jeff and Lynn are laughing.

"It's not funny!" I yell. "We're supposed to stand for democracy and all that, but everywhere we go there are these Nazis — the CIA feeding striking truckers in Chile, American military advisors helping soldiers murder college students in Bolivia, U.S. narcs training Ecuadorians to make illegal arrests! Fascism — that's our major export. Why don't they put that in the fucking *Wall Street Journal?*"

Hope clears his throat. "I wouldn't call it fascism."

"Don't argue semantics with her," Jeff laughs. "She's got a degree in political science."

"Why, you could have been a diplomat," Hope teases. "Relax, Rosa. It's over. You'll be home in time for dinner."

John Hope shepherds us past security officials and across the tarmac to the big Braniff jet. At the top of the steps I turn to wave goodbye. His blond hair catches the light like the hair of the girl to whom I threw my SOS note. Hope's hair is very short. Hers was like Jo's; it formed a fuzzy halo around her face. I imagine myself returning to Ecuador, finding that girl, and telling her how her defiance, her refusal to get into the jeep when men with guns ordered her to do so, and her call to the embassy, led to our release. But of course it's only a fantasy. She will never know.

As we rise into the air, I look out at tropical mountains and twisting roads falling away below us. It is as if, following such a road, we failed to navigate a hairpin turn and went careening over the edge into one of Ecuador's tangled green canyons, then woke to find ourselves floating five thousand feet above. I want to laugh and say, "Where am I?" But it's not exactly funny.

John Hope said I was going home. If that's true, why do I feel less akin to this smiling American stewardess and her sterile plastic tray than to big Luz with her tin can of smoky tea?

I want to be free of illusions. But perhaps illusions about the country from which we come are like compasses — small sensory devices that help us find our way back to wherever we feel that sense of belonging. If so, perhaps I've lost too many of mine.

I watch Caribbean islands pass beneath us, then the Florida coastline, and know that soon now, we will be landing in a nation which no longer belongs to me, or I to it.

LEAVING HOME

California — The 'Seventies

I stand at the edge of the cliff taking great gulps of air spiced with anise, sage, sumac, and salt from the sea. For the first time since emerging from prison in Ecuador, I have enough.

I have come here knowing I can stay one month only, yet knowing, from first breath, that I have come home. It is a land shrouded in clouds of eucalyptus and grey-green chaparral above a never-changing, ever-changing shoreline, a place invisible to the twentieth century sweeping along the highway below.

How strange to follow an overgrown driveway up a steep hillside and see the Budwood Ranch emerge like Brigadoon out of the past. I don't mean that ancient past when the Chumash lived here, a life of leisure and abundance, weaving baskets and racing their red canoes. Nor do I mean the next era, which belonged to the conquistadors, and when natives began to call the place *Malibu* — "rough going;" that century they fought the slavery demanded by Spaniards, choosing instead to fight and die, hide and die, or in the case of women raped for the purpose of bearing mixed-blood "tame Indians," to self-abort and sometimes die with their unborn children. That past, like all but a few drops of Chumash blood, has long since soaked into the ground.

Another more recent history dates from the time this land came to be known as *Rancho Malibu*. A five-mile wide strip stretching for twenty-seven miles along the California coast, it was granted by the King of Spain to a single family, who passed it to another, and another, until, at the dawn of the twentieth century, it fell to one American woman. May Ringe and her armed *vaqueros* rode the boundaries of *Rancho Malibu* until 1923, fighting off the future. Then, family fortune spent, the old woman laid down and died. Along with the sound of clods hitting her coffin could be heard the noise of a highway being built across the Malibu, and the scratch of pens on documents that would break the ranch to bits.

The Budwood Ranch is one of those bits, 132 acres at the eastern end of Malibu. Its name comes from two men, Bud Abbott (of the Abbott and Costello comedy team) and a film producer, Sam Wood. It is this part of the past that I see when I come up the narrow driveway.

What I see are low stone walls, constructed by Mexicans with the knowledge of placing rocks that hold without mortar, walls now overgrown with chaparral and wildflowers. I see the big house, the little house, two cottages, and a stable, constructed by Abbott and Wood in 1923. The buildings have weathered to a soft bluish green that blends with the trees they planted fifty years ago.

The Budwood now belongs (on paper) to the Manocherians of New York. They in turn lease it to Jerry Ziegman, a TV scriptwriter from Nebraska. Because Jerry believes that creativity is insufficiently rewarded in America, he lets the old ranch buildings at giveaway rents to artists willing to live at the edge of poverty in order to pursue their vision. He takes one look at me and knows I am one of them.

"That cabin there at the top of the driveway is empty," he tells me, "but only for a month. Its tenant, a pianist, is away in Paris. I know he won't mind if you stay there till he returns."

Perhaps it is Jerry's nature that impels him to this generosity, or maybe he sees how haunted I am. Our return to the States from Ecuador has left me both relieved and raw.

My brother Duane had not sold the motorcycle as we asked, but used it for rounding up horses grazing in his orange grove. Amused and grateful, Jeff and I had climbed on the Honda and rode west. I needed to see my daughter.

When we arrived in Los Angeles Jo and John greeted us with a notable lack of enthusiasm. Neither their life nor their small apartment had room for us. However, the Hamptons' door, as always, was open. They put us up while we considered what to do.

The first thing I had done was write a letter to Marty Kramer's family, telling them about the arrest in Ecuador, and sending the $40 Marty lent us in Peru which we never had an opportunity to pay back. Months later I received a reply from Marty, postmarked New Hampshire, thanking us for contacting his parents, and explaining that it had taken his and Karen's families four months and $4,000 to get them out of prison.

I also contacted American Express. For weeks we had tried to get our travelers checks replaced. In response to my carefully detailed report, I received a curt note from American Express saying that the travellers checks wouldn't be replaced as long as "they are in the custody of the police."

"They are not in anybody's 'custody!'" I shouted over the phone. "They've been stolen by uniformed, card-carrying Interpol officers."

The clerk regretted that I was upset, but policy, after all, was policy.

The Hamptons recommended that we seek help from a local program called *Action TV* which specialized in going after businesses and bureaucracies that were jerking people around. I told American Express that this was what I intended to do. The following day we received a call saying we could pick up our replacement travelers checks any time.

During our stay with the Hamptons in their comfortable Canoga Park home, Jeff watched football games with Phil and I hung out with Grace, trying to unravel the mystery of how they sustained the intimacy of their happy marriage. Whatever it took, I felt that Jeff and I (or perhaps just I) did not have it.

Within a few weeks we each made decisions which I hoped would end a relationship that I never meant to be permanent but had no reason to abandon. Jeff went off to work at a ski area in Northern California, and I moved out to the Budwood.

A grand piano half-fills the cabin's one small room; the rest is a clutter of books and art belonging to the pianist. I clear a space for my typewriter and go to work. The unsteady table trembles under the regular beat of my typing and irregularly with the impact of big waves. It rains and rains. On Christmas morning sun rays through the clouds like a resurrection painting, and Gregorian chants from Jerry's outdoor speakers fill the air. The rabbi who lives in the big house lopes down to the beach with a surfboard under his arm.

There are others who live in the big house, now divided into four apartments: a jeweler named Neil with hair to his waist, and his roommate Bruce, a very blond, very shy college boy engrossed in esoteric Oriental languages; a painter called Jim, whose work and physical appearance are reminiscent of Van Gogh; the photographer Steve and his wife Lita, a French/Tunisian painter on the ascendancy in avant-garde circles. In the week since my arrival I have only glimpsed these neighbors, but can't think what Christmas might mean if I have no gifts for them. I bake a cheesecake for each household, line them up on the table to cool, then wander down to the beach to see what last night's storm washed ashore. I return to find Neil's acid-addled sheepdog Zanzibar standing on a chair, wolfing down the last of five cheesecakes that have taken me half a day to make.

Zanzibar runs out the door then turns and holds her ground, yapping an explanation which I'm sure has to do with the fact that Neil has inflicted his vegetarianism on her, and can't I see she's always hungry? We stand there nose to nose, she barking unrepentantly and I in furious tears. Neil trots up the path, takes the stone from my hand, and puts in its place a walnut shell. Its two halves are hinged. When I open it, there on a bit of velvet is a star sapphire bluer than the winter sky.

I meet Steve and Lita a few days later when she invites me to a fiesta to celebrate the publication of a book of Steve's artistic, anxiety-generated photographs. The house is filled with gypsies, and Steve, who lived two years in Spain among them, takes his guitar and plays flamenco with the finest. I watch his hands caress the strings and envy the woman who feels them on her body, though Lita tells me some long time later when they have gone their separate ways that it wasn't like that at all.

One morning I hear the uncommon sound of swearing, and go out to find the painter Jim standing in the carport, muttering over a hole torn in the top of his VW convertible. Muddy footprints and the overpowering musk of male raccoon explain the hole and why, of a mellon left in the car overnight, only its ripe sweet scent remains. Jim accepts my invitation to consolation coffee, and seeing me trying to rub the stiffness from my neck, sits down behind me and massages away the tension.

The last Budwood resident I meet is Bond. When the pianist returns from Paris he says, with a soft Alabama drawl, that he is glad to have me use his place and I'm welcome to stay a little longer if I wish.

What I wish is to never leave, and imagine, bare toes curling into the dirt, that if anyone tries to make me go I'll hide in the hills like those Chumash who couldn't bear to give up either their freedom or their land.

I walk up past the stable to Jerry's little house and stand in the patio under the big eucalyptus where some previous tenant, a Scientologist, has placed the Budwood's grand piano because its vibes, he said, were bad. Jerry is in process of refurbishing the piano, and looks up with a smile. He thinks I have come to say goodbye.

"Jerry, can I rent the cabin at the end of the garage?"

"What cabin?"

"You know. The one with no windows and a broken skylight, and bullet holes in the front wall."

"But Rosa, it isn't habitable — no plumbing or anything."

"It's better than a cave on the hillside."

Old summer houses are being torn down along Topanga Beach to create more public parking. Jim helps me scavenge wood, windows, plumbing, even a refrigerator. Jeff comes back, dissatisfied, from the mountains. He helps restore the cabin, then, although he has his own apartment in town, moves in. His presence makes me cramped and cranky, but he has more than squatter's rights. If Jeff hadn't been acquainted with Jerry from their boyhood days in Omaha I wouldn't be here now listening to Chopin floating from Bond's piano across the lavender in his yard and through my open window.

Steve and Lita hurry by, headed for the city in pursuit of artistic fame. The rabbi wanders in expecting to be offered coffee and not minding that he has interrupted my writing. Jim, wearing only beard and cut-offs, sees the door wide open and comes to chin himself on the rafters below that leaking skylight.

Zanzibar, still a thief but no longer an enemy, appears at the door for the scrap of meat I secretly feed her every day. The horse, who has a stable up the hill but no corral, nudges the dog aside and stands there at the edge of the carpet, head shoved through the doorway in silent, horsey communication with a herd of humans she accepts as her own. She is a wise old horse who comes and goes at will, but observes the boundaries of the Budwood as if it were an island in a shark-infested sea. Which of course it is.

Jo rarely visits me in Malibu, and seems irritable when I visit her. Still, I am glad to be here. Intuition tells me that her travels with John are drawing to an end. I want to be nearby when it happens, if only to tuck a first-aid kit in her backpack when she strikes out on her own. I doubt she'll need more than that. She has already completed one year of art school and almost two of college, and is as healthy as a seventeen-year-old can be. I turn my attention to writing, and wait.

It is springtime when I look up and see her standing in the doorway of my Malibu shack, blonde hair backlighted by a shimmering, sunlit sea.

"John's going to Tokyo," she announces. "He's been offered a teaching job there."

"Are you going with him?"

"No." Her face is swollen with what seems to be sulk, but I recognize it as days or more of tears, held back. "I hate cities, I hate pollution, I hate him being my only social life. Tokyo is bigger than L.A., and more polluted, and I don't speak the language so I'd be even more dependant there than I am here."

"What do you want to do?"

She continues to stand there, all pout and pent-up anger. Suddenly tears begin to flow like clear liquid from a broken blister. "That's just the trouble, don't you see? I have no skills and no talent."

I put my arms around her, but feel the resistance, so draw back and offer the sense of solid ground I think she has come for. "If we made a list of your skills and talents, I think you'd see you have a few. But never mind that now. What you want to do is choose."

Her strong shoulders sag. "Choose what?"

"I don't know what possibilities you've considered, but here are three I can offer. I can ask the tenants to vacate our house in Santa Monica, and you can live there till you finish college. Or I can sell the house and use the money to send you to any educational institution you can get into, anywhere in the world, to study anything you want. Or I can buy you a round-trip ticket to Tokyo so you can go with John and have the freedom to come back if it doesn't work out."

She stands in the doorway a moment longer, then says, "I gotta go. Exams tomorrow. I'll call you."

She disappears back into her life with John and I hear no more from her for several weeks. Then suddenly she is there, as before, in the open doorway of my cabin.

"I want to transfer to the University of California at Davis."

"UC Davis? Up near Sacramento?" Place names in the long hot valley of central California are hardly on my mental map. "Why?"

"It has the best vet school in the world in an area that doesn't snow."

"Oh." I try to sort out the likely threads of her reasoning. "I thought, I mean, you're so good at languages, and art ... I know you've done really well in school, but you've only had one science class. Are you sure you want to be a veterinarian?"

She flops down on the couch in the old confident way I remember from her childhood. "I could probably make a living with art but it's no challenge; like, it's just too easy. And what can you do with languages except teach or translate? I'd have to live in the city to get a good job."

She picks up a sheet of manuscript that has fallen to the floor and begins to doodle horses in the margin. "I want to live in a rural area. I can't just live on the land because I want expensive horses and they cost money. So I'll be a vet. You know I've always liked animals better than people." She flings the sketch aside. "Want to go horseback riding?"

We saddle the neighbor's horses and ride up the wild hillside behind my cottage. On the ridge we stop to let them graze on a patch of grass freshened by recent rains.

"What's happening with you and John?" I ask.

Jo fiddles with the bridle reins. I can see she hates my probing. "He feels trapped, and so do I."

"You think he doesn't love you anymore?"

"Not the way I need to be loved."

"And how is that?"

"I don't know." She turns her horse sharply and gallops up the mountainside, blonde mane flying.

Jo moves to central California and very nearly out of my life. Three years later I try to close the gap by buying us tickets to Europe for her twenty-first birthday, but the timing is all wrong. She is keen to explore the world, but not in the context of a dominating companion. The European jaunt merely whets her appetite. When she graduates from university six months later, she gives herself what she really needs. She joins the Peace Corps and, unburdened by man *or* mother, vanishes to Africa.

Two years later she is back in California to enroll in "the best vet school in the world where it doesn't snow." When I visit her she seems more tolerant than welcoming, and I am offended by how quickly she takes offense at anything I say. Our conversations become increasingly superficial. I try to look interested as she talks about classes and complains about teachers, then tell her what I've been writing, knowing she hasn't bothered to read most of my published articles. She lives with three cats that are never permitted outdoors. Had anyone asked during these years, we would have agreed that we had very little in common.

Yet on the wall above her desk, as on the wall above mine, there is a photograph of a young margay. I never ask why it is there, and she doesn't ask, on my brief visits, why I stare at it so long. With a silence like that between us, there is no way of knowing what each of us remember of the year we lived with Hopi.

Ultimately it is Jo who breaks the silence, not by speaking of the margay who has been a part of our memory so long that it has become part of us, but with a casual remark that obliquely acknowledges our inability to forget.

"Have you ever watched that TV show, *Wild Kingdom?*"

"Once or twice."

"There's a cowboy on it who used to live in Guyana. He says that besides jaguars and ocelots, Guyana has two different types of margays."

A month later I phone to tell her I am going to Guyana.

There is a long silence on the other end of the line. Then she asks, "Mind if I come along?"

TRAVELING WITH MY DAUGHTER

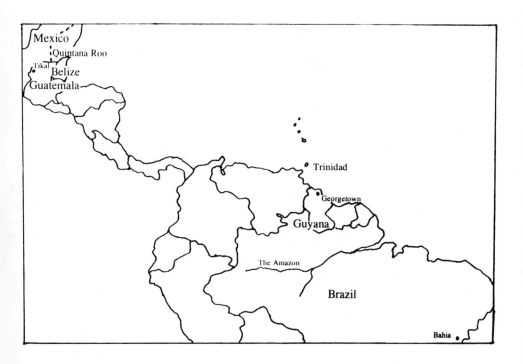

GUYANA

"Californians!" The official adds a spitting hiss at the end of the word. "What you want in Guyana?"

"A holiday," I say blandly.

I had intended to do more research before we left, but as usual, arrive knowing only what I gleaned from a guidebook on the flight down — a brief entry made even less informative by the fact that most of it was not about Guyana but about the Jonestown massacre.

"What kind of holiday?" His suspicion is well-founded, considering that Guyana has no tourist industry.

I might reply that we're looking for an exotic cat called a margay, which is listed in Appendix A of the international agreement which bans trade in endangered species, which we would like to have but wouldn't take from the jungle, and want to own although it's not allowed. But why confuse a bureaucrat with the truth when he already appears on the verge of refusing us entry because we have California addresses in our passports?

"I'm a veterinarian," Jo says coolly. "I plan to attend the Commonwealth Veterinarian Conference. This is my mother."

The official looks from her to me, comparing features. My brown hair is woven into a long braid against the heat. Although I am only five feet tall, I know that people do not perceive me as petite. Jo is taller by six inches, and also imposes a sense of strength. He looks into our eyes for a final confirmation of kinship. We stare back at him with blue and blue-green irises, conveying more confidence than either of us feel.

The man smiles unexpectedly. "Enjoy Guyana," he says, and brings his stamp down on our passports with a swift thud-thud.

In the taxi I ask Jo, "What veterinary conference?"

"I don't know," she replies cheerfully. "I heard a guy on the plane talking about it, complaining because it's being held in Guyana."

"Why do you suppose the official was so nasty when he saw we were from California?"

"They crazy," the taxi driver says over his shoulder.

Jo leans forward. "Sorry. What was that?"

"You didn't hear about Jonestown? Crazy Californians come down here and kill theyself in the jungle. Weren't no Guyanese at all except one nineteen-year-old boy they found tied up where Jones' people murdered him, and some Amerindian children left there by their parents for medical treatment. Some treatment! The way they show it on the news, and a lot of Jones' people being black, everybody think they Guyanese. I heard one Englishman say Jim Jones from Guyana. They already forget he from California."

We are on a heavily-trafficked highway which bears no resemblance to the steamy jungle scenes that blazed across the TV screen at the time of the massacre. We cross a wide brown river, pass through a derelict residential area, and cruise down a boulevard lined with Victorian mansions.

"Wow! So where do we hunt margays? In the rose gardens or out back on the croquet court?

"I thought Guyana was a communist country. I'm sure I read that somewhere."

"That Cheddi Jagan you thinkin' of, but he not communist," the taxi driver calls over his shoulder. "More like socialist. The British and Americans, they brought him down. Twenty-two years we stuck with their man Burnham. Now we got Comrade Hoyte. But Jagan, he a good man. They ever leave us alone, you see Cheddi gonna be the president of this Cooperative Republic of Guyana."

"What I want to know," I mutter that evening as we sit at the hotel bar, "is why we're spending our first night in this commie-socialist-cooperative-republic watching Dan Rather on the six o'clock news?"

Jo looks annoyed. She has missed my intended humor and registers it as a complaint. I turn back to the TV, wondering if this trip was a mistake. Certainly the last one we made together, to Europe, had done nothing to bring us closer. I'd sent her the airfare and Eurorail Pass as a combination twenty-first birthday/university graduation gift and said I'd meet her in Paris. I had expected her to cover the remaining trip expenses herself. She had arrived in Paris with $25, confident that whatever more she needed would come from somewhere. And so it had. While I counted pennies and borrowed from Jeff to cover her expenses, she took my fretting as evidence that I was a chronic complainer and hopelessly neurotic about money.

That was then and this is now, but I am still jittery about those criticisms she leveled at me a decade ago. As for the ones I hurled back at her about being self-centered and irresponsible, well ... little wonder we're both walking on eggshells, not sure of each other, or ourselves.

I'm still traveling on a tight budget, and dealing in foreign currency does make me nervous. But why work myself into a migraine over it? Jo uses the calculator on her wrist watch to figure exchange rates as efficiently as a international banker. I'll just turn my money over to her this trip, and let her do the juggling. My tension-generated grumpiness eases. I turn to smile at her.

"Look." Jo points to the television screen. In place of the usual TV commercial is a typed list of local activities. "The Guyana Veterinary Society is advertising an after lunch meeting tomorrow. Let's go see if we can get some information on wildlife."

When we arrive we learn that in Guyana an "after lunch" is not a meeting but a party which begins after lunch and lasts until dawn of the following day. The music is so loud it drowns out questions as well as answers, but eventually it becomes clear to someone (not us) who we want to see. A beautiful black woman with close-cropped curls is dragged off the dance floor and introduced as Dr. Karen Pilgrim, National Wildlife Director. She and Jo compare notes as best they can above the noise, and discover that they are the same age and graduated from different U.S. vet schools the same year. Then Dr. Pilgrim excuses herself and returns to the dance floor. Jo and I look at each other, shrug, and leave.

Back at the hotel we agree on one thing: we did not come all the way to Guyana to sit around a hotel. We are going into the rainforest, although we have no idea how to do this in a country with few roads, and rivers that turn into impassable rapids fifty miles inland. We are studying the map when the phone rings. It is Dr. Pilgrim.

"I'll come by in the morning," she says, "and take you around."

For two days Dr. Pilgrim drives us along just about every paved road in Guyana. As indicated on the map, these extend only a few miles beyond urban and suburban areas along the coast. She takes us to the museum, the botanical garden, and the zoo.

There are no native wildcats in the Georgetown zoo, only a solitary lion which Dr. Pilgrim tells us has been here ten years or so, a gift from the head of some African state. The lion paces continuously, pausing only when someone stops in front of his cage. He stands motionless now, staring out at us with gold killer eyes.

My mouth feels dry. "That cage ... it's way too small."

Karen leans languidly against a tree, a bit catlike herself, I am thinking; smooth, brown, and infinitely graceful in her movements.

"I had this idea of dredging canals in the botanical garden and making islands for the animals to live on. But no one was interested."

"As National Wildlife Director, couldn't you make it happen?" Jo, who envies Karen's position, sounds surprised.

"Guyana's not ready to take wildlife preservation seriously." Karen's smile carries neither humor nor sarcasm, but a placid acceptance which Jo and I do not understand. "Our government hasn't even signed the international accords prohibiting export of endangered species because it doesn't want to lose the foreign exchange."

"We'd like to get into the jungle," Jo says. "To see whatever we can of your wildlife. Is that possible?"

"There's an animal trader going up the Demerara River sometime in the next couple of days. I'll ask him to take you."

The trader is an expatriate German who buys exotic species from hunters and exports them to zoos in Europe. All day and into the night we motor along the Demerara River, stopping at clearings in the jungle to pick up tropical birds and reptiles.

"You hold that end," the German says to Jo, handing her the tail of a python. He tries to lay a tape measure against the snake, its price being determined by its length. The snake keeps coiling. I can't bear to watch.

"Don't worry. It's not dangerous," the trader assures me. To Jo he says, "If it gets a coil around your face, try to get your hands up so it doesn't cut off your wind. What've we got here? Nine feet, three inches?"

At each camp we broach the subject of margays, and from each hunter we get one of several answers that soon become repetitious. "Little cats? Oh yeah, lots of them. You wanna see some pelts?" Or, "Shoot 'em on sight, the little bastards. A dog take after one, it tear that dog to pieces. Can't afford to lose a good dog like that."

When we see Karen again, we thank her for arranging the trip, and try not to show our disappointment at not seeing any margays, but she senses it, and phones again the next day. "There's a trader named Cleo in town. They say she's got a margay."

Cleo is bony, fast-talking, and friendly. She simultaneously pours coffee, answers the phone, gives instructions to a workman building a crate for two sloths, and carries on a conversation with us.

"Oh yeah, I had a margay. Lot of trouble to catch one. You got to bait the trap with a live monkey, a young one, you know, that cries a lot. Then wait for the cat to pounce on it. Don't know how many traps the boys had to set. Took them over a month. We were going to make a video, that's what we wanted it for. But I had to go to Miami, and while I was gone the boys run out of rice and let it starve to death. Last week this was. Too bad you didn't get here sooner."

She splashes more coffee into our cups, yells at the workman, and lights a cigarette. "So you looking for a margay, are you? The boys can bring one in, I'm sure of that, if you got the time to wait and the money."

"No!" I say quickly. "We were just interested in seeing one."

"They're pretty rare," Jo remarks. "They're an endangered species."

Cleo scoffs. "Not in Guyana, they're not."

We escape Cleo's chaotic household and walk up the street past big houses more ramshackled than those on the main boulevard. "I've learned more about traffic in exotic species than I ever wanted to know," I grumble.

"We're lucky we came face to face with it this soon," Jo says thoughtfully. "The attitude that there are plenty of animals and they're not animals, really, just merchandise — you know what I mean?"

"You mean if we're not careful somebody's going to get the idea we're customers and kill a dozen monkeys trying to trap a margay for us."

"That's right." Jo pauses to scratch between the horns of a milk goat tethered in the weedy strip beside the boulevard. "But if we're not customers, what are we?"

"Hunters. Without guns. Without traps. With just ... imagination."

"Are we trying to recapture the past?"

"I don't think so. I don't know." I grin at her. "Whatever it is, it's been fun so far."

She cuts her eyes at me, and for a minute, I'm not sure how to read the look. Then I realize that it's one of relief. She has been as uncertain of my acceptance on this trip as I have been of hers. She takes my remark for approval — which it was.

"Yes," she agrees. "So far so good."

The remainder of our time in Guyana we keep our eyes open and our mouths shut. We catch rides down rutted roads with loggers and up rivers with gold miners. We see crocodiles and snakes and brilliant birds. But the only exotic cat we see in Guyana is the lion in the Georgetown zoo. When we return to the capital, we walk out to the zoo again.

When the lion sees us coming he stops pacing. His hot gold eyes follow our movements as if we are mice.

"It's inhumane, a cage that small," I fume. "If I had a key!"

"You'd let him out?" Jo scoffs. "Look at those eyes and tell me that if you had a key right now you'd open the door."

I am looking into the lion's eyes; I cannot look anywhere else. His desire for freedom, it seems, is dead. In its place, in place of everything he has lost, is the purest hatred I have ever seen. If ever he has the chance, there isn't the slightest doubt that he will kill first, then maybe, just maybe, remember freedom and run.

"I would! I'd leap onto his back and hang onto his mane and we'd be gone in a flash!"

Jo shakes her head at my nonsense. "This isn't the gentle lion god out of a C.S. Lewis story. All this old boy wants is vengeance."

"He deserves it!" I am furious with the Africans who have taken him captive, with the Guyanese who keep him here, and with myself. If I were half as bold as my fantasy the lion would not spend his life in a cage. He would be as free as I am or — I turn away, defeated by the truth of Jo's statement — we would both be dead.

We head for the zoo exit, not talking much. There is something in the lion's situation that takes us back to the time Hopi died, when there was nothing either of us could do, not even comfort each other. Is this what the margay search is all about? Our wanting to do it over again, only this time make it come out right, for the kitten and for each other?

We cross the botanical garden next to the zoo, stop at a broken traffic light, and wait for a flow of beat-up cars and a herd of zebu cattle to go past.

"What are we going to do?" Jo asks.

"What *are* we doing?"

"Uh ... hunting margays?" She flips me a grin that says, Stop fretting, Ma. You're just making things worse.

I grin back. "Oh yeah. For a minute I thought we were in the middle of a city breathing exhaust fumes, listening to a scratchy sound system blaring Christmas carols in hundred-degree heat. We're having an adventure, right?"

She arches an eyebrow at me. "You're the one who says adventure begins when you're not sure where the road you're on is taking you."

If I'm reading internal signs right, the road we're on, here on the outskirts of steamy Georgetown, Guyana, is taking us toward a relationship we haven't had before. Before we get home, two uncertain but independent women are each going to make a decision about the other's value as travel companion and friend. If adventure is not knowing how things will turn out, this trip can't be anything else.

BRAZIL

As the Amazon flows green beneath the wings of our plane, Jo talks about various lovers she has had since John. I marvel at how she manages to disentangle herself from men when they no longer meet her needs, but in a way that retains their affection. After John, there was a six-month fling with Dave, a boy her own age she'd known since junior high. Next it was Mauricio, a Salvadoran pre-med student we both adored, who lived with her until she graduated from university. She ended that affair, but not their friendship, when she went into the Peace Corps. I had hoped that she and Mauricio would get back together, but he'd recently married someone else.

"The wedding was beautiful," Jo sighed. "I cried all the way through it, and kept asking myself why I ever left him."

"Why did you?"

"He was insanely jealous."

"Ah." We both laugh.

"What about John?"

"What do you mean, what about John?"

"Was he jealous?"

"Well, sure. But mainly he was ..." She grimaces.

"What?"

"An education." There is a hint of resentment in Jo's voice and I think I know why. John was a teacher and being older, unconsciously parental. Leaving him had been more than a separation of lovers; it had been an act of rebellion.

Even so, he had gone on loving Jo, and was devastated when he returned from Japan and found she had a new boyfriend. Yet their friendship had survived, and when he invited us to visit, Jo said she wouldn't mind spending a few days with him and his Brazilian family.

"How often do you hear from him?"

"He wrote pretty often from Japan, and occasionally from Argentina, and then — was it Columbia? Anyway, he had hepatitis there and nearly died. Not much since he settled in Brazil. He really likes it there. Keeps saying how un-bourgeois it is. He's married to a local lady, and has two children." Jo grins mischievously. "How's that for un-bourgeois?"

John, for all the sideburns gone gray, looks more the boy than he did at twenty-five. Still skinny and slightly awkward, he does the socially correct things with an air of self-consciousness, like a high school student on a first date. He introduces us as "family" to his wife Marina. She enfolds us in a cadence of words as melodious as the *bosa nova*. She holds first Jo's face then mine in her hands to kiss.

"Welcome," she says in a way that leaves no doubt that she means it.

"We have another houseguest," John explains. "A Canadian, Robbie. I think you'll like him."

Soon after we arrive at the apartment, Robbie shows up carrying a shoe box with holes punched in the top. John looks at it with suspicion, Jo with interest. Robbie lifts off the lid. Inside are two incredibly tiny monkeys.

"Oh my god!" John groans. "Robbie, what have you done?"

Robbie looks hurt. "They were selling them in the market. Some ragamuffin boys had them tied up with dirty string in the hot sun, no water or anything. I couldn't just leave them!"

"Don't you know they'll just go out and catch some more?"

Jo cups one of the tiny creatures in each hand. "I had no idea such small monkeys existed. Are they native to this area?"

"I think so," John answers. "I've seen wild ones on Itaparica."

"That's an island just off shore, where we have a summer house. You can see it from here." Marina points across the bay.

For several days debates rages over what to do with the monkeys. Robbie will be leaving soon and cannot possibly take them. He wants to give them to John's small sons for pets, but Marina is concerned that they might transmit some disease to the children. However, the maid is charmed by them and asks John if she can have them for her children.

"I don't know," John equivocates. "They belong to Robbie."

"She has eleven kids," Marina frowns. "She needs a couple of monkeys like she needs another baby."

That evening as we sit in a restaurant having dinner, Jo asks John not to give the monkeys to the maid. "They'll need a special diet. And they're so fragile, being handled by all those children ... They'd have a better chance of survival if I took them back with me."

"You mean smuggle them back?" Marina asks.

"Why not?" Jo grins.

Robbie shakes his head. "I don't know what they'd do if they caught you bringing contraband monkeys into the States, but in Canada you'd probably lose your veterinary licence."

Jo smiles sweetly. "How on earth would they catch me?"

"There's *no way* to get through customs with those little devils," John says firmly.

Two hours later, as we are lingering over desert, Jo reaches into her blouse and extracts two very tiny, very sleepy monkeys.

"Oops. I thought they might be hungry, but I see they want to nap a little longer." Laughing at our amazement, she tucks them back into her cleavage, from whence comes not a sound for the rest of the evening.

At bedtime Jo and I sit out on the balcony and discuss the pros and cons of smuggling the monkeys into the U.S. Since they have already been captured and sold, we have no moral dilemma on that score; the damage has been done, and not by us. Nor have we any concerns about disease. As a veterinarian, Jo would obviously follow stringent quarantine procedures. On the other hand, could they survive if they were returned to the wild?

"The trouble is that we know absolutely nothing about this species. We don't even know how old these little guys are. John says the ones he's seen on Itaparica are tiny, so maybe ... who knows?"

"I took the risk for Hopi, but I was passionate about her. I don't have the same attachment to the monkeys. Do you?"

"Not really," Jo admits.

"Well, I think that's what it comes down to. Your desire to have them weighed against the risk you'd be taking."

"I wish we had time to stay and see to their release ourselves. That way we'd at least know if they are able to feed themselves, and whether wild monkeys in the area will tolerate them."

But we don't have time. We had not expected to find wildlife in the city, and had planned to spend only a few days with John, the rest of the trip in more remote parts of Brazil. We have at least two weeks more of traveling before we start back. We had come to Brazil via Miami, Guyana, and Trinidad, and our return tickets follow the same route.

"We'll have to clear customs not just at one border but three, you know. That makes it more or less three times the risk I took with Hopi. But it's up to you."

The day before we leave, John invites me to lunch at a former monastery in the old part of town. I ask him, in the cool, high-vaulted dining room, what he meant by calling us family. His nervous laugh rises from habit, but his eyes are serious.
"There's a bond with your first love that outlives the romance. No matter who you meet later or marry, in some ways you remain connected like, well, like siblings. There are just things you always remember, always know, about that person." John's long fingers move compulsively, drawing invisible, interconnected circles on the white tablecloth.
"It's no accident that I've never had a daughter," he says darkly. "Marina's — it was stillborn. We do pay. Even for what we couldn't have done differently."

Jo decides that she will not attempt to smuggle the monkeys back if John will promise to release them at Itaparica. He agrees, and does so, soon after our departure. Later he writes that the little creatures scampered around the yard of his island cottage for awhile, apparently happy, then climbed into a palm tree and disappeared.
I sometimes wonder whether I should have encouraged Jo to keep them. As it is, we will never know whether our decision gave them freedom, saved them from suffering, or brought them death.
On the flight home I tell Jo what John said about his daughter having been stillborn as some kind of retribution for the abortion.
Her normally modulated voice flares with contempt. "John and that Calvinistic God of his! How can he be so moralistic and self-indulgent at the same time?"
"I think he has some doubts, that's all," I defend feebly. "Don't you?"
"When I think I ought to be raising a child that's what I'll do. If John feels so guilty, why doesn't he adopt a starving street kid? There's certainly no shortage of them in Brazil."
I nod, agreeing completely, yet cannot escape a lump of tension, the punishing grip of John's vengeful god, on my neck.
Jo senses the tension, and lays a hand on my arm. "Everything that's happened," she says quietly, "played a part in making me who I am. And I like who I am."

QUINTANA ROO

In October 1989 I open a *National Geographic* and see, illustrating an article entitled "La Ruta Maya," a color photo of a magnificent margay. Three months later Jo and I fly to the Yucatán.

On the shore of Cenote Azul we lie in our hammocks looking up at stars blurred by the mesh of mosquito netting. I retell the story of coming here almost two decades earlier, of finding and crying and buying Hopichen. The following morning we go for a swim in the deep blue water, then sit on the bank remembering the margay.

"Would you really have taken her away from me?" I ask Jo.

"Probably. I think I hated you that year."

"Why?" Even now I am stung by the injustice of it.

"I don't know. Maybe because you were so sure of yourself."

"Me?" I laugh at the absurdity. "I've never been sure of anything. Except how easy it is to get trapped. So many times ..."

So many times I thought I had achieved the perfect balance of independence and connectedness, only to discover that what I'd taken as a connection was somebody's idea that I belonged to them. Better I let that pass. If I try to explain it to Jo, won't she point out that I treated her like that? Does she know I gave her exceptional freedoms to keep her from seeing me, and me seeing myself, as the trap? I shiver.

"You're cold." Jo touches my hair which has come loose from its braid and lays in wet tangles over my shoulders.

"When was I so sure of myself?"

"Like when you smuggled Hopi across the border. I said, 'What if they catch you?' and you said, 'I won't get caught.'"

"Well, I didn't, did I?"

"But what if they had discovered her? What would you've done?"

"I'd have made a run for it."

"They'd have shot you!" Her voice pitches high with indignation.

"What else could I do? Let them put her in a cage? No way! Her and you and me, it was all the same!"

There is a long silence. Then she asks, "Why did we go to Mexico that year anyway?"

"How else could I have let you drop out of school and take a grown man as a lover?"

"Teenagers do that sort of thing all the time."

"Not with parental approval. It's against the law."

Jo looks at me in surprise. "You mean you could have gone to jail?"

"And you could have gone to reform school."

"We both could've ended up in a cage."

"Yes." I grin at her. "So we ran away. Are you sorry?"

"About what?"

"Having so much freedom."

"I never thought about it like that."

I look at her, incredulous. "You never felt free?"

"Oh, I know I was in a way. But you always attached so much responsibility to it; I think I got the message right away that 'freedom' isn't just rah, rah, go ahead and do whatever you please."

"What do you mean?"

"Don't you remember when John and I decided to start sleeping together, how you made each of us tell you what we would do to prevent my getting pregnant, *and* what we'd do if it failed?" Her foot, dangling in the water, flicks a few drops at me. "And when I was in college, remember saying you'd help me get a car only if I took drivers' ed *and* a class in auto mechanics?"

"I remember you saying I was stingy. Calling me neurotic."

"Well, sure, the strings made me mad. And I suppose your strength, or at least your energy, intimidated me."

I wrap my arms around myself, feeling cold in spite of the warming air. "So what do you want — a different gene pool?"

"And have to go hunting by myself?" She hands me a towel. "For Pete's sake, we're in the tropics. Stop shivering, will you?"

BELIZE

We are standing in a beautiful room oppressive with death. It is the home of Bader Hassan, formerly an internationally-known jaguar hunter, more recently a man whose intimate knowledge of jaguars made him indispensable to the development of the world's first jaguar preserve.

"Assuming he left any jaguars to preserve," Jo whispers, gazing around at the jaguar hides tacked on walls and thrown across a gleaming hardwood floor.

"Belize still has the largest concentration of jaguars in the world. But this guy—"

Suddenly Bader is standing there, a compact man with tousled brown hair, face broad and ruddy, like a farmer's. He smiles at us in the watchful manner of a rural person who has knowledge which he doesn't expect a city person to understand.

"We're looking for someone to take us up the river," I explain. "People recommended you; they said you had a boat."

He does not answer promptly, but stands there assessing us. Then he replies with polite directness. "You couldn't afford it. It's a big boat, for groups going in a week at a time, like that."

"Are you a hunting guide then?" Jo asks. "You hunt jaguars?"

He responds simply, as to a child. "Not cats. That's against the law now. Except for science — catching them live and tagging them for study."

"Sounds dangerous." There is something electric in Jo's voice, not a challenge, but close.

"Yes. I lost one of my boys."

"A jaguar killed him?"

"No. Tommy-goff. The snake you call *fer de lance*."

"We'd like to see jungle cats," I tell him. "In the wild."

His reply carries the same note of patience-with-a-child. "I have lived in Belize and hunted the jaguar all my life, lady, and even I have seen jaguars in the wild no more than a dozen times. They see you but you don't see them." He smiles kindly. "But I will show you my own cats, if you like."

He takes us into a back yard with several cages. From one he looses a large brown puma. She rubs her head against his thigh and purrs.

"How long have you had her?" Jo asks.

"Since she was a kitten. We have to keep her penned at night because she kills the neighbors' chickens. Otherwise she's one of the family, same as the dogs. You can pet her."

I scratch behind the cougar's ears. She purrs and lifts her head to the touch.

"Have you ever felt a cougar's tongue?" He takes my hand and holds it to the animal's mouth. She drags a sandpaper tongue across the palm, then noses it away and takes Bader's hand into her mouth. She holds it between great white teeth and gnaws gently, carressingly.

"Have you ever domesticated a jaguar?" Jo asks.

"I've raised them. But nobody tames a jaguar. As soon as they get big, they're dangerous. They will kill."

"Like humans," I say.

He glances up at me. "Yes," he says. "Like us."

"How about margays?" Jo asks.

"I have one." He walks across the yard to another cage. A well-fed male margay growls at him. He stares at it a moment with a slightly bewildered expression, the look of a person who knows a lot, but not quite enough to make sense of the situation at hand.

"I raised this one from a kitten. He was the sweetest little thing. Lived right in the house for, I don't know, a couple years. Then we went away on vacation and I had to leave him with a caretaker, in a cage. When we got back, it was like he couldn't stand the sight of me. He was still affectionate with my wife, but whenever I came in the room, he'd jump me. I thought he'd get over it but he never did. Never forgave me for locking him up. I finally had to put him out here. He was just too dangerous."

As Bader walks us to the gate, he tells us, "If you want to go up the river just for a day, maybe to the ruins of Lamanai, there's a Mennonite family that might take you."

"How do we find them?"

He points to a small road leading off the main highway through fields of sugarcane. "Just wait over there. When a sugarcane truck comes by, wave it down, and ask the driver to carry you to the second Mennonite farm past Guinea Grass."

We walk over to the road and wait. I peel an orange, thinking about Bader. "He didn't seem like a killer, did he?"

"What do you mean?" Jo asks.

"I think of a killer being hot with hatred, like the lion in the Guyana zoo. Either that or cold, with no feelings at all."

Jo gazes at the field of rippling green sugarcane. "It isn't a matter of having or not having feelings," she says finally. "You just have to be without feeling for the thing you're about to kill."

When the sugarcane truck lets us off at the Mennonite farm, it's as if we have been dropped into rural America of the 1920s. A woman and eight big daughters are out in the yard doing a massive family laundry. Jo and I approach to ask about the boat for hire, but they do not understand any language we speak. One of the girls calls for her father. He looks like any midwestern farmer in bib overalls, but speaks Spanish. Yes, he says, he has a boat which can take us up the river to the Lamanai ruins, but we will have to wait a couple of hours, until his sons return at lunch.

"What language do your wife and daughters speak?" Jo asks the man.

"German."

"Oh, are you from Germany?"

"My wife and I were born in Mexico, and our children all born here in Belize. My sons and I speak Spanish of necessity, but our women speak only German, the language of our forefathers."

"Don't your children go to school?" Jo asks.

"As the law requires," he replies stiffly.

"Would you rather they didn't?"

He purses his lips. "A little schooling does no harm. They learn to read. It is good to be able to read the Bible."

Jo and I park ourselves under a tree and watch the women, who keep their heads bent over their work.

"Do you see something peculiar about that laundry?" I ask Jo.

"You mean that antique wringer washer they're using?"

"No, the laundry itself."

She studies the long lines of pastel dresses, overalls, denim shirts, table clothes and towels drying in the breeze.

"There's no underwear," she says finally. "Not a single piece. What do you suppose that means? They wash it by hand, or they don't wear any?"

I tell her what I'd heard from an American woman who once lived near a Mennonite farm. She had been visited by twelve Mennonite elders who politely asked her to refrain from hanging her underthings in public view where they would "inflame the passions of our young men."

At noon four strapping boys arrive in a horse-drawn cart. The youngest, about eighteen, is designated to take us up the river.

"My wife will come with you," says the father, cutting a meaningful glance at Jo's halter top.

"You're going to be chaperoned, " I tease Jo. "How's that for adventure travel?"

"I'd say it's their son they're concerned about," she giggles. "I certainly wouldn't trust any young man whose passions can be inflamed by the sight of underwear on a clothesline!"

I smile at the big boy who is busy cranking the outboard motor. He blushes as if I have made a suggestive remark, and for the rest of the trip, keeps his eyes carefully averted.

It is not a straight-forward river run to Lamanai, but requires navigating through a maze of waterways that remind me of the Florida Everglades. The boy chooses not to walk through the Mayan ruins with us, but his mother follows along, studying the ancient stone faces with interest.

When we have finished exploring Lamanai, the guide offers to show us the colonial ruins of Indian Church, about half a mile away. Hiking along the river to Indian Church, we come upon what looks to be the camp of at least a hundred people, although there is no one around. The shelters are no more than unwalled palm thatch roofs on poles. There are no mud ovens for baking, only the simple stone circle of a campfire outside each shelter. There are not even bits of plastic debris or the old tin cans one often finds recycled as cooking utensils in such places. The only thing that resembles dishes are stacks of clean coconut hulls and pointed sticks. I am intrigued by the level of primitiveness. Even in the Amazon one finds hammocks. Here, it appears, the people sleep on piles of leaves. I ask our guide what sort of people they are.

"Salvadorans," he says. "There are many in Belize now, who have come to escape the war."

"Where is everybody?"

"On the river, fishing."

"Everybody?"

"Either that or in the forest, looking for food." He clicks his tongue. "You can see they have nothing. This is how they come — with nothing."

As the Mennonite woman walks beside me I feel her longing to communicate but there is nothing I can do other than smile — an expression which she does not return. Finally she points to herself and flashes fingers indicating a number. I realize she is telling me her age. I sign to her that mine is the same. She clamps her lips, as if to keep a smile from passing them, but her eyes show delight. She then points to Jo, and asks in sign language how many children I have. Just one, I tell her. She looks at me in astonishment and, allowing the smile to slip out, signs that she has twelve.

When we return to the farm, she shouts for her family and has all twelve children stand in a row, from eldest to youngest. She points proudly to each one, saying the child's name and holding up fingers to indicate age. Jo and I smile, but they only stare at us, solemn-faced. Smiling, it seems, is too frivolous an activity to be acceptable in this culture.

Jo and I are following no particular itinerary. We leave Belize City in the late morning, on a bus chosen at random. It is filled with local people — blacks, Mayans, Salvadoran refugees, and Mennonite men in their pastel shirts and denim overalls.

"There's a zoo coming up soon," says Jo, one finger in the guide book, the other on our map. "No towns nearby. Looks like it's right out in the bush. Let's take a look."

"Zoos make me sick. It's like staring at prison inmates."

"Zoos are very important," Jo says huffily. "Without them and the consciousness they bring to people about animals, half the endangered species we know would already be wiped out."

"That's what zoo-keepers tell themselves because they don't want to face the fact that they're jailers," I retort.

Jo stands up and pulls her pack from the overhead rack. "If you want to go on, that's fine with me. Where shall we meet?"

I sigh, reach for my pack, and follow her off the bus.

It is unbearably hot. The jungle has been cleared for miles around, its thin soil briefly farmed, then abandoned to regrow into scruffy, waist-high brush. A clump of trees — presumably the zoo — is visible a mile off.

"Nice they put it in a rural area like this," Jo says with maddening cheeriness. "Remember that Brazilian army zoo we stumbled on in the Amazon, all those animals they used for jungle warfare training?"

I remember, and know what she is driving at. The military zoo had every species of jungle cat in the Western Hemisphere, all in good health and placid as domestic animals. The instructors, who used them to show Brazilian army recruits from the city and North American soldiers down for jungle warfare training what wildlife they could expect to encounter in the Amazon, showed no fear of cougars and jaguars, let alone smaller species like ocelots and margays. Why should they? After all, these were men who conducted classes in the killing of poisonous snakes with bare hands and how to wrestle crocodiles in the water. One instructor had let his three-year-old daughter tumble about with a puma as if it were a big dog. When Jo asked whether the animal was trustworthy, he had shrugged and said that all the big cats in the zoo were accustomed to being handled. I am thinking now that Jo remembers the puma's sleek complacency, and imagines it to be some sort of ideal in human/animal relations. What I remember are the cages, which as in every other zoo, were iron bar cells.

The Belize Zoo is nothing like what I imagined. Large patches of native vegetation are fenced with chicken wire, giving the place the feel of a weedy farm. Each pen has a hand-painted sign emphasizing that wild animals should not be caged. One cage contains three margays, and a sign explaining that they have been donated by people who thought they were "cute" but grew tired of them because, like most wild animals, they do not make good pets. The little margays look strong and healthy. I wonder if they could survive in the wild or if, like Hopi, they were captured so young that they never learned to hunt.

The jaguar cage is as large as a corral. There are bushes and trees in it, but no jaguars. We ask an attendant where the big cats are.

"They escaped last week," she explains. "Two of them. We think they climbed high enough into one of the trees to leap over the fence. A farmer spotted them not far from here and shot them."

I turn away, feeling sick. "I'll meet you at the entrance," I tell Jo.

When Jo comes out a half hour later, I'm feeling better. I have read news clippings in the gift shop about the founding of the zoo, and want to tell her about Sharon Matola, the American "lion tamer" who came to Belize with a Mexican circus and started this, the only zoo in Belize, with jaguars abandoned by a British film company, and how Sharon accepts only native species already in captivity that are unfit for release into the wild, and uses them to dramatize the importance of preserving habitat.

As we walk back toward the highway Jo listens to the Sharon Matola story with interest and adds more. "Apparently a U.S. firm has designed a new zoo *pro bono*. Sharon's out raising money now to build it."

As we talk my energy drains away. Maybe it's the heat, or the fact that it's mid-afternoon and we haven't yet had lunch. Or an image, in my mind's eye, of the jaguars running for their lives across this sandy wasteland in search of the thick tropical forests which should have been here to provide them cover. My pensiveness oppresses Jo.

"You liked those funky chicken wire cages, didn't you?" she says crossly. "Or better yet, no cages at all. You don't even care that the jaguars got out and got killed. You think they're better off dead!"

"They are!" I flare. "I'm not even born to wildness and I'd rather be dead than caged. Just imagine what it's like for a wild animal. Humans are disgusting! They cage or kill every living thing they can get their hands on. Cage it or kill it, that's all they know!" I turn on Jo, truly furious. "You think that's the only choice there is — be caged or be dead!"

"The jaguars *are* dead! Hopi is dead!" Jo, who never shouts, is shouting. Her face is dangerously red.

"And *we* are alive, and free. But it could've been the other way around. A few seconds here, a few there, and Hopi might've made it. The jaguars might've gotten away. Haven't you ever had a close call? Do you want to live in a cage just so you'll be safer?"

"No." Jo kneels on the hot sand road, a strong woman melted like soft wax into the form of a sobbing child. "I just don't want things to die."

I lean over her, to provide what little shade I can from the blazing sun.

"Listen," I plead. "Listen to me. It's death that brings death. Not freedom."

Then I am crying, too, knowing that nothing so abstract as words can ease the anguish that batters us both when something we love has died.

GUATEMALA

Many travelers had told us that we should come to Tikal at full moon, but we ignored their inarticulate sputterings about "magic," "energy" and "spirits" of the ruins. Now that we are here, even though the moon is two nights past full, I understand why no one was able to convey the experience of Tikal in moonlight. Not even a vocabulary of mysticism can describe this ruined city the way it describes itself.

We sit on steps of a temple built to a jaguar god. Howler monkey cries and a symphony of other animal sounds swell in the fading light, then gradually die away. I think of Bader Hassan, how he transformed himself from jaguar hunter to jaguar protector; his understanding that humans and cats are equal in their ability to show affection and hold a grudge; their readiness to love and to kill. The air around us is warm and barely moving, like the breath of something close.

"Do you feel something?" Jo asks in a whisper.

"It's just the jaguar god prowling around." I make a joke of it, though the sense of presence is strong.

"Maybe it wants something from us."

"Like what?"

"I'm not sure. A scratch between the ears, maybe?"

Although it's dark, I know she's smiling.

We bus from Tikal to Flores, a provincial capital tightly packed onto a small island in Lake Petan-Itza. Along the way we pass a huge military installation and a mile-long line of conscripts being forced to run in the brutal sun at a pace set by men in a jeep. Once we are on the island Flores seems peaceful, its colonial charm only slightly corroded by the commonplace sight of armed men whose eyes everyone avoids.

We wander down to the lakeshore, but it's too contaminated for swimming. A boy with a boat for hire offers to take us to *el biotopo*.

Only when we disembark on the pretty little island do we realize that it is, in fact, a rather nasty zoo with cages far too small for the animals confined there. In one a jaguar lays on a floor long unwashed, mauling a bloody bone. In another cage, no larger than a bathtub, are two sickly margays. Suddenly the ecologically spectacular Petan region seems as brutal as Guatemalan politics. We trudge away, our fantasy quest feeling as pointless as the lives of those imprisoned margays.

Back in Flores Jo suggests lunch at *La Mesa Maya*. Although I have no appetite, I quickly agree. Maybe *La Mesa's* comic toucan hopping from table to table, boldly snatching fruit from diners' plates, will lift our spirits. I order orange juice and immediately the bird is on our table, its long beak reaching to the bottom of the glass, slurping noisily. Its wings, I notice, have been cut short so that it cannot fly.

I give up trying to eat and sit there glowering. "If I had some wire clippers I could make a hole in that margay cage."

"They'd just catch two more to replace them," Jo reasons.

But her reason is as ineffectual as my anger at countering our depression. We sit there crumbling half-hearted suggestions onto the table like stale bread. Maybe we should go to the far end of Lake Petan-Itza and hang our hammocks for a few days at *Gringo Perdido*. Maybe we should catch a bus out to Finca Ixobel. Maybe we should go back to Belize. Or just go home. What the hell are we doing here anyway? We fall silent, separated by memories that ache like old bones on a rainy day.

"What do you want to do this afternoon?"

A shrug. The silence hangs on.

"We should buy some postcards."

We drift along the sidewalk and into a small shop. Photographs of Tikal, ruins of washed-out grey stone against backgrounds of undistinguished green, capture nothing of its ambience. Cards picturing local wildlife are true in vividness of color, but what does the magnificent spotted cat reposing amid jungle foliage have to do with the sad little margays in their coffin-sized cage across the lake?

The owner, a soft-spoken bookish man, watches us hopefully from the corner of his eye. A schoolboy buys an eraser, and a tourist, complaining loudly about the roads, purchases a map. We dawdle, expelling discontent. At last we approach the counter with our cards. He sees that they are of animals and asks whether we have been to the zoo.

"Yeah," Jo mutters. "Too bad its margays are more dead than alive."

The man's reply is so unexpected that we look at one another, our eyes asking whether we have translated it correctly. Has fantasy collided with reality to create words which only we have heard?

The man smiles at our amazement and repeats the question. "Would you like to see my *tigrillo*? He is small, but *muy macho*."

When Elias closes up his shop that evening, we walk home with him. He is a *mestizo* but his wife Zonia is pure Mayan, a tiny woman barely taller than her children. She leads us to a cement block storeroom in the back yard. There, chained to a table leg, is a male margay the size of a large tomcat. Even before it issues a warning growl we draw back, gagged by the smell.

Zonia apologizes. It is unfortunate that the little tiger has to live in its own excrement, but as we can see, he is vicious. She can do no more than stand in the doorway and splash a bucket of water on the floor. Sometimes that just makes the mess worse.

Clearly this aggressive bundle of snarl is no household pet. Elias explains that a visiting professor from the University of Guatemala put out the word that he wanted to buy a jungle cat for "scientific purposes," so three months ago, when an Indian came to their door with this one, they bought it in hopes of reselling it. Regrettably, the professor has never returned.

"It eats more than both my children," Zonia frets. "And it's very dangerous. They're always wanting to touch it. One day I know it's going to hurt them."

Jo and I stand there exuding longing for the margay, while an equally powerful desire radiates from Elias and Zonia, a desire for us to take the cat away and leave in its place enough money to recoup what they have invested.

The children, a brother and sister of nine and ten, stand apart holding hands. The girl looks from one adult to another with open curiosity, waiting to see what will happen. But the boy stands tightly contained, fatalistic. He knows, before any of the adults have decided, that this little pet which he cannot pet but which he loves passionately will be taken away. Whatever discussions must be held, whatever deal struck, he already knows that this is how it will end.

"Do you mind if I examine him?" Jo asks.

She crouches on the floor just out of reach. The margay bares fang and claw, snarling threats to shred her flesh if she dares move into range. I have never seen my daughter as veterinarian-at-work, and am terrified as she moves infinitesimally closer. The cat leaps halfway up a broomstick leaning against the wall, and hangs there monkey-like but for the flailing razor claws. Jo waits, then moves an inch closer. Over the next hour her nearness, and eventually her touch along its ribs, pushes the margay to the limits of its fear but never over the line to attack.

At last she backs away. "He's sick. Probably malnutrition. In the wild they eat birds and small rodents, bones, stomach innards and all. They have to have all that for a balanced diet."

The disappointment in her voice forewarns Elias and Zonia. "We can't possibly take him. He would have to be tranquilized, and in his condition, a tranquilizer would kill him. Under that fur he's just a bag of bones. He won't live much longer in captivity."

"What can we do?" Elias asks, waving flies away from his face and stepping back from the stench of the room.

"There's a chance he'd survive in the wild," Jo answers carefully.

"Would you consider releasing him at Tikal?" I ask. "Hunting isn't allowed in the park, and there's plenty of game."

In the silence that follows my suggestion, I add the obvious. "Of course, nobody would get anything out of it."

"That's not true." Zonia's voice is gentle. "The little tiger would get his freedom. And we would get a clear conscience."

She reaches for her son but he evades her embrace and runs into the house.

It takes almost an hour for us to get what seems to be an unlimited number of angry teeth and slashing claws contained in a bag. From inside, the margay continues to strike like a snake at each shadow of movement, puncturing the burlap with fang and claw. My hands shake as I hold the bag shut and Jo, with steady fingers, makes it secure.

Only when the margay is bagged and portable does it occur to us that we have no idea what to do next. The family does not own a car. If we try to carry the bag into the street, nobody is going to believe that what we have inside is a chicken. No matter how we transport it, we risk being stopped by a military patrol. Getting caught in possession of an endangered species is a sure way to see the inside of a Guatemalan prison.

"Ask the governor for a transit permit," suggests Zonia.

Jo laughs. "Of course. Tell the governor we're in illegal possession of an endangered animal and— "

Something in my expression tells her that I don't perceive the plan as impossible just because it's dangerous. She wags a finger in mock accusation. "I know that look."

"What look?"

"My mother the criminal savior," She shakes her head, smiling. "So where do we find this governor?"

Although it's early evening, we are told at the *palacio* that the governor is still there. We explain our situation to a matronly secretary. Wearing a bemused smile, she vanishes into his office. A quarter hour ticks by. We have time to consider that, despite local tolerance for outlandish tourist costumes, tee-shirt and jeans smelling of dirty male margay are hardly suitable for an audience with a governor.

Half an hour passes before the secretary returns to announce, "The governor will see you now."

The governor sits behind a littered desk, a man of middle years with the energetic motions of youth. He acknowledges us without rising, and looks from one to another, waiting for us to explain ourselves. I tell the story of the family who bought the margay from a *campesino* for sale to a visiting professor who never came back. Jo picks up from there, describing the cat's condition and how it will not survive unless released back into the wild.

"We'll take it to Tikal and let it go if you'll give us a transit permit."

The governor calls his secretary and dictates a brief, appropriately worded document. "How will you get it to Tikal?" he asks.

"We were hoping you'd lend us a vehicle."

The governor does not answer. We see that this is a problem, but in Latino cultures men do not comfortably refuse to help women.

The secretary returns with the document. The governor signs it and passes it across the desk with a gesture that says this is the best he can do.

Jo ignores the gesture. "Do you have a vehicle which might take us to Tikal?" she asks. "We have no other way."

Had she phrased the question differently, asked whether it was possible, he might have replied that it was not. But as governor of the state, how can he say that he does not have a vehicle at his disposal? Of course he has one, and courtesy compels him to honor the request. Moments later we are clattering down the marble steps of the *palacio* with transit visa in hand and a promise of transportation to Tikal in the morning.

Our hotel room is not air-conditioned. With no breeze and not even a fan to stir the humid air, sleep is impossible. Each time I fall into a doze I feel myself trapped like the margay, inside a bag. I try to get up without disturbing Jo, but when I fling back the mosquito netting, she sits up, too. Knees touching between the beds, we rest our feet on the cool tile floor.

"Sometimes I'm like this at home," Jo says in a low voice. "When there's an animal at the clinic I'm worried about. I can't sleep until I get up and go check on it."

"Maybe we should have brought him with us."

"That would only have stressed him more. Anyway," she points to an open window. "There are no screens. Can you imagine how hot it would be in here with the windows closed?"

"Are you sure he's okay?"

Jo is silent and I understand. She has given me as much reassurance as she can. If we are to share this adventure, we must share this long night of uncertainty.

In the morning, a warning growl is enough to reassure us that the margay is not only alive but still full of fight. I get into the front seat of the governor's vehicle. Jo gingerly lowers the bag of snarling margay into my lap. The truck lurches into motion, chauffeured by an unhappy Guatemalan who has never seen a wildcat and never wants to see one, especially not this one, which for the next fifty miles hisses and lunges through the bag at his hand each time he reaches for the gear shift.

At Tikal we show the governor's letter to the park director, who sends us to the office of flora and fauna. But the chief of flora and fauna cannot be found and his student assistant doesn't want the responsibility of approving the margay's release.

Jo's sigh says she is losing patience. She reminds the assistant that the margay has been in the bag overnight without food or water. Doesn't he suppose his boss will be upset if he lets this rare animal lay here and die? The young man looks into Jo's accusing blue eyes, and wavers.

"There are other *tigrillos* in the park," a veteran ranger offers. "One this *macho* will certainly find a wife."

In the background, the chief's secretary begins to type a release form. Everyone relaxes. A decision has been made.

The assistant gets into the truck with us and directs our sullen driver down a rutted track through the rainforest. Ocelated turkeys flutter out of the path. Overhead, a male howler monkey gives a pretty good imitation of a jaguar growl.

We stop by the shore of a small lake, its dark water overhung with trees and a tangle of vines. In a clearing that ripples with butterflies and the iridescent wings of flying insects, I set the bag on the ground. Jo pulls it open. The margay catches her thumbs, both of them, and bites hard. She draws back, dripping blood.

The old driver, who must have believed it inevitable, fumbles in the glove compartment and pulls out a first-aid kit. Jo lays her hands in mine for bandaging. I look at her face to see if she is in pain, but she seems to have forgotten the injury. Her eyes are on the cat.

The margay crouches in the open bag, taking in great breaths of steamy jungle air. At last he slips out and moves stealthily toward the lake. When he is belly-deep in the dark water he stops, lowers his nose to his own reflection, and drinks.

Then he lifts his head and looks at us almost questioningly. No one moves. He growls softly. Then, without warning, the black-and-gold body stretches into a long arching leap into the jungle.

Our eyes cling to the spot where the margay's colors merged with the forest's shifting patterns of sun and shade. No one moves.

It is the old driver who makes the first sound. In a voice of quiet awe, he says, "Now it is of God."

Jo's hand touches mine, but lightly. The blood, spattered on both, is already beginning to dry.

It has just become clear to us that our hunt was not to capture something, but to let it go.

LEAVING HOME

Budwood — The 'Eighties

I've walked away from houses I've owned and men I've married with an ease that always left me a little ashamed. People and places were continuously being left behind, filed away in memory like photographs in an album I rarely looked at again. By the time I got to the Budwood, much as I wanted to stay, I figured I was just another transient in a transient time.

Most of those living on the Budwood when I came drifted away as the seventies wore on. Neil the jeweler was last seen with Zanzibar, disappearing down the driveway in a fifty-foot school bus. The rabbi either went to South America to buy emeralds for a lady or is practicing Zen Judaism at an ashram (or possibly both, this being California, where any spiritual combination is possible). Jim went to the south of France to paint in the heavy shadow of Van Gogh's ghost, and Jerry, that generous dreamer who imagined our community before it existed, was taken even further away by illness, into a private world of pain. Jeff was the last to go and in a rage; this when it came to him that the monogamy I never promised indeed did not exist, and in the course of my wanderings, I'd fallen in love with a Canadian man.

"Then why aren't you living in Canada?" asks Jo, when I make my usual stop at her house on a drive between British Columbia and California.

"I am — when I'm not living in Malibu."

"What's so special about Malibu?" Jo, who only summered there once or twice when she was in college, doesn't understand my attachment. She has just come from work, collapsed on the couch, and kicked off her shoes. A ferret squirms head-first into a sock, while another burrows under the sofa cushions. Three Abyssinian cats mock battle, squall, and chase each other around the room. The little Aussie sheepdog lies quietly amidst the chaos, watching Jo with adoring eyes.

"The beach."

"Canada doesn't have beaches?"

"All right then, the Budwood. I guess I'm in love with the place."

"You're talking land and not a man," Jo admonishes in her maddeningly rational way.

"So? At least the land doesn't sulk when I go away. And I can count on it being there when I come back."

Jo grins. "Yeah, but what about TMWMMM?" She hasn't met my Canadian friend yet, and still refers to him by an acronym of her own devising, which stands for The Man Who Mellowed My Mother.

"Traveling's not his thing. But he doesn't mind if I do. At least, that's what he says. If that's true ..." If that's true, he's more self-reliant than any mate I've ever had. "But it's really too soon to tell."

I capture a ferret trying to wriggle up inside my pant leg and gingerly hand it to her. It snuggles into the curve of her arm and allows itself to be stroked. There's no need to say more. Jo, having disentangled herself from a few possessive men by now, understands my doubts. Men who claim to admire our adventurousness find it annoying when it doesn't include them. Even if the one in Canada proves to be different, I can't imagine leaving the Budwood. But if I say that aloud, Jo will point out that I'm *always* leaving. Leaving to travel with her, leaving to travel alone, and of course, leaving to be with that man. Leaving but always returning, to the beach and the Budwood.

I no longer live in the little cottage Jerry permitted me to resurrect, but now nest in a more private place formerly occupied by the surfing rabbi. It is at the far end of the old ranch house, but later built, after the original occupants were gone and the place had metamorphosed into a beatnik coffee house. The duenna of the coffee house, Lorice, built this thirty-by-thirty room, all redwood and glass and great stone fireplace, and used it for performances. Anais Nin read here, and Alan Ginsberg and the rest; the Positano was famous in its day. I've never met Lorice, who before my time on the Budwood went off to New York to produce a little play (which later moved to Broadway) called *Hair*. But I know exactly how the ocean drew her imagination past the walls and windows, out to the horizon and beyond. It does the same for me.

Of the people who lived on the ranch when I first arrived, only Bruce and Bond remain. Others have come and gone. Two couples have stayed. Pamela, a struggling landscape architect, moved into the big house next door to me. A year or so later she was joined by Richard, a quietly lucid man with a career in academia and a hunger for the sea. Then David and Jacqui came for a summer and couldn't bear to leave. David is an American of my generation, a writer who worked his way across the South Pacific until he met Jacqui, a young and beautiful New Zealander. Jacqui doesn't seem daughterly to me, but familiar. Like Jo, she has an artistic bent, thoughtful blue eyes, and ways that are wiser than her years.

It's hard to say why we seven are addicted to the Budwood's funky charm. Maybe it's because this is the eighties, and what with holes in the ozone, poisons in the food chain, and guns in the street, the larger world seems less hospitable. Or maybe it's because we're heading into middle age and all of us are changing. David and Jacqui, unemployed screenwriters when they arrived, now make hundreds of thousands per year. Pamela has gone from an unknown freelancer to landscaping university campuses more prestigious than the one where her husband works. Bond and Bruce have become a couple, while I bounce from one job to another, and back and forth between here and that new man in Canada. Our differences and diversions should have destroyed any illusion we have about this being home and our being a family. But it may not be an illusion.

"Rosa," David bellows, coming up the path wrapped in a towel and covered in soapsuds, "You know when you put on the sprinkler the water in my shower cuts off. The least you could do is phone!"

"Pamela," Bond drawls with exaggerated Southern politeness, "If you must warm up your car before I'm up in the morning, is it really necessary to do it with the exhaust six feet from my window?"

"Who's been using pesticides in the garden?" I mutter. "You people have the environmental sensitivity of slugs!"

"If your damned dog craps on my lawn one more time ..."

This is not paradise but it is family. What we lack in compatibility we make up for in trust, especially where the children are concerned. David is raising a son from a previous marriage, and now he and Jacqui have a daughter. Pamela and Richard have a boy and a girl. For a time I shelter a beautiful foster child, whom Jacqui mentors and Pamela provides with an after-school job. Bond gives the children lessons in piano and French. Bruce lends his Oriental treasures for show-

and-tell days at school, and shares his knowledge of the Mac. I teach them to ride the horse.

One child for whom I have a special affinity is Pamela's daughter, Julia, who at age five declares herself a vegetarian. One day I meet her on the hillside weeping because her family is having salmon for dinner.

"Don't worry. Your parents won't make you eat it," I assure her.

"No, but they're going to eat it."

Knowing her self-imposed dietary restrictions are like mine, based on a love of animals, I try to console her. "But Julia, darling, lots of people who care about animals eat fish."

"I don't know why," she sobs. "Fish have feelings, too."

I put my arms around her, having no answer for a child whose empathy for living things is so much greater than my own.

In a culture of exploding fragments, we are an anachronism. We have become attached, to a place and to each other. I'd say we are rooted here, but how could we have taken root when distant lords grant occupancy only month-to-month? How can it be said that anything is rooted on this rain-eroded hillside with waves just below, gnawing at the rocks?

I like swimming far out into the bay. From there I see not just the weathered dot that shelters me, but the whole of Budwood sprawled across the mountainside. Besides being home to humans, it belongs to hawks and hummingbirds, garden-raiding deer, and tribes of coyotes. There is a family of raccoons we call the Gang of Seven, opossums that regularly eat the soap from our outdoor showers, and a cougar who, on the rare occasions he chooses to show himself, does so in broad daylight, drinking from the horse trough or standing outside David's studio with a fresh-killed rabbit in his mouth. The animals accept our tenancy and we theirs, except in the case of certain rattlesnakes who believe that our path is their rightful place to sun. Fear once had us killing them, but now we simply call Animal Control and have them taken alive to a wilder place. About the only things we regularly murder are ants, biting flies, and black widow spiders. Nobody's respect for life extends to them.

The only recurring dream I've ever had started soon after I came here. In the dream I'm on my patio, looking toward the ocean. Far off I see a great purple swell, the gathering of an enormous wave. The color is ominous but I'm not afraid. No wave could reach this hilltop. Not until it crests do I see that I am wrong. It will strike with all its force and wash us all away.

When I am in some far place and think of losing Budwood, I pack my bag and come home. I know Los Angeles will hit me like diesel fumes from the back of a bus and if it's summertime, traffic will be gridlocked on Pacific Coast Highway. But when I come up Budwood's winding driveway and reach the curve where sage and sea breeze meet, I remember why I came back. It's worth being here for the smell alone. And when I'm here and think that someday I might lose it all, I study the maps that cover my wall, then go outside and plant a tree.

When a magazine assignment takes me to Mexico to do an article on a group called the Flying Samaritans, Jacqui asks to come along. I need pictures for this piece and my camera work is always hit-and-miss. Jacqui is a good photographer, and good company as well.

Volunteer pilots fly us and a Samaritan medical team to an isolated ranch in the middle of Baja. The ranch belongs to a seventy-seven-year-old *grande dame*, Señora Josefina Ziniga. When the trans-peninsular highway was routed across her land she demanded and got not money but a paved landing strip, one of the best in Baja. She allows the Samaritans to operate a clinic out of a small building on her ranch.

Lunch, served at a long table under a thatch-roofed shed, is basic local fare: tortillas and beans and sweet black coffee. It's January and time for the rains, which haven't started yet. A cold wind howls, rattling the thatch above our heads. Except for a few ranch hands there's no one around, but within an hour of our landing, the yard is filled with battered cars and pickups overflowing with patients and their families. Some have driven two or three hours for this infrequent chance to see a doctor or have their children receive immunization shots from a nurse. They wait a discreet distance until the doctor finishes lunch, then trail him across the road to the clinic.

The team processes thirty-six patients during the afternoon. The cement block building being used as a clinic has neither water nor electricity. I wonder what will happen if patients remain when daylight is gone. It's well after sunset when the last one, a young woman, gets in to see the doctor.

"Assistance," he calls. "She needs a pelvic. I think she's pregnant."

"How can you do an examination?" I ask the doctor. "Isn't it too dark?"

"Not if I can get somebody to hold the flashlight."

Jacqui and I wake at daybreak to find that the rainy season has arrived. We make a dash across the ranch yard and take shelter under the palm-thatched roof. The doctors and nurses bolt their breakfast and head for the clinic where patients are already waiting. I ask for another cup of coffee, and talk to the pilots.

The medical people I understand. Being needed is what they're all about, and clearly the need is here. But the pilots are a mystery to me. Most of them served in Vietnam, and now work in the military-industrial complex. One is in charge of the manufacture of surface-to-air missiles. Besides flying medical teams to Baja one weekend a month, he flies volunteer doctors to a Navajo reservation on another, on the third takes supplies to an orphanage in Mexico, and on the fourth weekend of each month, teaches Sunday school at a juvenile detention center in Los Angeles.

Doesn't he find an inconsistency between all these humanitarian activities and building weapons of mass destruction?

"Nope. The stronger America is militarily, the more peaceful the world will be."

It's what he believes and although I don't agree, I'm not inclined to challenge it. Something more than his blindness is bothering me, something that has to do with myself. I have always held humanitarian values. My closest friends up on the Budwood are the same. Yet I doubt that between us we spend four weekends a year doing things for strangers in need that could make the world a more humane and less hurtful place.

John phones. He and his Brazilian family are going to be the States for a short while. While Marina and the children visit his parents in Pennsylvania, he wants to fly out to California for a few days to see as many of the "old gang" as might be around. I call Barbara, who has long since escaped her oppressive husband and now lives happily with a younger man in the desert east of L.A. She greets the idea of a reunion with enthusiasm, as does Jo, who suggests we gather at Malibu, and says she'll be bringing her current boyfriend Aiden.

With a houseful of visitors, I hadn't expected that Jo and I would have any time alone. But there comes an hour when the others have either gone down to the beach or not yet arrived that we find ourselves sitting under the bougainvillea in the patio, splitting the last croissant and speaking of things under the surface.

"Where's Jeff?" Jo queries.

"He lives in a condo fifteen miles or so up the beach. He'll be here tonight," I tell her. "And tomorrow night we're all going to his place for dinner."

"I like Jeff," she remarks, and after a moment's silence, "Why did you break up with him anyway?"

"The real question is why we stayed together so long. He was never my version of the perfect man."

"The perfect man?" Her voice is amused. "Who would that be?"

"Oh, one who appreciates my strengths, tolerates my weaknesses, reduces my tension level, and doesn't bore me."

Jo gazes up into the bougainvillea blossoms. Her thoughtful silence tells me she is mentally measuring both present and past lovers against those criteria. Finally she says, "Aiden actually scores pretty high on all four." She reaches across the table and flicks a croissant crumb off my face. "What about Derek? How much of it do you get from him?"

"All of it, so far." I walk to the edge of the patio and look down at the beach, the beach I will someday have to leave if I ever decide to live full-time with the man who gives me everything.

"I always thought you and Jeff had a lot in common, the traveling and all that."

"Surface stuff. It's what's underneath that counts. Mind you, Jeff never bored me and I don't think I bored him. But we drove each other's tension levels right through the ceiling. At close quarters, we weren't all that good for each other."

"So he's okay about the breakup?"

"Depends on what you mean by okay. If I were to look for a term to describe Jeff's reaction, it would be something like 'suppressed fury.'"

Jo laughs. "At least it's suppressed. That's something."

"Yeah," I grin. "That's something."

The others come trooping back from the beach and Barbara turns her camera on us in various combinations. Later I see that her snapshots have captured more clearly than words Jo's present relationship with both John and Aiden. Barbara catches Jo and John at opposite ends of the kitchen table, his face serious and lecturing, hers stubborn, resistant to whatever view he is expounding. What the camera doesn't reveal but is obvious to those of us listening is that Jo is taking some pleasure in their sparring. John's firmly-held views attracted her once and gave her something solid against which to test her own ideas. But when she could not prevail over him or he over her they must have grown tired of the game and drifted apart. Now, behind them on the wall and separating them in the photo, is a map entitled "The World."

In the picture of Jo and Aiden, he stands peering out from behind her, his arms wrapped warmly about her. Captured is the sense that this shy man feels most comfortable with Jo's chunky, muscular body interposed between himself and the world, while she feels more confident with his arms around her than she ever felt without them.

We collect at Jeff's place the following night for a gourmet meal he has spent most of the afternoon preparing. When I had first mentioned the reunion he made negative noises, claiming not to have much interest in any of us anymore. Yet he had called Steve and tried to talk him into coming down from San Francisco (an invitation declined, as Steve explained that his wife was uncomfortable with any reminders of his life before they met). Instead, we're joined by Valerie, who left San Miguel to attend university in Los Angeles. She now holds two masters degrees, one in social work and one in urban planning, and has just adopted a beautiful half-black baby.

"It's the best thing I've ever done," Valerie tells Jo, referring not to her academic achievements but to the adoption.

Jo listens raptly to Valerie's account of the joys of motherhood. I can see that she's hungry for the same experience, but sufficiently self-aware to realize she's not ready to take that step yet. Jo knows, and seems to have always known, what's right for her and when.

On balance it is a strange weekend, one that highlights our differences while demonstrating that bonds formed during the year we taught high school dropouts in Los Angeles and the year we educated ourselves in Mexico have survived, withstanding time, distance, and changes we couldn't have anticipated.

I've been writing for more than a decade now, and still don't earn a decent living from it. I am a subsistence writer like my parents were subsistence farmers, often finding that ends don't meet and having to take on another job until the bills are paid.

My criteria for choosing a job vary a lot. Right now it's summertime and I'm not disposed to drive into the city. Rand Corporation, a so-called "think tank," is located just up the coast. Rand doesn't have an immediate opening for a research assistant, but it does have some clerical positions, and a locker room with showers. At lunchtime I can walk across the street to the beach for a swim, and see the Budwood where it curves around the bay eight miles to the north.

Half the research done at Rand is said to be on domestic issues. The other half is military-related. I don't want to participate in military research, and request an assignment in Latin American Affairs. I am told that I can interview for a position when there is an opening in that section, but right now I'm needed in Terrorism. Dr. Jenkins is a world authority on the subject, and his department has just begun to publish a monthly magazine for those working in the field.

I do not work for Dr. Jenkins directly, but for the resident expert on terrorists, a silver-haired, German-accented man named Conrad. To get a feel for the department's focus, I read everything in the previous month's *Journal on Terrorism*. There is one article on the IRA, one on the Palestinians, one on liberation theologists in Latin America, and five on domestic animal rights groups. The articles note that as of yet no one has been killed by an animal rights activist, and property damage has been minimal, but these people are fanatics and their organizations bear watching.

The Terrorism Department is one where the status of support staff is somewhat above a desk chair, but definitely below personal computers, which are just beginning to come on the scene and have a certain prestige. It is a week before Conrad bothers to say hello and I have a chance to ask him for a definition of terrorism.

He taps a forefinger against pursed lips, and says, "Vell, zat is a problem. Ve don't exactly have one."

A few days later Conrad brings me an essay which he says is to be the lead article in the next issue of the *Journal*. He has been calling Miami Cubans all week, so I expect it to have something to do with their activities. But no. The piece is, or is meant to be, a definition of terrorism. At first I can't make heads or tails of it, but eventually a kind of logic emerges. I see the dilemma.

"Conrad," I ask, "Was the taking of hostages at the Munich Olympics terrorism?"

"Sure it vas."

"Was the CIA's trying to kill Castro terrorism?"

"No, dat vas, uh, counter-terrorism."

"Was the French blowing up the Rainbow Warrior terrorism?"

"Ya, dat vas state-sponsored terrorism."

"Was the U.S. mining of Nicaraguan harbors terrorism?"

"No. Dat vas — vell, dat vas something else."

I'm beginning to understand the think tank definition of terrorism, and why Rand's experts are having so much trouble articulating it. What they're trying to formulate is a definition which includes all politically-motivated acts of violence short of war — except those of the government funding this study.

One day a friendly woman with short brown hair appears at my desk and tells me I am to come with her to meet Irv Cohen, who needs a new administrative assistant because she, Margaret, is planning to leave.

"Mr. Cohen is a wonderful man," she assures me. "But he has a hard time keeping an administrative assistant because he hates giving orders. He just mumbles, and leaves it up to you to figure out what he wants."

This sounds good to me; I hate being micro-managed. We walk down one of Rand Corporation's block-long corridors, one I have never had an occasion to explore. Margaret stops at a locked glass door, and lays her hand against an electronic box. The door clicks open.

"Where are we going?"

"Into a security area."

"You mean military? I don't want to work in military research. I told them that in personnel. What does Mr. Cohen do anyway?"

"Air base resupply. You know, our bases have to have food, toilet paper, all sorts of things. Ask Mr. Cohen. He'll explain it."

Mr. Cohen is a large, shaggy-haired man with the jowls and sad brown eyes of a St. Bernard. Kindness emanates from him as he goes over my résumé and tells me how much he appreciates that someone with my background is willing to work for him. I'm not yet sure I am willing to work for him, but after a month of being treated like squeaky office furniture, I am grateful to be recognized as a *homo sapiens*.

"This seems like a strange thing to be developing," I remark. "The U.S. military has had big air bases since World War Two. I should think it already has a sophisticated resupply system."

"It did have, when air bases were in safe places behind the lines. Resupply under those circumstances was only a matter of sending in truckloads of whatever was needed. Then came the nuclear age, and there were no safe places." Mr. Cohen pauses, waiting for me to get the point. "Remember SAC?"

"Strategic Air Command? Planes poised to bomb the Soviet Union if they ever launch nuclear warheads against us? What does that have to do with resupplying the bases?"

"The nuclear-war premise was that there would be no base to come back to. So it was no longer necessary to have a wartime resupply system." Mr. Cohen is gazing at me with the delight a kindly professor takes in watching a student grasp his point and make connections.

I am making a connection, and it is making my stomach turn. "Are we talking about Reagan's idea of winnable nuclear war?"

"Yes, of course. But only if we are prepared."

"Only if there is a system to supply the bases with food and toilet paper while this nuclear war is going on."

He beams. "So you understand now what we are doing."

What Irv Cohen is doing, now with my assistance, is managing the biggest government research contract that Rand Corporation has ever had. So far I am the least useful person on his staff because as yet I do not have a security clearance. I can't even go to the bathroom alone. As long as I'm on this side of the glass doors, doors which do not yet open to my palm print, I must have an escort everywhere I go. Fortunately that escort is Margaret, whom I like a lot. She shows me how to make travel arrangements for Mr. Cohen, confirm appointments with the heads of NATO, and pick up the amount of foreign exchange he will need in each country. She explains how to make hotel reservations for visiting Pentagon officials, reserve conference rooms, order buffet luncheons, and prepare viewgraphs for Mr. Cohen's presentation on how air bases are to be resupplied while the nation is under nuclear attack.

It's the viewgraphs that bother me most. To make a viewgraph I must type the points to be made by the speaker onto sheets of paper, then take those papers to the photo lab which reproduces them on transparencies so they can be projected onto a wall. In this way the points, being presented orally and visually at the same time, will be more easily remembered. The points have to do with how much of what can be delivered how fast to bases that are running low on supplies. There is nothing on the viewgraphs about food or toilet paper. What I see and remember in the wee hours when I should be sleeping but cannot, are statistics on how efficiently air bases can be resupplied with spare parts, new bombers, and of course, bombs.

I go to the Latin Affairs Department to see if they are hiring research assistants this month. Well, not just yet, the bright young department chief tells me cheerfully, but soon. His researchers are becoming increasingly busy, and new research projects are anticipated.

"In what area?" I ask, wondering how long it will take to get a transfer.

"Well, most of our research is related to more or less the same thing now. How to make the Contras more effective."

"I thought only domestic research was done on this side of Rand."

"This is domestic. I mean, the U.S. is not at war with Nicaragua or anything like that."

When I hired on at Rand two months ago I was told that transfers were easy and my qualifications would give me a shot at a variety of positions in that middle range between secretarial and the professional researchers. I am no longer going to the beach at noon, but now use my lunch hour to interview in the various departments which have job openings posted. No one offers me anything.

When Margaret discovers what I am up to, she explains why. "Irv Cohen likes you, and right now, he's the most important department head at Rand. Nobody would dare take you away from him."

I'm not sure I can take myself away from Irv Cohen. There is something about facing those kind, sad eyes and saying, "Mr. Cohen, I don't want to work for you" that makes me want to cry. In the end I behave like any coward. While Irv is away in Europe meeting with the heads of NATO to discuss the winnable nuclear war, I write a letter of resignation. In it I tell him that during my two months at Rand Corporation I have come to understand the definition of terrorism. Terrorism, whether state-sponsored or otherwise, is a politically-motivated act intended to kill or maim, which makes no distinction between innocent bystanders and those defined as the enemy. In my lifetime, from London to Hiroshima to Vietnam to the villages of El Salvador, bombs dropped from planes have been the ultimate weapon of terror. I don't know what he tells himself to sleep at night, but whatever it is, it doesn't work for me.

I've dreamed about that wave again but this time it wasn't the same. This time I was on horseback riding down from the deer meadow, with the others who live here on horses behind me. I glanced back and saw, coming over the ridge from the north and west, an enormous purple wave that reached halfway to the meridian. The wave curled down on us and we all, horses and riders, were washed over the edge into a canyon.

I'm leaving for Latin America tonight. I'll plant a tree before I go.

TRAVELING ALONE

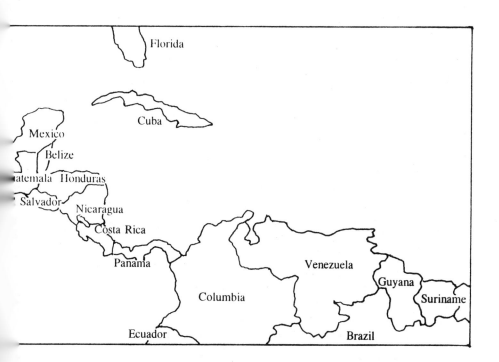

A PRESIDENTIAL WHIM

Mexico 1975

It seems so long ago that I lay on that Yucatán beach watching the horizon, considering what it might be like to go beyond my own imagination and experience the truly unknown. Such a long time since I climbed aboard a small plane, the destination of which I did not know, with a newspaper photographer I'd only just met. When our plane circled for a landing, I saw that its destination was a place I had been before: Palenque, ceremonial center of the ancient Mayans. I had come along only to have a destination, not caring what it was nor minding that it turned out to be somewhere I had already been. Still, I would have preferred a strange one, because strange places even more than familiar ones had brought me to where I wanted to be.

Where I wanted to be was in the "real Mexico" — a place I failed to find in San Miguel's trendy expatriate community. Not until this trip, with its weeks of drifting through parts of Mexico that foreigners rarely visit, passing time with school teachers, bee keepers, traveling salesmen, and Mayan children; sleeping on a hard wooden bench in a camp of unfriendly highland *indios,* in a hammock strung between palms on a Caribbean beach, and in an airport terminal locked up for the night, had I begun to touch realities, remote from my own life, that were truly Mexican. Here beyond the boundaries of my known world was where I wanted to be, not merely to escape my life but to think about it and try to figure out what had gone wrong.

Little by little I came to realize that the sense of entrapment that drove me to take this strange walkabout wasn't a figment of my imagination. I became aware of an invisible cultural web. Attitudes not of my making, beliefs I would not have thought I held, had somehow ensnared me and limited everything — expectations, imagination, curiosity, and courage.

It was not as if, understanding this, I suddenly sprang free. Indeed, it would take years to break enough fetters to live in a way that felt both responsible and unrestricted. This, though, was a beginning, and how it began was this: alone and moving at random, I simply walked through one strand of the web after another.

The plane bumps to a stop on Palenque's grass strip runway. I jump down into the thick of a press corps which is following the president of Mexico on a junket through the state of Chiapas. The hour is early, the air sweet with jungle smells. The ruins are closed to everyone except the presidential party. In the customary way of reporters covering a celebrity, we hang about waiting for the newsmaker of the day to appear.

I sit down on the bottom step of steep stairs leading to the Temple of Inscriptions and listen to the journalists' irreverent banter. A five-inch-long grasshopper with glittering wings crawls slowly up and over the toe of my sneaker. So engrossed am I in the grasshopper's progress that I do not hear feet descending the stairs until two polished black shoes pause on the step just above. I look up into the amused eyes of Luis Echeverría Alvarez, President of Mexico.

I stand up quickly but before I can move aside his arm drops around my shoulder. "Where do you come from?" he asks.

"Uh, Canada," I reply, British Columbia having been the last place I stayed before this particular trip to Mexico.

He smiles warmly and makes a short statement which I understand at once is not for me but for the media machines now whirring around us. He expresses admiration for Canada and appreciation that I have come so far afield in order to see parts of Mexico that my compatriots rarely visit.

Although I have been a freelance journalist for several years, and often spend time in Canada, I hadn't meant to create the illusion that I was a Canadian journalist here to cover the president's tour of Chiapas. However, in the full glare of the media I haven't the nerve to correct the false impression. In any case, it's over in seconds. The president and his party move on, followed by the press.

I slip away in the opposite direction, down an overgrown path where I can savor my mini-adventure in private. I am still chuckling when a short, perspiring man trots into view. He waves his handkerchief, mops his balding head, and gasps, "Oh, thank goodness, I've found you!"

I see by his shiny shoes and elegantly embroidered white-on-white *guyabera*, the shirt worn for formal daytime occasions here in the tropics, that he is from the presidential party. I feel a clutch of fear. Has he discovered that I am not of the official press corps? Am I about to be evicted from the park in full view of everyone?

He says, in perfect English, "I am the governor of Chiapas. The president wishes you to join his entourage."

I am relieved but not overwhelmed by the invitation because I don't completely understand it. I think that my unofficial status has been discovered, and I am merely being invited to join the press corps. Not until we reach the presidential party and I am formally introduced to President Echeverría do I realize that for the duration of this junket I am to be a part of his *personal* entourage. He says he regrets that there is no space for me in his helicopter, but thinks I will find the occupants of the second helicopter — two cabinet ministers, the director of the Mexican Coffee Institute, and Mexico's ambassador to the U.N. — agreeable traveling companions.

My small bag is passed up into the helicopter. The pilot takes my hand to assist me up. I hesitate, inhibited by another of those invisible strands, a mental image of the contents of my bag: dirty jeans, underwear, and t-shirts. A lifelong tangle of social admonishments clamor that it is impossible to travel in this company with no clean clothing apart from the fresh blouse and denim shorts I donned in the airport washroom an hour ago. Then I do what I have been doing all through these weeks of drifting. I simply push past that inhibition and find myself sitting next to the ambassador, surprised at how easy it really was.

Moments after the chopper lifts off it is descending to Agua Azul, a river through the rainforest which spills in white cataracts from one blue pool to the next. I have been here before, swam nude in these pools. But today, with fifty high government officials, an equal number of reporters, and a hundred Indians from surrounding *ejidos*, there is no swimming, nude or otherwise. At least I am comfortable in my "inappropriate" shorts. The men, in their short-sleeved cotton *guyaberas* also look fresh, but the four women in the presidential party, all wearing expensive suits with narrow lined skirts, nylons, high heels, and excesses of jewelry, stand in the heat on first one foot then another with makeup melting down their faces in rivulets of perspiration. The irritable way they glance away when our eyes meet tells me that more than nationality separates us now.

The president walks away from the crowd and stands in a rainbow mist rising from a small waterfall, then returns to a spread of tropical fruits which the Indians have prepared. Earlier I heard reporters complaining that because Echeverría doesn't drink there will be no free booze, nor even steak at tonight's banquet, since the president is also vegetarian. I admire such common-sense simplicity, and I admire how he moves among the people; the way he smiles directly into the eyes of an Indian woman who passes him a plate of fruit, drops a casual hand on the shoulder of a child who has toddled up and grasped him by the pant leg, or grips the gnarled, rootlike fingers of a local farmer. I also like his extraordinarily tranquil face, though I don't know what to make of it, as I have seen little in this chaotic, wealth-imbalanced country that might incline a leader to tranquility.

Mentally I make fun of myself for falling so quickly under the spell of Echeverría's quiet charisma. On the other hand, living in Malibu and working on various political campaigns, I have met my share of celebrities and political leaders, most of whom seemed rather ordinary. Being charmed by this particular man, I decide, is simply part of the fun of this particular adventure.

Soon we are in the air again, circling over hydroelectric projects under construction, new roads, and drainage systems. We land in San Cristóbal de las Casas to see, among other things, a government farm where rabbits are being raised as a source of protein for malnourished Indians. The president disembarks into a crowd of waiting dignitaries, but the officials are shoved aside by Gertrude Blom, a seventy-year-old Swiss anthropologist who has devoted her life to the study and protection of the region's indigenous people, particularly the gentle, jungle-dwelling Lacondóns.

Without preamble, Madam Blom tells the president that the rain-forest is being destroyed by outsiders, that he must take steps *immediately*. "Now, Mr. President, now, or all will be lost!"

The president replies that he is well aware of the plight of the indigenous peoples of Chiapas; indeed, the reason he has brought so many high government officials with him on this trip is so that they can gain a better understanding of what is needed. Already, roads are being built to any number of isolated villages.

The old lady cuts him off with an imperious wave of her walking stick. "And who will use the roads, Mr. President? I will tell you. In a village where not one person owns a vehicle, only the Coca Cola truck will use that road. What the people need is not contact with the outside world but self-sufficiency. Instruction in the raising of vegetables, because you see, they only raise coffee now, and a little corn. They have lost the old ways, and no longer are able to feed themselves."

"We are looking into the distribution of fertilizer —"

"Not fertilizer, Mr. President, composting! Self-sufficiency! Education!" She pounds her walking stick on the ground for emphasis.

"But are our indigenous people ready?"

"They are ready," she nods her white head vigorously. "I assure you, Mr. President, they are ready!"

Behind her, cabinet ministers chuckle and local officials look annoyed. I make a mental note to look up Gertrude Blom the next time I come to Chiapas.

We reach the rabbit farm and are briefed by its manager. The rabbits are doing well and multiplying rapidly. Unfortunately, the indigenous people are not accustomed to eating rabbits, and well, one must understand that in societies ruled by tradition and superstition, it is difficult to introduce new things. However, rabbit meat is being served to Indian children in the schools, so although it may take years, eventually it will be accepted.

I wander through the barn looking at big white rabbits in little cages. An Indian man moves from one to another, filling water containers. This is one of the people who, we have just heard, will not eat rabbit flesh. I ask him whether he has ever tasted it. He says he has.

"You didn't like it?"

It was okay, he admits. But not good food for *indios*.

"Why not?"

Continuing to fill the water pans, never looking directly at me, the man replies, "The *ladinos* do not pay *indios* enough for their products that *indios* can afford to buy *ladino* food. It is better that we do not develop a taste for white men's food."

I think of the well-dressed white men outside (as well as Indian workers inside) listening to a well-dressed white man saying that Indians are too superstitious and tradition-bound to adopt this new and better food. Perhaps the Indian's shrewd economic analysis has not occurred to the president's men — or perhaps it has, but they find their own explanation less embarrassing.

We switch from helicopters to a private jet which takes us to the border between Mexico and Guatemala. As we land in the city of Tapachula where we are to spend the night, we see such crowds gathered that all roads leading to the airport are gridlocked. The welcoming party, trapped in traffic, is not on hand to greet the president. I recall a TV clip of a top Nixon aide who was infuriated because a golf cart wasn't on hand to carry him across the lawn at San Clemente. I wait for Mexican officials to show their irritation but no one does. In sweltering, 100-degree-plus heat, Echeverría starts walking, followed by Vice-President López Portillo, the Chief Justice of the Supreme Court, half the National Cabinet, the U.N. ambassador, the governor of Chiapas, heads of agencies, directors of banks, and fifty reporters. Somewhere in the swirling mob I know are four security agents. Where they are now I have no idea but I am close enough to the president to see that they are not clustered around him. I wonder if it is one of Fate's little jokes that the more security a person has, the more often threats are made on his life. If this is true, I have little to fear in the company of this president.

We arrive at our hotel, an elegant structure built in the Spanish style of rooms that open onto a cool central courtyard. We gather in this oasis of pools, waterfalls, and tropical flowers, discussing politics and perspectives on the day's events, until someone glances at his wrist watch and mentions that the banquet for the president of Guatemala begins in twenty minutes. Banquet? What banquet? Suddenly those voices in my head are screeching again, insisting that I cannot, simply cannot, attend an evening banquet in denim shorts and running shoes.

"Oh, too bad," I say lamely. "My bag wasn't brought from the plane. I have nothing to wear."

"I sent someone back for mine." The ambassador motions toward his room. Through the open door an aide can be seen hanging up a dozen shirts. "Anything there you'd like to wear?"

His teasing grin turns it into the sort of challenge my friends and I used to put to each other as teenagers. ("Dare you to go to the Halloween party dressed so you look pregnant." "Dare you to go to his wedding in hot pants.") I know I'm too old for this sort of reaction, but it seems as natural as our laughter. I walk into his room, scan the row of beautifully tailored shirts, and pull out a blue silk which looks as if it will come to just above my knees. Holding it against my body, I turn back to the ambassador. He nods approvingly.

I disappear into my own room. It fits even better than I had imagined. Stockings are hardly essential, but those sneakers! I trot into the lobby where a bored young desk clerk sits swinging her sandaled feet. I explain my dilemma, and offer her the price of a pair of shoes if she will trade her white sandals for my once-white sneakers, just for the evening. She knows about our luggage not arriving, and agrees immediately. It must be fate, she giggles, that our feet are the same size.

I walk through the banquet hall to my table with more confidence than I have ever felt. Blue is my color, silk is my fabric, straight brown hair and smooth brown legs my best features. A waiter enters, carrying an elaborate first course of fruit. As he bends low to serve the president, the president indicates that he is to serve me first. The men around me, who all share my wardrobe secret, can barely conceal their mirth.

"To the unisex look," teases the ambassador, lifting his glass. The ministers chortle.

"To the unisex look," they chorus. "Our president's favorite."

The following morning we tour a charming seaside cottage, a model, I'm told, of what the government intends to build for the poor of Chiapas. The president praises the Minister of Housing for the concept, which combines basic needs with economy and beauty. I am enchanted by the elegantly simple architecture and cool furnishings of locally woven hammocks and straw mats. As we tour the house, the president, who has not let a day pass without some small gesture of attentiveness, picks up a hand-carved statuette of a Chamula Indian and presents it to me. I dispense with propriety and hug him. I feel his thrill as the warmth of my body passes through our thin cotton shirts and merges with the warmth of his.

We walk back to the waiting helicopters and lift off. I am bubbling enthusiasm. A minister cuts me short with an angry torrent of Spanish. "You think such houses should be built for the indigenous population? Houses with private kitchens for families whose drinking water is contaminated with tuberculous? Houses with flush toilets in villages that have no drainage, no running water closer than the river?"

"You're the Minister of Housing," I retort, embarrassed at not having seen for myself what he has just pointed out. "If it isn't an appropriate model, why didn't you build a better one?"

He throws up his hands up in a gesture of God-spare-me-from-this-fool. "That house isn't a model for the poor of Chiapas. It's a model to make our president happy. Don't you suppose he knows that?"

"Not necessarily." I think of the rabbits, and how no one told the president the real reason for why the Indians would not eat them. "He has to rely on others to advise him. If you don't tell him the truth, who will?"

The U.N. ambassador pats my arm. "You do not understand the Mexican political system, Rosita. In Canada you have a prime minister. In the U.S. you have a president. In Mexico, we have a god. One does not tell God how his universe is to be designed."

It may be true that Echeverría is a Mexican version of Marie Antoinette, wondering why breadless peasants don't just eat cake, but what was she speaking from if not ignorance? I have no way of telling whether President Echeverría believes such houses will someday be built by his government for poor families, or if he knows it to be an illusion. In either case, these cynical men have done their part to create and maintain the illusion. I am angry with them for it, and I am angry because the truth they aren't bothering to conceal from me will eventually force me to give up my own illusions about the only political leader I have ever really liked.

"Why are you telling me this?" I ask suspiciously. "Is this what you want journalists to write?"

The Director of the Coffee Institute yawns. "The Mexican press writes whatever we tell them. You will write whatever you want, which, because the president has been kind to you, will probably be kind to him. Few Mexicans will ever see it, not even the president, unless it is sure to please him."

The last place we visit is a rural site where government outreach workers bring quality sperm to farmers for artificial insemination, in an effort to upgrade local cattle stocks. I am pleased to see that here Echeverría not only listens to local officials but moves among the farmers and asks individuals whether the program is helping them. The farmers speak eloquently and without hesitation. Their main complaint is that the government team comes only once a fortnight. No one can predict when the cow will come into heat, and as the president knows, a cow can only be bred at the time of her own choosing. The president nods gravely. Back inside the building, President Echeverría says to the director of the artificial insemination program, "We must modify this program. In the future, each farmer will be given the sperm needed to inseminate his own cows when the time is right."

The director looks aghast. "But Mr. President, the sperm can only be kept alive in special low-temperature thermoses."

"Then each farmer shall have such a thermos."

"But these thermoses—" The program director sounds panicky. "They are made only in Switzerland. By what technology—"

"Mexican technology," the president says curtly, and strides out of the room.

"Impossible, impossible!" exclaims the program director to those of us still standing there. "A thermos that holds the temperature to forty degrees below zero — Mexico has no such technology! What shall I do?"

An elderly Mexican journalist and advisor to four presidents including Echeverría, puts an arm around the director's shoulders. "Just continue doing what you have been doing," he says softly.

"But how can I? The president said—"

"Yes," says the old advisor. "God has spoken. But does God ever look back?"

I leave the presidential entourage to follow the Director of the Mexican Coffee Institute to El Salvador to observe and write about his efforts to form an OPEC-type cartel of coffee-producing countries. A few weeks later, I return to Mexico City to attend the International Year of the Woman conference. There I receive an invitation from god-the-president to a banquet being given at the National Palace for foreign delegates to the conference.

There is a marked contrast between the male-dominated crowd that followed President Echeverría through Chiapas and the gathering of mainly women here in the palace. Most of the several hundred guests are wives of important men. During the conference I had listened, unimpressed, to the women's speeches. The majority merely parroted clichés that reflected the political aims of their spouses. Only Mrs. Echeverría made a positive impression on me, for she dared, in this Catholic country, to insist on the necessity of family planning.

I pass through a crowd of East Indian women in exquisite silk saris, African women with magnificent headdresses, European women in gowns of elaborate brocades, and Latina women, Mrs. Echeverría among them, in long full-skirted dresses covered with exquisite embroidery. The invitation had said that the evening's dress was to be "native costume." The women return my smiles and do not look askance at my black jeans and turtleneck. Perhaps they are as amused as I am with the thought that this is as close as a North American can get to "native costume."

The tables are beautifully laid, each with a clay candelabra in the shape of what Mexicans call the "tree of life," its branches decorated with vines, leaves, and birds. Entertainment is provided by Mexico's famous Ballet Folklorico. At my table, a Mexican dignitary whom I had met in Chiapas grumbles that this simple-minded president thinks he personally discovered *folklorico*. What's more, failure to serve wine at a banquet for such distinguished international guests is a disgrace, don't I agree?

"Well, some of the guests," I indicate the Egyptian wife of Anwar Sadat at the next table, "may be Muslims who would find alcohol offensive."

The dignitary gives me a suspicious look, brings his water glass to his crotch, and surreptitiously fills it from a flask.

After the meal we adjourn to a salon where I thank the president for his hospitality, still wishing, damn it, that I did not find him so attractive.

As I pass back through the dining hall on my way out, a heavily-accented voice calls, "You speak Spanish, yes? Vill you please to help me?"

A large Dutch woman in a brocade gown is struggling with a small Mexican waiter. She clings to one side of a clay candelabra, he to the other.

"You see," pants the woman, "It is no goot — not glazed. The melted vax cannot be removed. They vill throw it away. Tell him I vant to keep."

I translate her request to the waiter, and translate his response back to her. "He says, Fifty pesos, please."

"Ah!" Nodding vigorously, she lets go the candelabra and fishes in her jeweled handbag. The little waiter gives me a grateful smile.

Suddenly a supervisor descends on us with a look that sends the waiter scurrying. "A misunderstanding! Take it, please." He waves away the woman's money and presents the candelabra to her with a flourish. He grabs another candelabra and shoves it at me.

"No, thank you." I try to push it away.

"Take it, I insist! A memento from the President of Mexico."

A memento, yes, of both the generosity of Mexico's president and the poverty of its underpaid working class. I will accept a clay candelabra from the palace of a clay-footed president to remind me, always, of what is real and what is illusionary in Mexico.

I turn back for a last look at the man, standing in a pool of light with hundreds of brilliantly dressed women floating like flowers around him. He is watching me, smiling. What intrigues him is my unconventionality, which I have brought to his palace in the form of a braless turtleneck, black jeans, and long straight hair. He must think that this is how I've always been.

If there weren't so many people between us I'd go back and find a way to thank him for the loan of his magic carpet. It has helped me get to a freer place than I've ever been before.

BEYOND PREDICTABILITY

Costa Rica, 1979

It has been four years since I traveled with the president of Mexico. I have made other trips since, to the Caribbean, to Europe, and many to Canada. I've been back to Mexico, too — once to cover the building of the giant Chicoasén dam in Chiapas, once to write about coffee growers in Guerrero, once to visit a friend in prison, and then just passing through with Mark and Kathy, young friends from Omaha, en route to Costa Rica.

The trip with Mark and Kathy I knew was a mistake by the time we reached Southern Mexico. Mark's four-wheel drive jeep never left the pavement of the Pan American highway unless it was to look for a pharmacy where they could buy drugs which in the States could be gotten only by prescription, or some idyllic beach, there to lie about stoned for days on end. As we neared the Mexico–Guatemala border, my smoldering dissatisfaction with the nature of our travels flared up.

"Look, I'm not crossing an international border with marijuana in the vehicle! I've seen the inside of a Latin American jail once, and believe me, once is enough."

"Oh, Rosa, you are so fucking up-tight," Mark moaned.

"Rosa's right," Kathy announced. "We shouldn't go through customs with dope in the car. Let's smoke it all before we get there."

They were in the process of doing this when, passing the last joint between them, it was dropped and rolled under the seat. The smell rose like burning incense. Kathy searched but couldn't find it, while Mark continued to drive. The border loomed ahead.

Faced with a choice of jumping out of a moving vehicle or pulling up to a checkpoint wreathed in marijuana smoke, I opened the door to jump. Mark saw I was serious and stopped the jeep. They found and smoked the last joint. The border crossing was without incident, as was the next one, from Guatemala into El Salvador.

The light-hearted way they moved from country to country, focusing on their own "good time" rather than the culture and diversity around them, was pretty much how I had traveled on my first trip to Mexico. I had been on the move as they were now, to get away (but not really away) from my own culture. I had not been seeking or even very interested in what lay beyond. But those weeks of random, solitary travel that preceded my trip with the president had changed my way of traveling, and changed me, in ways I was only beginning to understand.

In El Salvador we spent a couple of days camped on a popular black sand beach, dining regularly at a cafe operated by an American surfer. I had no objections to Mark and Kathy's drug use, but my non-use was an affront to them. They accused me of being unwilling to take risks.

In fact, that was precisely my problem on this trip: the lack of risk-taking. I was tired of floating on fat rubber tires through country after country, bored with sitting in cafés while my companions browsed the local pharmacy for some new high, sick of watching them bargain with locals for handmade crafts while smiling at the vendors' malnourished children, then cruising away in a Toyota space ship fueled by our relative wealth.

It came to me, there in the surfer's café on the beach at La Libertad, that the problem with this trip was that their definition of risk-taking and mine was not the same.

As we headed south again on the Pan Am Highway, I saw a sign for San Salvador's international airport. "Let me out here," I said.

They looked at me, astonished. And hurt. "What about Costa Rica?" asked Mark. "Don't you want to see the Switzerland of Central America?"

"Another time. Drop me at the airport. I want to go home."

Two years later I plan a trip — alone — to Costa Rica. A friend, seeing a brochure on my desk that shows the usual idyllic beach scene, murmurs enviously, "Costa Rica. Looks like the sort of place a person could really relax."

"Umhum." I am already feeling the excitement that builds when I prepare for a trip, knowing I am soon to abandon the routines of home and work, rush for the airport, and feel the scoop of air under the wings of the plane. I haven't the slightest intention of trading that high for "relaxation" when I get there.

By now I have a whole bag of travel tricks to keep the adrenalin flowing. The first is to have no itinerary nor any advance reservations.

I like not knowing where I will be sleeping the first night away from home, like it that there will be days when no one I know will know where I am. This was a risk I never felt justified in taking as long as Jo was dependant on me. Now that she is a university student capable of winging off on her own to places as exotic as Zaire, I indulge myself more and more often in the thrill that comes from letting go of familiar things. Each time I do, I feel the breaking of more strands of that invisible web, the falling away of more inhibitions.

Certainly there are levels of freedom I haven't attained, some I don't even want. But these days I seem to fetter myself with fewer and fewer excuses. I no longer sink into apathy when monotony closes in. As a hunter might shoulder his rifle and go stalking wild game, I shoulder my backpack and stalk adventure.

I know where it lurks. The place I'll find it — or more likely, it will spring on me — is somewhere beyond predictability. The less predictable I make my trip, the more likely I will experience facets of life (and of myself) that I never imagined.

The process itself has by now become routine, like the familiar trail one starts out on to reach more distant, unmapped places. My small pack just fits under an airline seat, a seat near the front of the plane. I'm among the first in line at customs, and out of the airport before other passengers' luggage has reached the carousel. I ask the cab driver to recommend a place to stay, somewhere interesting that's not in anybody's guidebook. Whether a jewel or a pit doesn't much matter. What I'm after is that element of surprise.

After checking in I go out and walk randomly through the city, adjusting my ear to its voices, my body to its temperature, my pulse to its rhythms. As I ramble I collect maps, brochures, and newspapers. The first evening finds me flopped across a bed littered with materials I've collected, studying the lay of the land.

Parts of the "Switzerland of Central America" are, as promised, extremely beautiful. During my first days in Costa Rica I climb 1,600 feet up into the cloud forest of Monteverde Nature Reserve and look for (but do not see) quetzal birds. I take an excruciatingly slow, choo-choo kind of train down to Limon on the Caribbean coast, and then across to Puntarenas on the Pacific. In the capital I even succumb to an Egg McMuffin under the Golden Arches.

It is at McDonald's, a favorite lunch spot for lively young professionals, that I meet Gustave and Paula. They invite me out to their ranch for a weekend of horseback riding.

Though we ride western, Paula wears English-style riding clothes. She is a plump woman, sitting her horse in the graceful, relaxed way of a girl who learned to ride young. Gustave is thin and looks elegant on horseback, but rides with a competitive edge, urging us to gallop along wooded trails where there are overhanging branches to be avoided, and down slopes so steep it would be difficult for a horse to recover from a stumble. Paula is the better rider, which I suspect accounts for Gustave's recklessness.

We pass the day in light-hearted banter, but that evening, as we sit in the den watching the news on their big color TV, Gustave's mood turns sour. The lead story is the war in Nicaragua, covered in greater detail here than in the States. Images of corpses mutilated by Somoza's National Guard flash across the screen. The dictator is bombing his own capital. Managua's streets are filled with rubble and blood.

"He's hysterical," said Gustave with disgust. "He's done for." In an aside to me he grumbles, "Your government certainly backs some beauties."

What am I supposed to say? That U.S. support of three generations of Somoza family dictators has escaped my notice, and went undetected as well by my parents and grandparents? In a way, that's probably true. We might have noticed, but not like Gustave and Paula are noticing. For them, the war is happening just across the border, maybe two hours north of here. "Didn't Carter cut off aid to Somoza for human rights violations?" I ask hopefully.

"Oh, yes." Gustave sneers. "Then worked out a deal with the Israelis to supply the weapons."

I hate his sarcasm. Even more, I hate it that I do not know whether what he says is true.

Although Gustave's annoyance is directed toward the U.S. for what he terms "pouring fire on fire," neither he nor Paula show sympathy for the Nicaraguans.

"It's not surprising they've lived under dictatorship so long," Paula remarks. "They're very uneducated people."

I wonder how much education she thinks it takes to be opposed to a ruler as brutal as Somoza. But I don't ask. I have encountered this same attitude among many Costa Ricans - an appreciation for the fact that they are better off than other Central Americans, combined with a conviction that it is because they are better people.

At the end of the newscast, the television and their interest in politics click off simultaneously. Dinner conversation is about a sailing regatta they plan to attend next day. They urge me to come along.

I know it would be fun, as the horseback riding has been fun, but none of this is very different from what I might have done if I had stayed home. I am nagged by the feeling that I have left but haven't gone anywhere — or at least haven't arrived anywhere — yet. They are offering me a diversion, which I as a foreigner would repay by being their diversion. Being diverted, being someone else's diversion — this too I could have had at home. I thank them but claim that I have reservations at a resort on Playa Tamarindo and must go on in order to maintain my (imaginary) itinerary.

I spend the following night in a hotel near La Cruz. Outside passes the Pan American Highway. A bus south could take one to Panama. A bus north could take one — in about fifteen minutes — to Nicaragua.

There is excitement in the hotel lobby when I check in. Everyone is watching television and there are two radios blaring. Somoza has fled. He flew out this morning, taking with him, it is said, the entire national airline and virtually every liquid asset from every bank in Nicaragua.

I go to my room and sit looking out at the tropical foliage. It is very tranquil. Yet just to the north a people have overthrown a tyrant. Hype and romanticism aside, how often do real people overthrow real tyrants? How often am I this close to where real history is happening?

Although the bed is comfortable I don't sleep much. A little after four a.m. I get dressed, brush my teeth, and repack my bag. In the lobby the desk clerk sleeps with his head on the counter. He sits up when I cross the room.

"Is there a bus to the Nicaraguan border?" I asked.

"Not at this hour, *Señorita*."

"Is there a taxi?"

"Not at this hour, *Señorita*."

He speaks courteously, without interest or curiosity. But when I start for the door he calls after me, "You're not going out at this hour, are you, *Señorita*?"

"Is it dangerous? I've heard there's very little crime in Costa Rica."

"No Costa Rican will molest you, but there are many refugees in the our country just now, many Nicaraguans. Who knows what might happen?"

I smile and step out into the night. Not knowing what might happen is exactly what I've come for.

THE END OF A WAR BEGINNING

Nicaragua 1979

The Nicaraguan border is only ten kilometers or so, an easy two-hour walk in the cool of the morning. I pass a few houses, and sometimes hear the reassuring sounds of a family stirring inside. I keep looking for dawn light but fog holds it back. Houses become fewer. Soon there are none. Jungle odors of sweetness and decay press in on me. The highway is more isolated than I had expected. Maybe walking wasn't such a good idea after all. Okay, so I'm beginning to feel spooked. What sounds like footsteps behind me is probably my imagination. I listen again and don't hear anything. Then I do. The heavy, measured tread grows more distinct. I walk faster, but my legs are not long. The person behind is coming closer. I look back and catch the outline of a figure larger than myself. By now I am almost running. Still the footsteps come closer, until they are just behind me. Then they slow down, and I know it is for a reason: the walker is watching me. The person hangs there, still behind and a little to the side; close enough to pass, or grab me. Finally I can bear the tension no longer. Whatever is about to happen, I want to see it coming.

I turn sharply. The walker's steps falter and so do mine. I am staring into the curious brown eyes of a very young woman. Relief explodes across my face.

"*Buenos dias!*" I cry.

"*Buenos dias.*" She moves past with a firm, man-like stride, then slows her pace to match mine. Perhaps she too wants company for the walk along this empty, dawn-grey highway.

She asks why I am going to Nicaragua and I answer honestly. "I don't know. I just want to see the end of the war."

She takes a sudden, joyous breath. "So do I!"

Her name is Sabina. She says she is seventeen and has been a Sandinista guerrilla for three years. She had been in Costa Rica for treatment of a wound. Nothing serious, she claims, pushing back the collar of her shirt to show me a bandage, but infection was a danger. Anyway, it was a promise she made to her brother, that if she ever got wounded, she'd try to get to Costa Rica, where they have antibiotics.

Where is her brother now, I ask. Is he older or younger?

"My twin. He died. Two years ago. From infection, after they amputated his leg."

She looks straight ahead and walks a little faster. It crosses my mind that it isn't hate or anger or fear that makes good soldiers, good killers. It is this absence of feeling which I sense in the girl walking next to me.

It has become lighter. The fog is lifting. Suddenly the sun blazes over the treetops, so hot that we cross the highway to stay in the shade. Traffic is increasing. It is now a steady flow toward Nicaragua. There are trucks and pick-ups and old cars filled with children piled on top of parents piled on top of household goods. Some are singing. Others laugh and wave. They call out to each other and to us. "Is he really gone? Did they see him go? Is it true? Is it over?"

A mile or so from the border we reach the end of a line of traffic which is not moving. We walk on until a bus rumbles by, not taking its place in the line but moving ahead up the wrong side of the road.

People in the waiting cars shout as the bus passes, "*Nuestra ninos! Heroes de la revolución! Viva Sandino!*"

"Sabina!" yells the bus driver, grinding to a stop.

"Come on," Sabina nudges me. "We can ride."

My feet touch the metal step of the old school bus. I take a deep breath and plunge aboard like a scuba diver splashing off the side of a boat into that different world so close but out of sight just below the surface. This is it. I have my adventure.

The bus is jammed with kids, all wearing uniforms or some part of a uniform. An image shatters in my head. Everyone knows that the Sandinistas are mainly students, but in my mind's eye I had seen a revolutionary cadre of *university* students. It never occurred to me how very few university students there are in countries like Nicaragua. Not one person on this bus, including the driver, appears old enough to have been in college. They are all children. Wounded children.

Sabina moves down the aisle asking and fielding questions in the same breath. "I'm fine. How's your arm? Isabel was in San José with me, but couldn't leave the hospital. Where's Carla? Pepe's getting released tomorrow; he'll come as soon as he can. Has anybody seen Miguel?"

I stand at the front of the bus clinging to the back of a seat in which sits a boy who must weigh all of eighty pounds. One eye is heavily bandaged. The other stares at me with frank curiosity.

"How's your eye?" I ask.

"Gone," he says. And with an impish grin, asks, "How old are you?" I blush. "Thirty-nine. And you?"

"Fourteen," he says. "Almost."

At the border Sabina says, "I left my gun here. I have to go get it." She vanishes into a crowd of laughing, shouting teenagers. I start to follow, but soon lose her. It's like being in a college town after a victorious football game. Everyone wears green army fatigues and red-and-black scarves — their team's colors. The exhilaration is contagious.

I head for the office to get my passport stamped. At the entrance a stout boy lifts a smaller one up to hang a shoe shine kit, the sort little boys run after you with in poor countries. On the side of the shoeshine box are hand-painted words which translate: *"This will not be the future of our children."* They are, after all, celebrating something more important than a football game.

Inside I discover why traffic is not moving. The old bureaucracy has been displaced. There is as yet no new one to do even such a simple thing as open the border to homebound Nicaraguans. When no one offers to process my documents I go looking for Sabina. I don't want her to think I'm following her, but I don't know what to do.

Behind the building is a community of tents, a military encampment of sorts, and swarms of young people. I love the look of them. Berets tilted rakishly over bright eyes, dark curls against the red-and-black scarves, they are a thousand Che Guevara posters come alive. I doubt there's any reason to be frightened by all these milling, happy kids, but it makes me nervous to be around so many people carrying guns. Some of them glance at me as I pass. Their stares are curious. Not necessarily friendly.

I can't find Sabina so I go back into the office. There are a dozen people behind the desk. None pay me any attention. It occurs to me that they might be ignoring me because they don't know what to do. I walk around the counter and speak to a young woman leaning on the stalk of her rifle.

"Look," I smile, holding out my passport. "It needs a stamp."

She stares blankly at the passport. I pick up a stamp from the counter, adjust it for 19 July, and hand it to the boy with whom she is flirting.

"*Correcto*," he says, peering at the date on the stamp.

"What about this?" The girl holds up a list which shows names, dates of entry, passport numbers. "It has to be typed."

"I'll do it." I sit down at the typewriter and with half a dozen teenagers hanging over my shoulders, fill in the information.

"*Correcto*," they chorus, comparing what I put on the form with what is on my passport, proofing it word by word as I type.

"*Gracias.*" I pick up my passport and start for the door. Outside the line of cars is still motionless. The sun, much hotter now, blazes through windshields. Children whimper. I point to the waiting cars. "What about them? Shouldn't you let them in, too?"

They look at each other uncertainly. "I don't think so," one boy says finally. "There could be terrorists among them."

"Terrorists don't travel with babies," I counter. "Look, it's hot, and there's no place to get water."

As the words come out of my mouth I see their eyes, which had been so good-natured, grow hostile. Suddenly I realize how inappropriate it is for me, a North American and an adult, to say anything that might be construed as criticism. I back toward the door, praying to get through it before they decide to exercise their new authority in some unpleasant way.

At the door I raise my camera for a photograph of the shoeshine box, thinking it might please them. As I focus on the words, "This will not be the future of our children," tears come to my eyes. Their *children's* future? What about their own? Most of them aren't old enough to be married, to have held a job, or even finished school. What are they but kids themselves, in charge of a country? Who will help them? Do they even know they need help?

I lower the camera and see Sabina, a pistol now stuck in the waistband of her green fatigues. "There's space in a car going to Managua," she says. "You want to come along?"

I squeeze into the back seat with Sabina and two boys, Paco and Felipe. Two sixteen-year-old girls, Chita and María, sit next to the driver, giggling and flirting. They tell me they left school three months earlier, during Easter break, to join the Sandinistas. I ask what will happen now that the war is over.

"That's for *Los Viejos* to decide," the driver says over his shoulder. The Old Ones, he explains, are that handful of Sandinista leaders in their late twenties, thirties, a few even in their forties, who this very day are in the capital organizing a new government. Nicaragua's real problem has been the war and the Somozas. With the war ended and the Somoza family gone, life is wide open; Nicaraguans can do anything, be anything. Paco and Sabina agree. As for themselves, they are going back to school.

"What about you?" I ask Felipe, who has remained silent through the discussion.

He shrugs. It seems he isn't going to answer, but suddenly he begins speaking in a voice so low and Spanish so rapid I have difficulty following. "The problem is that we don't have a model. Who will we be like? Certainly not the U.S. or the Soviet Union; that's impossible. Honduras? Salvador? They're the same as Nicaragua was under Somoza. Costa Rica's better, but not much. It's just a slightly less poor banana republic. What about Cuba? I went to Cuba for training last year and I learned — oh, I learned many things. We love Fidel, you know. He's like a big brother to us. But his government, no, Cuba's style is not for us. The Nicaraguan spirit is too free. Even for the good of the nation we couldn't stand that much control of our lives."

The others chatter agreement. "Yes, yes. Nicaraguans love their independence. We want to come and go as we please, dance all night if we like. Cuba is fine for Cubans, but it wouldn't work here."

The car bounces into the ditch to detour around a Cessna crashed on the highway.

"You see," Felipe points. "A plane like that, it's not very big. But it would take a long time to build one if you didn't have a model."

We stop at a roadblock. A lanky, sweet-faced boy smiles through the open window and waves us on without bothering to check documents. He holds a machine gun in his hand, and in the same hand, a bunch of luscious green fruit of a type I had never seen. The camera lays in my lap, and as the car pulls away I spontaneously lift it and photograph the boy's face, framed as it is by the fruit and the gun-barrel.

An instant later the driver glances into his rear-view mirror and hits the brakes. We slam forward. He throws the car into reverse and begins backing up. I look back and see what he had seen: the sweet-faced boy down on one knee, his machine gun trained on our car.

The boy jerks open the door, gestures at me with his gun, and yells something I do not understand. Is he telling me to get out? Is he going to shoot me? I am paralyzed with fear.

"Camera!" he shouts, whacking my camera with the gunbarrel. "What are you taking pictures of?"

"Oh!" I begin to cry and then to laugh. "The fruit. I've never seen that kind before. I just took a picture of the fruit!"

"The fruit?" He looks baffled, then down to where I point, to the cluster still dangling from the hand that holds the gun. "Oh, haven't you ever seen _____ before?" He says a word I don't recognize and can't later remember.

"No, never. Do you want it?" I hold the camera out to him.

"No, no," he laughs. "Here, have some!" He tosses a handful of the grape-like fruit into my lap.

"Thank you," I say humbly.

"It's nothing." He smiles and waves us on.

Paco says something equating the intelligence of North Americans with cows. The girls in the front seat giggle. Sabina looks out the window, her jaw set in a hard line. I offer to share the fruit but no one responds. It is as if I am no longer there.

My throat is so dry it hurts to swallow. The temperature must be close to one hundred degrees. What am I doing here, packed body-to-body with a bunch of kids who, with justification, hate me? I close my eyes, feeling nauseous. For the moment, I've had all the adventure I can stomach. When I get to Managua I'll go directly to the airport and catch a plane back to a nice, air-conditioned hotel in Costa Rica.

We stop at a small store. The shelves are bare. Sabina asks a woman behind the counter, "Anything to drink?"

The woman disappears into the back and returns with a pail of water and a dipper. I am afraid to drink the water. I ask if I she has anything in a bottle. She shakes her head.

Paco leers at me. "Haven't you heard? Somoza bombed our Coca Cola plant." He zooms his hand through the air. "Nerrrrrrrrrrro — KABOOM!"

Everyone laughs. I try to smile, but don't quite make it. Their laughter is not at Paco's clowning but at me, and not because I'm funny but because I'm stupid. I walk outside. The sun is unbearably hot. Is there any way back to Costa Rica? I haven't seen any buses. Passing cars are packed. I am not lost; I am trapped.

Sabina comes out of the store. She holds out a dipper brimming with water. I take it. The instant it touches my lips I forget the dire consequences that might result from drinking impure water. It is so cool and sweet it brings tears to my eyes.

"Thanks." I hand back the dipper and whisper, "I'm really sorry."

She stares at the dipper for a minute, thinking thoughts which cause her face to change from that of a soldier to a young girl and back again. "It's not that we're anti-American," she says finally. "But it's been hard for us, you know."

I nod but can't speak. My emotions are pulling me too many ways.

The others come out. Paco opens the car door for me. Felipe offers me a piece of chewing gum. I see again how young they are. Too young to stay angry when we are, after all, on the way to a victory celebration.

On the outskirts of Managua, Sabina gives the driver directions to a barracks where she will rejoin her regiment. I want her to know how much I appreciate her having been my friend, or at least my guide, this far. I hold out a poster of Sandino bought at the border.

"Can I have your autograph? You're the first Sandinista I ever met."

She takes a stubby pencil from her pocket and in Spanish writes, *"From Sabina to my companion of the road. Don't forget us."*

The crowds in Managua are the same as those at the border, only larger and noisier. It is such a TV war-victory scene that it hardly seems real, yet because my mental image of such celebrations was formed by movies and television, this is exactly what I was expecting. Attractive young people in clean creased uniforms swirl through the crowd. Speeches, laughter, and music spill from everywhere. International media are omnipresent, packaging the scene for those not lucky enough to be here.

I wander into a park. In the heat of the day we sprawl on the grass, talking, laughing, floating on the moment. Every teenager seems to have a gun, which still makes me uneasy. As we talk I find myself asking, "Where did you get that gun?"

Almost every reply is the same. The Israeli-made machine guns are like their uniforms, clean and new. They were issued earlier today from supply depots abandoned by Somoza's National Guard.

After awhile I go to look for a hotel room. Some hotels are centers of military activity. Others swarm with foreign press. There are no vacancies. When I try to get something to eat in a hotel coffee shop, I am told that they are only serving their own guests. Other cafés are closed. Perhaps I could find a room or a restaurant in another part of the city, but as far as I can tell, there are no buses or taxis running.

Someone gives me directions to a market and I walk there to buy some fruit. In the vast space which should have been crowded with stalls, there are only a few. Each has a line of women and children waiting to buy whatever is for sale. I queue up for some oranges. When it is my turn, I hold out a dollar and ask for three oranges.

"There isn't enough," says the vendor.

Not enough? Maybe she doesn't understand. "I only want three. Not three kilos. Just three oranges."

The woman behind me pushes past and begins selecting the fruit. "There isn't enough!" she repeats sharply.

"One orange then!" I cry indignantly.

The vendor ignores me.

"I haven't had anything to eat all day!" Is that my voice, whining?

The women in line whisper to each other. Are they saying I don't belong here? But why? I turn away, feeling dizzy.

A little girl touches my arm. I look down and she hands me an orange. I take it gratefully, and hold out the money to her. She gives it a wide-eyed look and flees to her mother who is standing nearby with a bag of oranges she has just bought. I start toward the mother, smiling, but she hurries away, tugging the child with her.

Suddenly I ache with exhaustion. My ten-pound backpack feels as if it weighs fifty. How many miles have I walked today? Can it possibly get any hotter? Nothing, but nothing, appeals to me quite so much as a short, air-conditioned flight back to that air-conditioned hotel in Costa Rica.

The atmosphere at the airport is the same as in the city, except that here there are many more guns. There are no clerks at the airline counters. I spot a mechanic at the desk of the Nicaraguan airline, and ask where I might find out about flights.

He smiles broadly, but his voice is pure malice. "Where are the flights? The question, *Señorita,* is where are the planes?"

Then I remember what I heard on the radio: Somoza has stolen the entire national airline. All those planes are now parked in Miami.

The airport coffee shop is open but serving only Sandinista soldiers. I go out to the highway and look across at what until recently was a luxury hotel. It now seems to be a command center. Military personnel come and go. Maybe I could get food at the restaurant there, but I haven't the nerve to ask. I'll take my chances with a woman selling pineapples by the side of the road.

There is no line at her stand, and she does not seem to mind when I ask her to cut one for me. She whacks off the top and with a few flicks of the machete, removes the spiky peeling and sections the juicy gold fruit into wedges. I sit on the curb and eat the whole thing. Then wipe the stickiness off my hands and try to figure out what to do.

With no transportation to scout for a place to stay, going back into the city doesn't seem like a good idea. According to the map, I am on the Pan American Highway. It isn't all that far to Honduras. Two, maybe three hours, five at the most? How bad can things be, I reason, if I am no more than half a day from a country where things are still working?

An old Chevrolet with a bunch of kids like those I rode with earlier stops to buy pineapple. I ask if I can ride with them. A plump girl of fifteen, with a rifle stuck between her knees, tosses the gun up on the ledge behind the back seat and squeezes over to make room. Her name is Gloria. She is from a village ten miles away, which is as far as they are going.

"Where did you get your gun?" I ask.

"From a *Guardia*," Gloria replies, giving me the answer I will hear most often from now on. "There's no other way. You want a gun, you must kill a *Guardia* and take his gun."

The next ride is short, and the one after that ends at a roadblock where a sentry asks me to give up my seat for somebody on crutches. While waiting for another ride I watch a nine-year-old boy pick at something between his front teeth with the sight on the barrel of his pistol.

"Where did you get your gun?" I ask, as much to make him take the damned thing out of his mouth as to find out the answer.

"It used to be my father's." He proudly hands it over for my inspection. I take it gingerly and see that there are bullets in at least four cylinders.

"You shouldn't put a loaded gun in your mouth." Embarrassed at having given be-careful advice to a child who carries a gun, I add, "Guns have to be kept dry or they, they rust, don't they?"

He takes the gun from me. Holding it against his abdomen, he carefully wipes the spittle off its barrel with the tail of his T-shirt.

The next ride takes me a fair distance, but turns off the highway in the middle of nowhere. It is hilly green terrain, tranquil and lovely in the golden light of late afternoon. But when an hour goes by without a single vehicle passing, I stop appreciating the scenery. Even at home dusk is a lonely time.

A jeep comes around the curve, slows, and stops. The relief I felt at its approach vanishes when I see that it carries four men wearing red-and-black Sandinista scarves.

"*Norteamericana?*"

"Si."

"Get in."

"No thanks," I say brightly, as if I have chosen to be on this god-forsaken stretch of road for the fun of it.

"What's the matter?" the driver calls sarcastically. "Is the little *gringa* afraid of Sandinistas?"

"No," I retort. "It's just not my habit to travel alone with four men."

Suddenly the two men in the back are out of the jeep, machine guns in hand, waving and shouting. For a second I think I am being assaulted.

"Stupid *gringa*!" they yell. "Don't you know the difference between a *Guardia* and a *Sandinista*? Don't you know what it means to be a revolutionary? The women are our comrades, our equals! Revolutionaries aren't *macho* pigs! We have respect for women!"

There is more but with the two of them plus the two in the front seat shouting simultaneously, I don't catch every word. The main point is clear enough.

"Okay, okay," I laugh nervously, and climb in over the tailgate.

"Hold this," says one soldier, plopping an ugly machine gun in my lap. He picks up another and turns away to scan the dusk-darkened mountains.

The men are in their early twenties but the wariness in their eyes makes them look much older. They tell me that they have been fighting in the mountains for the past five years. The tone in their voices, like the look in their eyes, is different from that of the youngsters I met in the south and around Managua. I sense that for these soldiers hunting and being hunted is more than a daily activity. It has become their sensory reaction to life; their pulse-beat.

"It isn't over yet, you know," says the driver. "There are plenty of *Guardia* in the mountains around here who haven't surrendered yet."

Suddenly I see clearly where I am. I am not in the victory picture which reporters at this very moment are packaging for delivery to the world's TV viewers, but on its underside. Here there are no celebrating winners, but bitter losers hiding in dark hills, not wanting the war to end like this but wanting, still, to kill.

The night closes in, very dark. The canvas-topped jeep winds its way along slowly, headlights illuminating only a few feet of the narrow mountain road. Moment by moment the tension increases. Perhaps each of us are imagining the jeep's lights as they might appear to a *Guardia* out there in the darkness, through the cross-hairs of his gunsight. I look down at the machine gun in my lap.

"I'm afraid," I say in a voice as thin as a child's. "I don't know how to use this."

"Maybe you won't have to," says the soldier next to me. But his eyes, incessantly sweeping the dark, brush-covered hillside, are not reassuring.

"When will it be over?" I ask.
"What?"
"The war."
Minutes passed, and nobody answers.
Then one of them speaks. "Who knows?"

It is very late when we breast a hill and glimpse a twinkle of lights ahead. "This is the last town before the border," explains the driver. "You'll have to spend the night here."

As if by magic a motel sign looms out of the darkness.

"Yes," I say eagerly. "I'll get out here."

They exchange glances, but say nothing. The jeep stops. I thank them for the ride.

"*Buenos noches, gringita.*"

As they pull away I hear them laughing but I don't care. The motel looks very modern, splendid in the moonlight.

When I push open the door it is not the expected coolness of air-conditioning that greets me but a hot, sickening smell. Even before my eyes adjust to the light I know that I am still on the underside of the victory picture. Here in the harsh glare of florescent lights there are no parades.

In beds and on pallets on the floor, covers are thrown back to expose young, thin bodies. In plain view are arms that aren't there, legs that aren't there, bandaged heads, bandaged groins, dressings in need of changing, and blood-stained sheets. I try to turn away but there is no place to turn. All over the lobby, along the hallway, in the rooms, and out in the patio are wounded people — young faces that seem younger because even against the white sheets they are so pale.

Someone touches my shoulder. "*Señorita?* What are you doing here?" A tall captain is looking down at me.

"A room," I whisper. "Where is the nearest ... hotel?"

"You're North American?"

"A journalist. I came for the victory celebration."

"You'll be able to find something in town." His hand gently clasps my bare arm as he walks me outside.

I look in the direction he points and see the town a kilometer or so off the highway. I think of the *Guardia* who haven't surrendered yet. I do not want to walk down that dark road alone.

His fine-boned fingers close over mine, warm and comforting. I know he knows what I am willing to pay to not be alone anymore tonight. Even in the half-light I can see that his eyes are dark-circled with fatigue. The way his hand trembles tells me that he needs a night of anesthetic against the pain of all those bleeding kids even more than I need the illusion of his protection.

I feel him weighing the idea, whether to come with me and if so, for how long. Then I see something which has been in other gazes that have followed me all day. In a moment as desolate as I have ever known, I suddenly understand what it is.

I am passing through a nation where perceptions of "us" and "them" have been honed by war. They are the "us" and I am the "them." It shows now in the captain's eyes as it has in others, a kind of curiosity mingled with indifference. My throat constricts as if touched by a knife.

"You don't think there will be any shooting tonight, do you?" I try to sound casual but my voice is faint.

For a moment he says nothing. Then replies, "If there are any snipers around you'd be safer walking alone than with me." The hand is withdrawn. "Come back tomorrow and I'll find you a ride to the border."

I force myself out of the circle of light and down the dark road. He stands there, watching me walk away. I hope he regrets his decision, that he remembers and fantasizes for a long time about the hours we might have spent together the night the war ended.

But no, he will not remember it that way. Mingled with the desire in his eyes there was that other thing. As I disappear into the darkness he will be musing that if a *Guardia* bullet finds its way into my body it will be only just. After all, the *Guardia* got their weapons from Them, and I am one of Them.

At the end of the road I find a small war-ravaged town. Radios blare speeches, cheers, and music from Managua but the streets are totally empty. Everyone is inside, still behind barricaded doors because there are *Guardia* in the hills who haven't yet laid down their arms.

A woman shows me to a cement room as cold and bare as a cell. The room's heavy door, though barred from the inside, fails to convey the sense of security I would have drawn from a man's warm body. I lie awake waiting for morning, and sleep, and wake, and wait.

During the night I hear gunfire, or what I think is gunfire. Perhaps only fireworks. Or prescient dreams of another war, just beginning.

THE TRAINING OF A TOUROIST

Suriname 1990

It is tedious but commonplace to spend one's first moments in a new country standing in line while an immigration official squints at each passport as if the signature is forged and the photograph resembles that of a well-known terrorist. But when the ferry from Guyana docks on the Suriname side of the river, I find no squinty-eyed officials waiting to check passports, nor any posted instructions. I follow other passengers from the boat into a barren room. They sit down on hard wooden benches facing an empty table. I do likewise without the slightest idea of what to expect.

After a twenty-minute wait, three men in military uniforms stride in and sit down at the table. One barks a name. A woman passenger steps forward and stands before the military police as if at a court martial. The middle MP squints at her passport and snaps a question. The woman replies softly. He orders her to speak up. Thus every question and every answer is heard by everyone in the room. As these exchanges are in Dutch I don't understand them, but I suppose they are the usual questions asked by immigration officials the world over.

Interrogations continue until each of the hundred passengers have been processed. I and a Dutch missionary traveling with her elderly father are the last called. For reasons I do not understand, they are denied entry.

When it's my turn, I stand before the three MPs and answer the questions they put to me in broken English. I explain that I intend to spend a week in the capital, then go to the eastern border town of Albina and catch a boat to French Guiana.

"Too many tourists in Albina," growls one MP. "Take de plane."

I can make no sense of the MP's ridiculous statement, and figure it's none of his business anyway. Once past this petty army bureaucrat, I'll travel where and how I please.

Like most North Americans I travel with the assumption that I know where I am going and, unlike my earlier travels, am now well-informed enough to know what to expect when I get there. From research I have done on this former Dutch colony, I've learned that most of its less-than-a-million people live in towns near the coast, surrounded by rice paddies and sugar plantations. The nation's vast jungle hinterland is uninhabited except for a small indigenous population known throughout the Guianas as Amerindians, and a few "Bush Negroes" — descendants of runaway slaves.

A four-hour bus ride past well-tended farms interspersed with marshes glittering with bird life brings me to Paramaribo, capital of Suriname. I am enchanted with the solid, Old Europe look of its Dutch colonial architecture. Never have my travels taken me to a place so meticulously clean. At the budget-priced guest house where I'm staying, crisp, ironed sheets are replaced each morning with fresh ones, the floors are scrubbed daily, and everyone's shoes are parked Dutch fashion outside the door. Food in open-air markets is fly-free, wrapped in plastic or kept in glass cases. Restaurants serve an aromatic blend of East Indian–Indonesian–African–Creole cuisine.

A few hours into my first morning, the pleasure at having discovered such an untouristed jewel is interrupted by a sharp "Nay!" from a soldier. He wags his finger to indicate that it is not allowed to do what I am doing, which is sitting on the seawall.

I get up and move. A block further on, I lift my camera to capture a photogenic ferryboat. Before I can snap the shutter, another soldier materializes and informs me that if I do this subversive thing, my camera will be confiscated.

I know Suriname had a military coup in 1980, and under pressure from the Dutch, elections were held in 1987. A new president was installed, by which I supposed Suriname had regained a civilian government. It looks as if this is another of those places where a democratically elected president gets the ceremonial functions while an authoritarian military keeps the power.

Paramaribo under military "order" is not nearly as inviting as a city of such innate charm should have been. I decide not to stay a whole week, but shall go on to Albina where, according to my guide book, I will find a ferry to French Guiana.

I ask people for directions to Albina but get no response except "Nay!" and a discouraging shake of the head.

Does this mean that there is no bus? That they don't understand me? Or don't know how to reach a town which is only one hundred kilometers away? I hail a taxi, confident that any cabby's English will be better than my Dutch.

When I ask the taxi driver how much the two-hour trip will cost he astonishes me by replying, "Nay, nay! It's hot in Albina now. Touroists make too much trouble."

The next taxi driver I approach reacts even more strangely. "Me no!" he says sharply. "I don't like touroists."

Frustration comes easy when temperature and humidity are in the nineties. When the next cab stops I get in and say in my most comanding voice, "Take me to Albina."

The driver swivels around in his seat and laughs out loud. "No can do dat, my frien'. Maybe dey let you pass, but me, I black, same as Bush Negro; the military call me touroist and I don't go nowhere for sure."

At this moment my ear fine-tunes the "taki-taki" English spoken here. The word they are pronouncing "tour-o-ist," which I had been translating as "tourist" is actually *terrorist*.

"What *terrorists?*"

The driver shrugs. "Well, de military call all dem Bush Negroes touroists, but de Bush Negroes dey fighting for all us. Dey don't want de military same as nobody don't want de military. We can't fight; we be killed for sure. Dem fight and run to de bush, don't most of 'em be caught. Only if dey be caught, dey killed, and dey towns like Albina be burn to de ground. Das why all deese refugees here in Paramaribo. You don't never see dat befo' because Bush Negroes, dey don't like de city; dey don't work for no man but dey-selfs."

As so often happens, things take on an entirely different and more comprehensible shape in the light of a little information. One whole wing of the guest house where I am staying is crowded with black families. I have seen them cooking in the courtyard, and watched Rotary Club buses coming to pick up the children. When I ask about this I learn that both the lodging provided by the guest house and service club outings for the children are part of a city-wide pattern of generosity toward Bush Negroes refugees. The desk clerk's explanation is an echo of the taxi driver's words. "The Bush Negros fighting our fight."

"We were a Dutch colony," says a pretty, pudgy Javanese woman I meet in a pastry shop. "Five years of independence, and wham! Just like that, the military stole our democracy. The president went off to exile in Holland, and what have we got? A puppet president and runaway inflation." She bites into her eclair with a look of inexpressible sadness. "All my children have emigrated to Holland."

She also claims that the revolt against the military is being carried out by Bush Negroes because it is easier for them to escape capture in the jungle. However, I visit a Dutchman who offers another explanation.

"These Bush Negroes, they don't give a flip who's in power as long as you leave them alone. But after the military got arms from Khadafi via the New Jewel movement in Grenada — there's a left-right connection to make your head swim — the soldiers just had to push somebody around. Bush Negroes do some light smuggling, cigarettes, canned goods, stuff like that, from French Guiana; have done for years. The army decided to put a stop to it. Now it's women who do the smuggling. You'd think the stupidest person in the world could see that if you start hassling Bush Negro women you're going to anger Bush Negro men, but the army didn't figure that out. So now they've got a full-scale revolution on their hands."

"What about the Amerindians?" I asked.

"Ask my wife; she's Amerindian."

We are sitting at a table in their cleanly-raked, white sand yard. His wife hacks a pineapple from a spiky plant growing nearby, brings it to the table, and begins to pare it with a machete. She hands us each a slice and sits down. Her four-year-old son leans against her.

"Amerindians and Bush Negroes have always gotten along," she says evasively. "There's enough room in the jungle for everybody."

"Our friend wants to know how it is now," her husband admonishes. "Not how it's been for the last three centuries."

She looks out across the yard. Finally she says, "Amerindians don't like to fight. But the military drafted some into this Delta Force, they call it. They want Amerindians to track Bush Negroes in the jungle because your ordinary soldier, he can't do that." She pauses. "You understand, there's nothing an Amerindian can't find in the jungle, if it's there."

To the child she says, "Bring us some napkins, son, to wipe our hands."

When the child has disappeared into the house, she continues. "Where my parents live, last September, two soldiers came by in a tank on their way from one base to another. For no reason, they blew up the village. An eighteen-year-old girl and her baby, asleep in a hammock, were killed. The papers say there will be a trial, but who knows? Because of this, some Amerindians have joined the Bush Negroes. So you see, they are on both sides now."

The child returns with the napkins. She takes one and wipes a trickle of pineapple juice off his uptilted face.

"Times change," she says quietly.

I am working on an article about Suriname and I don't want to leave the country without visiting at least one of its famous nature reserves, preferably the 149,000-acre Raleigh Falls reserve deep in the jungle, or Brownsberg, a pristine rainforest reserve not far from the capital.

"Sorry," says Anita, the forestry department official who arranges its eco-tours. "All the facilities have been burned at Raleigh Falls, and Brownsberg has been declared off limits because according to the military, the area is controlled by terrorists."

Anita, whose parents came to Suriname as indentured servants from Indonesia, has a passion for the jungle that I have not seen in others here in the Paramaribo. She senses my frustration at getting to see no more of Suriname than the narrow, cultivated strip along the coast, and sits there tapping her pencil.

"You should meet Edward," she says suddenly. As we walk down the hall to his office she explains that Edward is a thirty-seven-year-veteran of the forestry service, a man of Jewish/African/Dutch/Amerindian descent. "In other words," she laughs, "he's pure Surinamese."

As soon as she tells Edward what I want, he offers to use his forestry pass to take me into the off-limits rainforest. He waves away my offer to pay. "I bring de truck, 'Nita bring de food, you fill de gas tank. We all have a good time."

"You're a tourist," Anita says by way of explaining this act of pure hospitality. "We can't let the war stop you from seeing all the most beautiful parts of Suriname."

"What about the terrorists?" I ask.

"Dat military word," Edward sniffs. "Don't mean nothing to us."

After a day in the rainforest, we drive into a Bush Negro village. Here, instead of the village being destroyed, it is the military compound that has been burned to the ground. Otherwise there is no sign of conflict.

We take shelter from the sun under the thatch roof of a café. The place looks pretty primitive and I am wondering about sanitation when a barefoot black girl of about twelve strolls out with a large pan of dirty dishes balanced on her head. She off-loads the dishes onto a wooden table in the middle of the sand yard and fills the pan with water from a nearby spigot. With undivided attention, she carefully scrubs each dish, then scrubs the table, then dumps the soapy water over her feet. She refills the pan with clean water, rinses the dishes, rinses the table, and rinses her feet. I decide that this is a higher level of sanitation than one is exposed to in the average First World restaurant, so enjoy my meal and suffer no ill effects.

On the way back to Paramaribo we pass a train over on its side with tall grass growing up through the windows. I mention that according to my guidebook Suriname still has one train, a steam engine relic built in 1904 to haul people in and out of the gold fields. I hope to take a trip on it before I leave.

"Dat's it." Edward jerks his thumb at the overturned train. "Murdered."

"Who? The engineer?"

"Not de engineer. De train." The old forester sighs. "Soldiers not de smartest people. Dey want to inspect de train for dem dey call turoists so dey yell to halt. De crew put on brake, but train no stop on de spot like a car; it got to run on a few meters. Soldiers get mad at train cause it still moving, and start shootin' with dem machine guns. De crew get bullets in dey legs, but de train she boiler shot plumb to death. She don't never gonna run no more."

How is it that I who pay attention to foreign affairs, subscribe to both mainstream and alternative publications, and carry an expensive up-to-date travel guide, have arrived in Suriname totally ignorant of the fact that there is an armed struggle in process?

"I didn't know there was a war here," I say crossly. "I've never seen anything about it in the news."

"Why would anybody in your country care?" Anita asks softly. "It's only our people being hurt."

Edward pushes his spectacles up on his nose and smiles. "Suriname don't have it so bad. Where the U.S. fixin' things, lota more people gettin' killed."

I think of how Surinamese citizens are outraged that one Amerindian woman and her baby were killed and one Bush Negro town burned. When I compare this to the devastation I have seen in Nicaragua, the thousands of refugees in El Salvador, the massacres of Indians in Guatemala, the bombed suburbs of Panama, all countries where "the U.S. fixin' things," I don't know how to answer.

Anita glances at my unhappy face. "Don't think about it." She pats my hand with her own, delicate as a Javanese dancer. "You're a tourist; you came to have a good time."

It's true that I travel for pleasure. But where is the joy when every trip opens onto a new vista of violence, and not even in the jungle do I find anyone who admires the nation of my birth?

Is "don't think about it" the only solution? Or is there something I should be doing?

RAMBOS AND REALITIES

El Salvador 1991

San Salvador's sleek new Tower of Democracy looms on the screen. Some passengers watching the in-flight video burst into laughter. Those of us who haven't been to the country recently don't get the joke, and won't, until we see the actual building.

I am en route to El Salvador, working with a Malibu group called Earth Trust Foundation which is providing support to refugees made homeless by the war. I have been to El Salvador before, but not for quite a while.

Fifteen years ago I jeeped the Pan American Highway as far as El Salvador with Mark and Kathy, careening from one beach and pharmaceutical high to the next. Later that same year I flew to San Salvador in a private jet with the director of the Mexican Coffee Institute and stayed at Hotel Camino Real in the heart of the capital, the only North American journalist allowed to observe the formation of an OPEC-type coffee cartel. In 1979 I was again in El Salvador, hitchhiking north from Nicaragua after the Sandinista victory. I fell ill and was taken in by a farm family. I came back to visit them a few years later, but they had disappeared. No one at the military compound which stood where the farm had been could tell me what had become of them.

Each of those visits left me with a different sense of El Salvador, and all of them together did not prepare me for this trip. What war does to people is one thing. What a decade of it does is something else.

As I cross the city with my host, an American priest, he points out the Tower of Democracy, built by a government that has been at war against its own people for more than a decade. The black glass-and-steel skyscraper stands in splendid isolation but many of its dark windows no longer reflect the sun. They are broken and covered with cardboard. I ask the priest what happened.

"Somebody blew it up."

A few days later I pass the building again in a taxi. I ask the Salvadoran driver, "What happened to your Tower of Democracy?"

He looks up at the building and replies, as if asking a question, "In El Salvador there is another reality?"

I soon realize that what happened to the Tower of Democracy has also happened to El Salvador. Somebody blew it up. And there *is* another reality.

I am a guest at a house where Jesuit volunteers, a sort of Catholic Peace Corps, stay when they're in the city. Most of them work in rural areas with recently repatriated refugees. They carry identification cards which describe them as missionaries, although liberation theology gives them leeway and encouragement to be community organizers as well.

The communities where they work are made up of Salvadoran people whose villages were destroyed by the Salvadoran military, sometimes the army, sometimes the air force, sometimes both. Survivors fled into neighboring countries, usually empty-handed. Some hid in the forests, living in primitive camps like the one I saw in Belize. More often they were ferreted out by the authorities of the country they had entered and confined in UN-sponsored refugee camps. Years passed. Living as prisoners in these camps eventually became as intolerable to them as the war. One by one, refugee groups decided to go home. Most returned as they had fled, empty-handed.

I visit several communities and am appalled by their beaten-down appearance. But Anna, a young volunteer from Spain, describes a different reality. "It used to be that when soldiers came into the village people hid because they all have memories of these terrible atrocities that caused them to flee in the first place. But now when they see the soldiers coming somebody rings a bell and everybody comes out. We surround the soldiers. If they try to take someone, we all go. We don't allow them to take just one."

I ask Anna whether she also encounters guerillas. She says yes, men from both sides come into the refugee camps. They cannot be distinguished by their uniforms. Government troops often dress as FMLN guerillas in order to ferret out sympathizers, and the guerillas, having no money to buy uniforms, wear whatever they can get.

"So how do you know which is which?"

"I look into their eyes." Anna stares intently into mine. "If they are military, there is this Rambo thing because the military training, it makes boys into Rambos." She squeezes a fist against her chest. "A tension comes inside me."

Later, back at the volunteers' house in the city, I step into the street as three boy soldiers clump past, camouflage uniforms and hot black boots on a hot afternoon, fingers curled on the triggers of their automatic rifles. By the tight, jabbing way they move, it seems that at any second they will kick in a door or shoot someone. I choose another route to the park. When I arrive I see them there, just having lunch. There was no purpose to the way they moved, any more than there is a purpose to the way they look at me now, eyes hard, no smile in response to mine. It is simply the Rambo way, transferred from the cinema jungle of Vietnam to the suburban streets of San Salvador.

The quickest route from the volunteers' house to downtown is through a neighborhood of lovely homes belonging to high-ranking military personnel. There are ten-foot cement walls around these homes. Along the tops of the walls are coils of razor barbed wire, the kind used around the perimeters of prisons. Each end of the street is heavily guarded. Soldiers point their guns at passing traffic and stare hard, transmitting a tension which says that this is their jungle and the enemy is everywhere.

Before coming here I had been shown a video of a camp where the Salvadoran government had confined a group of repatriated refugees who, in defiant memory of an archbishop murdered by the military, call themselves Ciudad Romero. The campsite, a treeless plateau formerly used as a bombing range, offers no possibility of farming, fishing, or any type of self-sufficient activity. It is this helpless community that our group in Malibu wants to help.

The first thing I learn about these refugees is that they are not so helpless as we imagined. Father Kelly, a priest from San Francisco, tells us that Ciudad Romero's leaders got permission from a disbanded cooperative to take over its abandoned three-hundred-acre farm, and then, family by family, quietly moved there. This has greatly upset the government but because of the attention repatriated refugees are getting from international groups like ourselves it dares not use force to bring them back to the assigned camp. Instead, the army has established a roadblock on the dirt track leading to the farm. Its objective is to keep the people of Ciudad Romero confined there and to prevent other refugees from joining them.

The priest drives out to the farm not knowing whether he will be able to get past the roadblock or how safe we will be once we get there.

Along the highway we see hundreds of soldiers, many of them the so-called "special forces," with faces painted black so that they appear more intimidating. I am not reassured by a billboard which proclaims,

> WELCOME TO USULUTÁN
> THE SIXTH INFANTRY BRIGADE
> SALUTES YOU
> RESPECTS YOU and
> PROTECTS YOU

As Father Kelly feared, there is trouble at the roadblock. Just ahead of his jeep are three large trucks piled high with the belongings of a second group of refugees called Nueva Esperanza. They want to join the Ciudad Romero group already at the farm. They are insisting that the soldiers have no right to prevent them from going where they please in their own country. The soldiers, who have their orders and their guns, are implacable.

Suddenly, women leap down from the trucks and start rolling away the boulders that block the road. Soldiers rush at them shouting, holding automatic rifles to their heads, but perhaps because of the priest and foreigners watching, they hold their fire.

The instant the road is cleared of rocks, the lead truck, driven by a teenage girl, moves forward. The second one follows. But the third refugee truck, just ahead of Kelly's jeep, will not start. A soldier walks back and shoots out the tires.

Men, women, and children pull what they can carry off the disabled truck and walk down the dirt track chanting, *"No passe atras!"*

"That's a Sandinista slogan," Kelly translates. "It means 'Not one step back!'"

"Dirty Commies!" the soldiers yell after the departing refugees.

The people of Ciudad Romero have only been on the farm a couple of days. They do not have tents but are living under blue plastic sheets donated by the United Nations High Commission for Refugees. When we arrive, fires are burning, rice and tortillas cooking. Children carry water from the creek half a mile away.

Ciudad Romero has moved repeatedly in the past six months. First it moved by boat and on foot from a camp on Panama's Caribbean coast to the capital city. There 635 refugees camped on the street in front of the embassy. The winter rains began but they stayed on. For two months they negotiated with the Salvadoran government for the right to return to their own country.

A teenager named Alberto, old enough to remember life in El Salvador before the war, tells me he thought they would return to the farm where they had originally lived. Or better yet, they might be allowed to settle on the coast where they could have a fishing cooperative and enjoy El Salvador's beautiful black sand beaches. Instead, the government had forced them onto a waterless plateau of blazing sun and blowing dust, where they refused to stay.

"I dreamed of coming back since I was five years old," Alberto recalls. "But that place with no trees, it was not what I dreamed. It was not my country." He gazes across the brush-covered land where the community is now encamped. "There is water here," he says. "We can farm. My father will teach me."

Four friends from Malibu have arrived, bringing with them medicine and clothing. Scores of Malibu children have sent letters and gifts to the children of Ciudad Romero. We had planned to distribute these at school but children who have moved four times in the past six months (most recently the day before yesterday) do not attend school. Children are as busy as their parents, carrying water from the river, collecting sticks from the surrounding bush to keep cook fires going, grinding corn for tortillas, and looking after younger siblings. Nevertheless, word gets around and on Saturday morning about fifty youngsters show up to receive their mail.

Among the gifts sent from Malibu are notebooks, pens, and crayons. When these have been distributed the children lay the tablets in their laps and write to their pen-pals in Malibu. The letters are brief and, like those they received, are decorated with drawings. The most common image is that of a home. Some sketch the camp where they now live. Others draw the house they would like to have. One child draws a simple outline of a house with no details except, on one side, a large water faucet.

There are many sketches of a truck which the community has just purchased and which is its only vehicle. The third most common drawing is that of a helicopter. One child whose page is filled with pictures has labeled each thing: Mother. Dog. Duck. Tent. Hovering above the mother, the dog, the duck, the tent, is a helicopter which he has labeled: WAR.

Two days later we see the frightened faces of these same children looking up at a Huey helicopter as it circles low over the camp, machine guns protruding. But this particular Saturday is for kicking the soccer balls sent from Malibu and blowing rainbow soap bubbles into the sky, a morning for forgetting about helicopters and what they mean.

The children tell me that this farm is nicer than that plateau where the government made them live. I cannot imagine. During the day shade temperature hangs in the nineties. I can't bring myself to wash in the creek where Ciudad Romero's 635 people, plus the 350 from Nueva Esperanza, now encamped on the opposite bank, are bathing, drinking, and doing laundry. If this is nicer what could it have been like there?

I hear of a well at a farm a mile distant, with clear cool water and friendly owners. When the temperature drops a little in late afternoon I brave the fierce biting black flies and go there to bathe.

I am shampooing, pouring buckets of water over my head, when I look up and see three men and one teenage girl in green fatigues, carrying rifles. I ask the farmer's wife if they are guerillas.

"They are community defenders," she replies evasively.

I study them closely. All I can tell for sure is that their eyes are not Rambo. The girl walks toward the well unscrewing the cap of her canteen. I draw a fresh bucket of water and fill it for her. We are about the same size and have the same brown hair. From a distance might we be taken for mother and daughter?

"Are you a combatant?" I ask.

She giggles. "Is a monkey a combatant?"

I later learn that this teenager is engaged in one of the most dangerous of all clandestine activities. She climbs palm trees to get coconuts for the medics who, lacking plasma, use the milk for transfusions in the field. The military knows that coconuts are used for this purpose, so the groves are guarded. When they see a person clinging to the slender trunk they shoot to kill.

Another day I go with friends from Malibu to meet formally with a guerilla spokesman. He explains that the FMLN has always believed that a reasonable distribution of land must be Salvador's first priority. But now demilitarization is even more important because no positive social change can take place as long as the population is being harassed by its own military. One of the Malibu people, a veteran of Korea whose most formative experience in that war was the rebuilding of villages destroyed by the fighting, asks the FMLN officer if it wouldn't be better for their cause if they excluded the Communists.

The young man smiles slightly but answers seriously. "We are aware that North Americans think of communists as evil people. But if we have nothing to eat and someone who finds a little food brings it back for all to share, that is communism, too."

The American veteran, whose sympathies for the poor run very deep, looks uncertain.

The FMLN spokesperson seems to understand. He adds in a quiet, non-judgmental voice, "Perhaps because we have so little, we don't fear sharing as you do."

I walk back to the Land Rover half-blinded with tears. Whatever the meeting has been for the others, for me it is pure *deja vu*; another place and time but the same earnest, non-dogmatic humanitarianism I encountered among the Sandinistas in 1979. We already know what happened to them. Why should it be different here in El Salvador? What odds does anyone give this twelve thousand boy-girl army against fifty-four thousand U.S.-backed Rambos?

On Sunday morning I ford the stream to become acquainted with the refugees of Nueva Esperanza. I want to interview Father Angel, a Spanish Dominican who was the priest of their village at the time of the military massacre and remained with them throughout a decade of exile. I find the padre with pant legs rolled up and a shovel in his hands. There has been a great rainstorm in the night and everyone is busy trenching around their campsites to drain away the water.

I help awhile, then sit down to chat with his wife, Soledad. ("We don't talk about it," another priest had explained, "but since they have four children it's hard to think of her as anything else.") Soledad is a wiry blonde with clear green eyes. She talks about the atrocities that forced them to flee in 1981.

"The soldiers took members of our families and cut them to pieces and threw the pieces about in the corn fields, forcing us to spend days gathering the bodies for burial. Later they returned and when they saw we hadn't left they burned our food, the corn and rice and beans, every grain they could find, and poisoned the wells. We were forced to run with no food, nothing, across the border into Honduras. Fifteen months we were there, living on green mangos. The children born in that time were *nacido muerto.*"

I don't understand the Spanish phrase she uses and ask her to repeat it. The priest, who has been listening, outraged at the memory, shouts in English, "They never saw the light of day!"

"The Hondurans tried to drive us out, too. We were running and hiding with no place to go," Soledad continues. "Finally the Sandanistas allowed us to settle in Nicaragua. They gave us land to farm, plus credits for seeds and equipment. It was hard, clearing wild land from scratch, but at least we lived like humans instead of hunted animals."

I look around the dirt-floored tent, flooded from the previous night's rains, and do not understand what possessed them to leave Nicaragua, where they had been safe, to return to a country which is still making war upon its own people.

"Why did we leave Nicaragua? Because when the Sandinistas lost the election, the Chamorro government wanted us gone. We had no choice."

"But with the war here still so hot! Like yesterday, when you were moving the stones and the soldiers stuck their guns in your face — weren't you afraid?"

Soledad looks at me for a long moment. Her green eyes, it seems, are almost too steady. "What more can they do to us?"

I sit with my note pad on my knee, unable to find words to express what I am beginning to understand, which is that this other reality, which I keep glimpsing, is perhaps much larger than I thought.

Back in the capital I make an appointment with Kevin Johnson, Director of the U.S. Embassy's Political Department, for a briefing. En route to the embassy my taxi detours around the Tower of Democracy in such a way that I see the side with the most blown-out windows.

"What happened to that building?" I ask.

The driver replies in a voice edged with bitterness. "The military constructed it as a symbol. So it becomes a symbol."

Is the U.S. embassy a symbol, too, I wonder, as I search for the entrance to the grey fortress decorated by block-long smears of anti-American graffiti? I cross the chain-and-post barricade which protects the high cement wall which protects the windowless building which houses embassy offices, and pass through various gates and checkpoints to my meeting with Kevin Johnson, who will explain to me how the U.S. taxpayers' money is being spent here in El Salvador.

"Three quarters of U.S. aid goes to non-military purposes," Johnson informs me, with the air of one pleased to set the record straight. He hands me a booklet filled with glossy photos of bridges and hydroelectric projects built with U.S. dollars. A four-color bar chart prominently graphs the small amounts designated to "food for peace," "disaster relief," and "surplus dairy products for humanitarian purposes." The booklet does not offer figures for U.S. military aid. Neither does Mr. Johnson. However, I have already obtained those figures from my congressman, and know that in the past three years the U.S. gave El Salvador $348 million in direct military aid, plus another $500 million in indirect military assistance.

I haven't come here to argue numbers. I simply remark that during this visit I have observed soldiers pointing U.S. weapons at unarmed people and U.S. helicopters over-flying refugee camps, and I have heard (although not seen) that in the north they are dropping U.S. bombs from U.S. planes. But I have not seen *any* form of U.S. aid being offered to the thousands of people made homeless by the war.

Johnson throws up his hands in exasperation. "We'd like to help but these repatriated refugees are refusing assistance unless it comes through the United Nations or other international agencies. They simply won't take anything from the Salvadoran or U.S. governments." He looks righteously annoyed. "Sometimes it seems like they'd almost rather see their children starve."

"Can we really expect people to trust a government that continues to finance a military which continues to harass them?" I ask. I tell the ambassador's political advisor about soldiers sticking guns in the faces of the women of Nueva Esperanza and shooting out the tires of their truck so that they had to carry their belongings on their backs.

Johnson says he has not heard about that, but surely I can understand the army's belief that it must have some control over these people! The refugees have returned "with a very bad attitude, the attitude that they will be self-sufficient and independent, countries within the country."

I ask whether the U.S. views such self-government as subversive.

Johnson replies that it is certainly something which the Salvadoran government is not likely to tolerate.

"The United Nations went to a lot of trouble to negotiate a site for these people, and they agreed to live there. Now they've sneaked away to live in an area where the government believes they'll be used as part of an arms supply route to the guerillas. I'm not saying it's true but the military believes it. This is very embarrassing for the United Nations!"

I think, but do not say, that it must be very embarrassing for our government to have destitute refugees insisting that they would rather starve than accept help from the U.S.

On my last day in El Salvador I go to the University of Central America and ask a gardener if he can show me where on the quiet suburban campus the six Jesuits, their cook, and the cook's daughter were murdered.

He leads me to a small brick courtyard and begins to detail the atrocities, how the priests were dragged from their beds, and how the head of one was smashed against the brick wall by a soldier crying, "There are the brains of your revolution!"

Suddenly I do not want to be here, do not want any more mental images of middle-aged teachers being slaughtered by jeering young Rambos. All I want to imagine — but dare not ask if it's true — is that the mother was killed first, and did not see the things they did to her daughter Selina.

I turn away. "How long have you worked here?" I ask the gardener.

His reply is barely audible. "I am working here a long time. Until I die. It is my mission, to keep alive this garden and the memory of my wife and daughter."

He asks if I want to see where the Jesuits lived, where his wife and daughter normally did not sleep, but where he sent them that night for safety, because of the military offensive. I tell him that I would rather be here in the garden. The roses are very beautiful.

"These I planted," he says. "Red for the Jesuits, and yellow for my wife and daughter." He looks at the flowers as if he sees their faces. Perhaps he does.

Looking at his, it occurs to me that I have never been any place where so many individual faces appear so wholly good or evil. It's as if the great neutral masses have been driven out — or changed. What remains are faces so cruel that no humanity is visible in them, and others of such profound goodness that they seem to exist on another plane.

Maybe this is because no one can remain in El Salvador without choosing to do things which may cost them their lives, or making choices which cost others theirs. This is what I think makes people's faces they way they are. Whichever they have chosen, it shows.

I leave El Salvador glad to be going, away from the madness of a nation making war upon itself, a nation of Rambos who believe that they are its reality and its future. It is hopeless.

Yet I take with me bits of hope: memories of individuals who refuse to submit to terror and defy the purveyors of it, people whose courage has created another reality.

FINCA IXOBEL

Guatemala 1992

It was a hard trip, ninety hours of driving from Malibu to El Salvador to deliver a four-wheel drive pickup loaded with tools and vitamins to Ciudad Romero and Nueva Esperanza.

Mission accomplished, I bussed up through Honduras to visit the Mayan ruins of Copan, then on to Tikal in Guatemala. I am more than a little road-weary, and know of only one place in this part of the world where a traveler can truly rest.

For hours the bus tears recklessly along an unpaved road as rocky as a dry river bed, scattering dogs, chickens, and children in each tiny community through which it passes. It is an hour past dark when I finally pull my pack from the overhead rack and ask the driver to let me off. The last village was two kilometers back. There is nothing to mark this spot except a small wooden sign that reads "Finca Ixobel" and a dirt track leading into the woods.

It seems miraculous that in the midst of a sweltering jungle I am standing in a cool pine forest. What I will find when I have walked a mile truly is a miracle: the kind that springs from love in unexpected places.

Not everyone who comes to Finca Ixobel knows that what created this ranch was the affection two people felt for the place and each other. Mike DeVine was an Iowa boy just out of the navy. Carol was the California girl he loved and married. In keeping with the spirit of the seventies they backpacked through Mexico and on to Central America. In the wild Petan region of Guatemala they came upon a pine forest in the midst of the jungle. There by their own hard labor they built the ranch called Finca Ixobel.

Naturally friends came to visit. Those friends told their friends about the ranch's pine-scented woods so pleasant for camping, the free-roaming jaguarundi and toucan that ate from the same dish as the dogs and cats, horseback rides to ruins that were in nobody's guide book, and welcoming hammocks strung on the wide veranda. Each year more visitors made the rough overland journey to Finca Ixobel. Exhausted, they would stumble off the bus just as I have and after a few deep breaths of cool forest air, stride off down the track leading to the ranch.

I don't know the DeVines personally but by now that doesn't matter. Most of the people sitting around the long dining table when I push open the screen door are like myself, friends of friends of friends or outright strangers. I drop my pack on the floor, slip into a bathroom to wash up, and help myself from a sideboard of steaming dishes. Everything is grown on the premises, cooked or baked in the kitchen; there's no better food in all of Guatemala. At the table there are perhaps twenty guests conversing in many languages. A freckle-faced girl slides over to make room for me.

"Hi. You traveling alone?"

"Yes."

"Me, too. All the way from Alaska. This is the best place I've found so far."

"How long have you been here?"

"A week."

"Are Mike and Carol around?"

"Who?"

"The owners."

"Oh. I wondered who's in charge. Like, there's a man named Juan you talk to if you want a horse or a guide to the caves, and a German woman in charge of the kitchen. And that dreamy Chilean over there in the white pants and sandals, he's the one people pay when they leave. But it's not like anybody's 'the boss,' you know what I mean?"

I know what she means. After dinner I pick up the notebook laying on the sideboard, find a clean page, and write my name at the top. Under it I write: *dinner* and *camping*. This is how accounts have been kept here for I don't know how many years. Guests keep track of what they use, and pay when they're ready to leave.

In the morning I add *coffee*, *cinnamon bun*, and *guide to river cave* to my list. Half a dozen others come along on the two-hour hike to the cave. It's a rough walk and we are drenched with sweat by the time we arrive, glad to change into swim suits. Some have brought flashlights. I light a candle. We slip into the icy water and paddle into the darkness of the cave. It is delicious, spooky, and for me, always a bit claustrophobic, downright terrifying. But I paddle along with the others and eventually come out shivering with cold and satisfaction.

Back at the ranch I nap for an hour in my tent, which I have pitched in the pasture. There are other options — thatch-roofed shelters where one can hang a hammock, a couple of tree houses built thirty feet up in big pines, sometimes even a room available in the ranch house. Everything at Finca Ixobel is open, based on trust.

Toward sunset I go up to the ranch house veranda and find an unoccupied hammock. Nearby a young man is writing post cards home to Norway, and a beer-guzzling Australian is butchering French phrases in an attempt to impress a girl from Quebec. A hysterically funny volleyball game is going on in the yard. In addition to the usual teams, two free-flying parrots have formed their own team with its own rule, which is to attack whoever has the ball. The German woman comes out of the kitchen and sits down on the porch railing near me.

I point to the birds. "If those parrots repeat every name they're called, they must have a huge vocabulary of multilingual profanity."

"They're too preoccupied with thinking up new ways to torment the guests to do much talking." She smiles. "When did you arrive?"

"Just last night. Are Mike and Carol around?"

She looks at me oddly. "You haven't heard?"

"Heard what?"

"Mike's dead."

There is something about the way she says it that sends a chill down my spine. "What happened?"

"We're not supposed to talk about it." She gets up to move away. "You wouldn't understand. This is Guatemala."

I understand more than she suspects, because I am a journalist and this is not my first but my fifth trip to Guatemala. I know that it was in Guatemala that the phrase *los disaparicidos* was coined to describe people who had disappeared; that the military and the death squads are one; that entire villages have been massacred with impunity; that right now the international media are reporting the murder by police of large numbers of street children in Guatemala City. I have friends working with religious and human rights groups who tell me that Guatemala, the most beautiful country in Central America, is also the most violent.

What I don't understand is how this violence reached Finca Ixobel; how it could have taken the life of an easy-going farm boy grown middle-aged, who so disliked conflict that he'd leave the room when heated political discussions broke out, who forever seemed to be petting a kitten, passing it off to one of the guests, and picking up another one to make it purr.

I walk back to my tent among the trees, trying to comprehend the incomprehensible. The forest is dark now. There is no sound except a whisper of breeze through the pines, and a whisper of verse by Edna St. Vincent Milay running through my head:

> *This little life from here to there*
> *Who lives it safely anywhere?*
> *The tidal wave devours the shore*
> *There are no islands anymore.*

I refuse to ask what happened. I don't want details of what I know (because this is Guatemala) was a brutal death. But little by little details drip out, leaving images that stain like blood. Mike had left the village two kilometers away, headed for home. But never reached Finca Ixobel. The next morning searchers found his Ford club wagon hidden in the bush beside the road. Mike was leaning against the back tire. His head had been all but severed from his body.

Carol had hired a detective and in time several things were discovered. Neighbors had seen him turn off the road and head up the lane to the ranch. Moments later they had seen the Ford come out again. Some whispered that soldiers had been lying in wait, and some had seen more: something so terrifying that men who thought they might be identified as witnesses left the area for fear of being killed. Carol would tell me later that it was Indian women living in little huts along the lane who found the courage to come forward and tell what they had seen.

When Carol announced that she planned to bring her husband's murderers to justice, no one of any political persuasion believed she could succeed. Most of them believed that she would be killed if she tried. For the thousands of crimes committed against civilians by the Guatemalan military, not one soldier had ever been convicted.

In Guatemala it is not the state but an individual who must lay criminal charges. Carol DeVine, a small brown-eyed woman who had lived all her adult life under the wing of Mike's protective love, surrounded by friends and the rural tranquility of Finca Ixobel, journeyed to the capital and there laid charges against members of the most vindictive military in Latin America.

Carol received death threats, as did the friends with whom she stayed while the case wended its way through court. But she stood her ground and her friends stood theirs. U.S. government interest in the case may have been what prevented those threats being carried out.

The U.S. ambassador to Guatemala had talked to Carol, and sent two attachés from the embassy to question Colonel Alpirez, head of the army base near Finca Ixobel. Colonel Alpirez refused to cooperate.

Said Ambassador Stroock, "Here was a peaceful American citizen murdered by an army we were sending aid to. I just figured that this was something the average American taxpayer wouldn't stand for."

In December, six months after Mike's death, the White House impounded three million dollars a year in aid to the Guatemalan army, saying it would not release the money until the Guatemala courts demonstrated a willingness to "seek justice" in the case of Mike DeVine.

At that, the trial went forward. Eight soldiers were convicted of the murder, and sentenced to thirty years in prison.

Carol is in the capital appealing the case, which is why I do not find her at Finca Ixobel on this visit. She is appealing the case because she is not satisfied with the outcome. She wants not only the men who murdered her husband, but the officer who ordered it.

Several months later she and her daughter María visit me in Malibu. I am seeking permission to write a film script based on their story. Carol is cautiously interested, but María studies me with cool dark eyes.

"I've never known anybody who had a movie made about their life who was satisfied with it. Besides, my mother still lives in Guatemala and the case against Captain Contreras is still before the court. A film could mess up the case. Or it could get her killed."

I offer several reasons for wanting to turn their story into a film, but María's few weigh more than all of mine. Like my own daughter, she says little but what she says carries the weight of reason.

Carol senses my disappointment and says I must visit Finca Ixobel again when she is there and she will let me read some of Mike's letters. I am grateful for the offer, not because I intend to pursue the idea of a movie but because I hope someday to have a friendship with her that reflects the depth of my respect.

Not long afterwards I hear on the radio that Captain Contreras has been convicted and sentenced to prison for twelve years. It is newsworthy in that he is the first Guatemalan officer ever convicted for human rights violations.

Two weeks later the six o'clock news carries another small item from Guatemala. Captain Contreras, confined in a military prison for the murder of Mike DeVine, has disappeared. Those in charge of the prison say they have no idea how he escaped. I stand at my window looking out at the ocean, aching for Carol DeVine.

A year passes and another. Again I stand at the window, a different window in a different country. In my hand is a copy of *The New York Times,* dated April 2, 1995. Its front-page article, entitled "In Guatemala's Dark Heart, CIA Tied to Death and Aid," reveals that Julio Roberto Alpirez, a colonel in the Guatemalan army *and* a CIA employee, was the senior officer who not only ordered but personally supervised the murder of Mike DeVine.

Someone will have sent Carol a copy of the article. She will have read it perhaps a week ago. I cannot imagine her anguish as she fitted together yet another piece in the picture of how Mike died. I only know that as she laid aside the paper, she would still be asking the question she asked that June morning five years ago. Why?

Some will say later that it was because Mike had come upon soldiers illegally cutting mahogany trees in the rainforest, and they were afraid he would reveal their dirty little secret. But who will ever really know? And what difference does it make now?

Tears slide down my cheeks like wet spring snow against the windowpane. If I did not travel as I do, this news item would be meaningless to me, just one more drop in a flood of details arising from injustices around the world. But I have been to Finca Ixobel; I have met Carol and her daughter María. There is no way to avoid this sadness.

Yet there is more to this than sadness. If I hadn't traveled so far afield I would not know what I know about courage, wouldn't know that this quality of the human spirit lives in the soul of so many ordinary people. I would not have seen how many ways and for how many reasons it emerges to take a stand against what Camus called "the human order of terror."

I remember Carol DeVine, her farmwife face framed by short dark hair, looking away when I told her that she was brave and her actions heroic. Her politely distant gaze seemed to say that such grandiose words have nothing to do with who she is or what she has done.

I find myself remembering the artist Sally in Mexico who, after facing down an intruder and being shot five times, returned to live in San Miguel. I remember Virginia in El Salvador, who as a teenager pulled wounded combatants from under fire and gave transfusions of coconut milk in place of plasma which she did not have. I remember green-eyed Soledad rolling boulders out of the road and shouting at the soldiers, "Not one step back!"

Then there was that pretty Javanese woman in Suriname who advised me to travel for pleasure and not think of unpleasant things. I thought then that it was good advice which I should try to follow.

I now understand that for me this is not possible. I travel to see the world as it is, not as it appears on postcards or from the terrace of a luxury hotel. I would not say that I am drawn to dangerous places, but life is a dangerous place. And it is there, in the shadow of love and violence, that I come face to face with courage.

LEAVING HOME

The Budwood 1993

A desert wind, blowing hard, pushes the fire toward the sea. I sit on my patio with a map of the Santa Monica mountains spread on the table. Informed by the radio moment to moment, I follow the path of the fire across the map with my finger. Once in awhile I walk around to the back of the house and look up into the hills. I can see the grey-yellow smoke mushrooming higher and higher. But the wind is blowing away from us. Budwood's air is crystal clear.

The fire is passing us by some distance to the north, moving instead toward Pepperdine University nine miles up the coast. I doubt that wealthy community has much to fear, though. Malibu's fire fighters are among the best, and more are being brought in from all over the state. They say that at least a thousand are already on hand to defend us.

"What should we do?" asks Pamela, who has come home from work to pack. Pamela's children attend school near Pepperdine but they are safe; they were evacuated two hours ago.

"The wind is blowing away from us. As long as the wind doesn't change, we're okay."

Fires flare up in Malibu every year but never here, never on the Budwood. The Budwood is charmed. It hasn't burned in a hundred years.

The monster fire has lengthened. It now stretches for miles, from Malibu's wild dry chaparral hills down to its millionaire communities on the coast. But the wind is still blowing away from us. I know that fire does not travel against the wind.

What I don't know is that great fires create their own backwind the way a boat sends water in its wake going the opposite direction. Even as the desert wind blows the fire away from us, another wind, the backwind, is pushing it toward us.

By mid-afternoon the pattern is discernable. One canyon after another is consumed, each nearer to us than the one before. Still there are so many homes between the fire and us, so many solid residential areas! Surely it will be stopped at Rambla Vista or Las Flores or Big Rock Canyon. How can we be in danger with a thousand firemen on hand, and more arriving every hour?

Jacqui hears on the radio that a friend in another part of Malibu has been caught in the flames and is now in hospital dying. I meet Jacqui on the driveway as she is putting her four-year-old in the car.

"Maya and I are going into Santa Monica to visit friends," she says in a casual voice. Jacqui is slender but strong. Her clear blue eyes have a haunted look and her face is pale as an invalid. Concealing grief and fear from the child seems to be taking all her strength.

A perfect leaf, perfect except that it's made of ash, floats down from the sky. I show it to Jacqui and Maya, and say goodbye.

Bruce tries to bring in vans to save the horse and Bond's pianos, but Pacific Coast Highway is closed to incoming traffic. Bruce leaves the vans and, evading police blockades, walks eight miles along the beach to get to the Budwood. He has come to help Bond pack and tell us what we already know: that we can take whatever we can carry, and nothing more. Once we leave we will not be allowed to return.

Night comes and the lights go out. In the near distance, fire is so brightly reflected in the billowing clouds of smoke that at times the clouds themselves seem to be made of fire. We bring what's left in our refrigerators to Pamela's house, and by candlelight have a last potluck supper. The dining table is big enough to hold us all but we eat standing up, plates in hand, and keep walking out on the porch to watch the approaching red cloud. We are together and we are not. What separates us is the one emotion we share: a sense that this night, this end, cannot be.

A truck comes up the driveway, the firetruck we have been waiting for. "You must evacuate. Now," the fireman says. And he drives away.

Aino, the Finnish writer whose French, English, and Portuguese songs I listened to up in Jerry's little house the first night I ever came to the Budwood, and who moved back here only two years ago, piles a few family heirlooms into her VW and heeds the official warning. She is followed by a nun from the smallest cabin who came just last year, and Derek's mother Doreen who arrived from Canada less than twenty-four hours ago. Doreen has been trying all day to get me to pack and all day I have been resisting. She doesn't understand. If I can't have the Budwood and all its wild things, my friends around me and this wide view of the sea, I don't want anything at all.

I phone Derek in British Columbia and tell him, "Don't worry, we're safe. We're evacuating." But I do not go.

Bond, who is deeply sentimental about personal possessions, runs a hand one last time over his precious pianos and says in a voice that has never lost its Southern drawl, "Well, you know, it's the living things that count." Then he puts on a white suit and black tie, and with his dog beside him, leads the horse down to the beach.

I go down to the highway and run along the row of fire engines that wait there, waiting for what I do not know. I beg the drivers to come and defend the Budwood, because the fire is now very close to the top of the ridge. Some say they must wait for orders. Others simply sit there staring through me with smoke-reddened eyes. Finally one glances up at the old big house perched at the edge of the cliff above us, and says, "We're going to let that one go."

From the depths of my soul comes a fatalism I never knew was part of me. It overwhelms and blots out the pro-active person I think I am, and leaves me wondering who it is inside my skin. Water pressure is non-existent so rationally speaking, there isn't much we can do. That doesn't change what I afterwards know for sure: that I would have lost far less of myself if I had tried.

I walk back up the driveway, past dark palms and along the path to my patio. I've always known that the most radical changes come without warning, and that in such a world, flexibility is a quality worth cultivating. But I'm not prepared for this.

Of the Budwood people, only David, Pamela, and I remain. We sit on the grass under a night sky made clear by the devastating wind, while red-and-white-hot clouds of smoke roll toward us. David has ashes in his grey hair and tears in his eyes. He opens a bottle of champagne he says is too good to be burnt, and we toast to a future somewhere beyond this hillside where none of us want to go.

We tell each other we won't take chances; we will leave as soon as we see the first tip of flame. But there is nothing tiptoe about this fire. It circles us on two sides and crests the ridge in a great red wave that reaches halfway to the meridian. From there it flows like lava, so swiftly that even the deer cannot outrun it. The Budwood is burning.

We flee to the beach and from the water's edge watch rivers of orange snake down through the chaparral, then follow the trunks of palm and eucalyptus trees upward like Roman candles. The trees sway as in a great storm. My roots are burning.

In the grey morning-after I walk up the driveway between stone walls engineered by Mexican men with the knowledge of placing rocks in such a way that come wind, rain, or fire, they have not needed mortar to last these seventy years. These stone walls and our chimneys remain, and boulders on the hillside, protruding like bones in a landscape stripped of every living thing.

From among the ashes of what last night was my home, where in one more month I would have lived for twenty years, I gather some small clay leaves, a bird, and vines twined about broken branches of what Mexicans call the Tree of Life. It is what remains of the candelabra given to me after a banquet at the National Palace in Mexico City. I have never really understood its symbolism — whether it means that there is no such thing as death, or that all things, while they live, are intertwined.

TRAVELING THROUGH TIME

CANCÚN TO CHIAPAS

It is one week since the fire. I sit on a beach and stare across the Caribbean, feeling the crash of each wave in my bones. This might be the winter of 1993, or it might be twenty-one years ago when I first glimpsed these turquoise waters. As long as I face straight ahead and do not let my gaze wander to sunbathing tourists that line the shore in both directions, it looks the same.

On that first visit two decades ago, there was only the sea, the sand, and sweet green jungle. Jeff and I and his brother Don and other friends had bounced along a dirt track in search of a campsite. We broke through the trees onto this long white beach at the same instant our wheels sunk out of sight in powdery sand. Hiking back toward the highway in search of help, we came upon a bulldozer cutting a swath through the jungle.

"What are you doing here?" I asked, and the driver had replied, "Building Cancún."

I wade into the bath-warm sea and swim far out, then, treading water, look back at the line of hideous hotels. Directly ahead is the one where we are staying, but only for one night, to catch up on sleep after a crowded red-eye flight. I am traveling with three women who have never seen this part of the world — Sara from Australia, Dianne from Canada, and her mother, Doreen, who lives on an island a ferry-ride away from Vancouver. I myself am two travelers: one with friends on their voyage of discovery, the other alone through a tangle of past and present time.

I swim back to the beach and fling myself down in the shade of a palm-thatched palapa. Four years after the bulldozer driver's forewarning, it was my sleeping on this beach under just such a palapa that caused me to be arrested. I smile up into the fronds, remembering how I had opened my eyes and seen a man squatting there, moonlight glinting on his badge.

"Excuse me, *Señorita,* but it is against the law to sleep on the beach here in the hotel zone. You are under arrest."

"Please don't arrest me," I begged. "I'm afraid of jails." Already I was on my feet, fumbling at the ropes of my hammock.

"I don't have to take you to jail," he said. "But I must arrest you." He reached up to loosen the knots and with a single deft movement, bundled and tied the hammock.

I followed him back to the patrol car with more than a little fear. If he didn't take me to jail, what would he do with me? A second police officer waited in the car. I explained to them how the plane had been four hours late so I had arrived after midnight, too tired to look for a hotel in Cancún which was, after all, so very new.

"You arrived after dark? You did not see our white sand beaches sparking in the sun? Darkness was already upon our Sea of Seven Colors?"

I had thought by the lilt of their Spanish that they were Mayan and now, hearing the unconscious poetry of their words, I was certain of it.

"Yes," I replied. "The sea and sand were dark."

They put me in the back seat of the car and continued their rounds. Cancún was not yet the horror it would become. It was only a village with unpaved streets, occasional running water, and sporadic electricity. Out here on the peninsula miles of jungle still separated a few large hotels. At each of these the policemen stopped and one or the other went to patrol the beach. They were quiet, saying little to me or to each other.

Day was breaking when they pulled off the highway and up a sand track with no hotel in sight. The driver shut off the motor, turned to me, and said, "This is the perfect place."

"For what?" I quavered, for although they were small men I knew I would have no chance against their guns.

He gestured toward a promontory, below which lay an empty stretch of sand. "To see our sea of seven colors, our beach as white as sugar, sparkling in the light. Go, quickly! The sun is rising."

They waited in the car while I climbed the knoll and sat there ten minutes or so watching the sun rise over their sea of seven colors. When I came back to the car they drove me to town and let me go.

I miss the sweetness of that young Cancún. We will leave here in the morning, before the sun rises over pavement and plaster of many hues.

I nag everyone into the rental car at dawn, only to discover that the car won't start because, when we came back from dinner last night, I left the headlights on. Doreen begins to fret.

"I'm a jinx," she mutters, inexplicably blaming herself.

"Nonsense," I laugh. "This is not a problem. It's an adventure!" Moments later a taxi driver comes over to see if he can help, gives us a start with jumper cables, and we are on our way.

We drive south to a Mayan ruin where I once met a legless Vietnam vet selling drugs, and penned a poem to my country that never got beyond the inside cover of my address book. Then on toward Cenote Azul where I camped and swam four years ago with my daughter, and told her the story of how, seventeen years before that, I found the margay kitten, Hopichen.

I don't want to merely follow in the track of previous trips, so on a whim, take a side road across a marshy waste to a fishing village on the coast.

"An adventure," I tell my uncertain companions. "We're looking for the old Quintana Roo."

The village is a cluster of cottages, one cafe, and a corral built out into the water where women, with their skirts tucked up, wade out to catch the seafood of their choice for lunch.

In the café we order shrimp and scrambled eggs, then sit watching the shimmer of sun on water and distant waves crashing on the reef. I notice that a young man at the next table, dressed in swim trunks and sandy feet, is listening to our conversation.

"It's a lovely beach," I remark. "Do you live here?"

"My family does."

"What do people here do for a living?"

"They fish."

I glance at his hands. "But you"re not a fisherman."

"I'm a marine biologist."

"Working from shore or off a ship?"

"After Christmas I'll be going out from Mazatlán to do some studies in the Sea of Cortés." He names the boat.

"That's one of Cousteau's teams, isn't it?"

He nods diffidently.

"Then you must speak French as well as English."

His eyes flash up to meet mine. "*Mais oui, je parle un peu,*" he grins.

"Come join us. We've only just arrived. Tell us a bit about the area."

Politely but without enthusiasm, he picks up his coffee and transfers himself to our table. I sense that while he appreciates the fact that I have not imagined him ignorant because he is a native, he has yet to see us as more than stereotypical tourists.

"This is my friend, Sara, a biomedical researcher from Australia, and my sister-in-law, Dianne, who majored in bio-geography." I toss off their scientific credentials with malicious satisfaction. "And my mother-in-law, Doreen, who has a degree in chemistry."

"Not a degree," Doreen interrupts. "I never finished my studies."

"Her hobby is astronomy," I conclude, ignoring the correction. "And your name is— ?"

The young man's expression is no longer one of bored politeness. "Netzahualcoyotl Segundo," he smiles, shaking hands all around.

"Netzahualcoyotl is no Mayan name. Your ancestors must be Chichimecan."

He laughs in surprise. "And you must be a spy, to know so much about me without being told."

"Worse than that," Sara cracks in her cheeky Australian accent. "Rosa's a journalist."

"What do you write about?"

"Anything that interests me. If we can rent some snorkeling equipment, maybe I'll write about the reef here at Majahual."

"Tourists rarely come here so there's no place to rent equipment. But I have two masks and snorkels in my car if you'd like to use them."

We walk across the hot sand to the water, where he shows Dianne and Sara how to use the equipment. Doreen wanders off in search of shells. Netzahualcoyotl and I sprawl on the beach. He tells me of his days as a student radical at the University of Mexico, how Salinas stole the presidential election from Cárdenas, and how NAFTA is driving the Indians of Chiapas to the brink of starvation. He is one of those people I meet so often in my travels whom I want for a friend always and am almost sure I will never see again.

We have dawdled too long on the coast. It's a long way to Palenque; nightfall catches us in the swampy lowlands of Campeche. Ditches along the narrow highway are full of water. Insects spatter against the windshield like rain. The sky is a dazzling canopy of stars. Near the horizon I see the North Star, the one I have used since childhood to find my way home.

Home is where none of us are going just now. For the duration of this trip we will share destinations, a different one every day. Then

Dianne will return to Vancouver. Doreen, rather than returning to her island, will fly to Australia to winter on the shore of the Coral Sea. Sara, who is from Australia, will make a painful journey back to Los Angeles to say goodbye to a man who, for all her passion, could not bring himself to love her. I will go back to Malibu to face again the truth that my Budwood home is no more.

I lean my head out the window, letting the moist warm wind tangle my hair as I search the sky for the Southern Cross. It is said that the ancient Polynesians used it for navigation but I don't know how since, like the other constellations, it's always on the move. I am about to ask Doreen to point it out when a gasp from Sara snaps my attention back to the highway. A truck is approaching at terrible speed, in our lane, head on.

Sara's slim brown hands grip the wheel. She aims the car like an arrow down a hopelessly narrow strip of grass between road and ditch. As the outside tires drop off the pavement the car rocks sickeningly sideways. Sara keeps her foot on the gas, keeps the forward momentum, and it doesn't roll. She holds the left two tires to the edge of the pavement as the truck roars by inches away, then brings the lurching car back onto the highway.

"He must have been drunk! Either that or asleep."

"Just another adventure," Sara says shakily.

"How much further to Palenque?" Doreen asks.

"Not far," I tell her. "Less than an hour."

"Good," she says in a small voice. "I think I've had about all the adventure I can handle for one day."

While Sara, Dianne, and Doreen explore the ruins of Palenque, I trail along in a cross-current of memories. I seek out a river beyond the ruins where, returning from the Yucatán with the margay kitten, Hopichen, Jeff and I had camped with an American couple and their big black doberman. I remember waking to find the margay gone and how I had panicked, knowing that if she had escaped into the forest I would never find her and she would never survive. I came upon the kitten in a small sandy clearing a hundred yards from camp. She was trying desperately to reach the concealing tangle of vegetation which she mistook for safety. At every turn her way was blocked by the doberman who, no matter which way the kitten scrambled, simply put its body in her path, and with one large paw, gently pushed her back.

I find the bend of the river where we slept that night but there is no forest here now; it has long been cleared away. I return to the ruins and sit down to wait for the others at the bottom of the steep stairs leading to the Temple of Inscriptions.

It was three years after camping there with Jeff and Hopichen that I flew to Palenque with the photographer from *La Prensa*. I smile, remembering how as I sat in this spot, polished black shoes had appeared a step or two above me and I had looked up to see the president of Mexico looking down at me. He had escorted me into the heart of the largest pyramid to admire the sarcophagus without protective bars blocking our view. Then we climbed to the top of the pyramid and looked out across the rainforest.

The president had said gravely, with only the tiniest hint of a smile in his eyes, "You know, my friend, there once was a Mayan ruler who came here at sunset. The instruction he gave his people at that hour was, 'If anybody telephones, tell them I'm not in.'"

We stop for a swim at Agua Azul. The turquoise pools, strung on a silver chain of cataracts, are now lined with little stalls selling native crafts. I climb to the one highest up and buy a bag. It is poorly made but the man says his wife weaves the fabric and sews the bags herself. I shake my head. The pattern is traditional but the fabric is machine-made. Sure, he says; they have a weaving machine in the house as well as a sewing machine. They no longer weave in the old slow way, although it is still his grandmother who selects the colors, for this not even his mother can do.

The road over the mountains from Palenque to San Cristóbal de las Casas is not the raw dirt road it was when I crossed with the teachers twenty years ago. But here we are stranded — Doreen, Dianne, Sara, and I — not far from where I spent a rainy night in a camp of hostile highland Indians. I have forgotten to buy gas before leaving Palenque. When a vehicle comes by I flag it down and ask directions to the nearest gas station. The Indian looks down from the cab of his truck and, after thinking it over, waves his hand in the direction we are headed. There, just around the bend, he says. That family might have some to sell.

I follow a narrow path through the bush until I come upon a hut built in the old way, an oval of small peeled logs supporting a palm-thatched roof. An Indian woman squats by an open fire. Behind her a naked infant lies on the earth floor waving thin brown arms in the air.

"Do you sell gasoline?" I ask.

She glances at me from the sides of her eyes, then down again without reply. I stand there feeling foolish. The hut hasn't even a kerosene lantern. The grinder she uses for making corn into meal is stone on stone. How on earth could I imagine she has gasoline? After a moment of silence I start back up the path. Then, for no reason I can think of, I retrace my steps and come the back way around her hut. There concealed in the bushes are barrels and barrels of gasoline.

When I appear again in her open doorway she does not even glance my way, but continues mashing small balls of dough into tortillas. I kneel down and say, "Our car is out of gas. Will you sell me some?"

The only sound is the rhythmic slap of bare hands flattening balls of dough. Moments pass and I speak again. "We are four women alone. My mother-in-law is with me. She is seventy years old."

Two more balls are slapped flat. Then she rises and without a word takes a can from outside the door and fills it with gasoline from one of the barrels. She pads silently up the path ahead of me to where the others are waiting in the car. She pours the gasoline into our tank then, holding out her hand, names the amount of money she wants. I pay her and thank her but she gives no sign of having heard.

Six weeks later, when the Indians of Chiapas rise up in armed rebellion against the abuse they have endured for centuries, I have a notion of what the Indian woman did not tell me. I suspect the gasoline was not for sale, that the barrels had been stockpiled for use by the Zapatistas in their just and hopeless war.

In San Cristóbal de las Casas we stay at the home of the old Swiss anthropologist, Gertrude Blom, where I have stayed many times since I first encountered her on the presidential tour. The meals served at *Casa Na-Bolom*, replete with organically-grown vegetables from well-tended gardens behind the house, are as delicious as ever. The guests are still a mixture of Lacandons from the jungle and scientists, diplomats, and other visitors from abroad. Once Gertrude would have dominated her guests with arrogant, knowledgeable conversation in five languages. Now, at ninety-one, she sits at the head of the table being spoon-fed by an attendant.

I last stayed here two years ago. On that occasion school children from several local Indian villages came through on a tour, the sprawling house with its three central courtyards having become a virtual museum of indigenous artifacts. The old anthropologist, who had been silent through dinner, hobbled out to address them. She spoke very briefly, then raised her carved cane into the air and shouted, "Your natural environment and your culture are your heritage! DEFEND THEM WITH YOUR LIFE."

Recently, though, Gertrude Blom has suffered a stroke and does not seem to recognize me. Nevertheless, I kneel beside her wheelchair and tell her how important I think her life's work has been, how I remember, almost two decades ago, her telling the president of Mexico that he must act quickly to save the rainforest of the Lacandons.

For a long moment her intense blue eyes stare into mine. Then she says, "Too late, Rosa. Too late." She brings her carved cane down with a hard thump on the tile floor.

She continues to speak but her sentences are a jumble of Spanish, English, German, French, and Mayan. I can make no sense of them and look up helplessly at the attendant.

"No one understands her," the attendant sighs. She leans over the old lady. "It's a pretty day, *Señora*. Shall we go out into the courtyard?"

Madam Blom, whose name in Mayan means "jaguar," will die three weeks hence. I watch her being wheeled away and know that at this very moment some people are teaching others how to accept death. Let them do it their way. No matter what god decrees it, I will never make peace with the cutting of forests, the crushing of life, or the vanishing of wisdom that comes from living. When my time comes I hope to go like Gertrude Blom, with rage in my eyes, thumping my cane as hard as I can.

We recross the Sierra Madre and drive back across the Yucatán peninsula, this time avoiding major ruins with their block-long lines of tour buses. We bounce through the bush to smaller sites where I have never been. Often we are the only ones there. As we climb over crumbled walls, now less decorated with man-made symbols than with small plants and great trees that have forced their way up through the cracks, it occurs to me that this sacred place is not destroyed. It has merely undergone a transformation in which human loss was nature's gain.

With this thought my heart unclenches, and here among these ancient stones, I scatter the still-warm ashes of Budwood.

CUBA JOURNAL

Belle Glade, Florida, 1950

    His name was José Martí, like the Cuban poet, but his boss called him Marty-Joe, and so did I. The summer I was eleven I often stood at his elbow while he painted. Scratching mosquito bites on one leg with the toenails of my other bare foot, I watched him letter signs and listened as his voice, a lilting mix of Cuban Spanish and southern drawl, painted vibrant pictures of the island of his birth. The faster he talked the faster he painted until at last he would drop the brush, leap to his feet, and dance hypnotically to some Afro-Cuban rhythm pounding inside his head. He merged into the scene his words had created, dancing with black and brown friends on a white sand beach after swimming in warm blue water and eating their fill of lobster boiled pink over driftwood fires that blazed all night. I could see the bodies swaying like palm trees, see the waves rolling in behind them, and the yellow-orange of the imaginary fire. While José danced, his smile was the widest, his teeth the whitest, his laughter the most joyful I'd ever known. I longed to be there with him, and at times felt I could be if only he would dance a little longer and hold out his hand. With jarring suddenness the dance would stop. He would sink back on the stool, fluid muscles bunched together, and I would see his face, still dripping sweat, harden into the mask of a sullen twenty-year-old. Without a word he would pick up a brush and start painting again.
    The abrupt way it ended always put me off balance, left me feeling as if something precious had been snatched and smashed. It was no use trying to re-engage him. He painted in silent fury and wouldn't speak again except to tell me to leave him alone; couldn't I see he had work to do?
    I would go then but all that summer I kept coming back, unable to resist those glimpses of a magical place called Cuba which he could not resist creating for me. It was my private fantasy that he would

someday return and take me with him. One afternoon I asked him outright, "Marty-Joe, you gonna go back to Cuba afterwhile?"

Without taking his eyes off the sign he was lettering, he said, "Rosita, you dirt poor. But your family have a pen full of chickens and a few head of cow. Folks in Cuba way more poor than that."

I was too stunned at being called "dirt poor" to absorb the comparison. I could only reply, in a voice made small by hurt and disappointment, "I thought you *wanted* to go back."

It seemed an eternity before the answer drifted over his shoulder. "Nobody wanna to go back to that kind of poor."

St. Augustine, Florida, 1960

I had been working three jobs; nine-to-five as a doctor's receptionist, weekends at a restaurant, and weekend nights as a cocktail waitress. The restaurant had just closed for the season, and I had quit the cocktail lounge. For the first time since Jo and I were on our own I had some savings. The doctor was taking a vacation and I was to have a week off.

I walked past the travel agency twice before getting up the nerve to go in. My friend Sylvia said it wouldn't cost anything to ask for information but I could tell it was going to cost something. The blonde woman at the desk, groomed to a plastic sheen, lifted her eyes slowly, in such a way as to see my feet first, then my hands. By the time her gaze reached my face she had already gleaned enough from the white waitress shoes and ringless fingers to decide what sort of romantic travel illusion I could afford.

"Vacation coming up?" she asked brightly. Before I could answer she had handed me a travel brochure showing a young couple on a beautiful beach. "How about Nassau? That's our least expensive."

"Do you have one on Cuba?" I asked tentatively.

"Dear, you don't want to go to Cuba. That awful Fidel Castro is in power. Why, when him and his bunch was in New York, they cleaned their boots on the hotel towels."

"How much would it cost?"

"What, dear?"

"Going to Cuba? And coming back."

"Honey, we do not send people to Cuba. I don't even think Americans are allowed to go there."

"Why not?"

"Because the government's afraid they'll get hurt. You don't want to go someplace and get hurt, do you?"

I didn't take a vacation. I went to Utah instead, and five years later to California, and five years after that, to Mexico. Eventually I visited many Caribbean islands, but never Cuba. Not because Washington forbade it but because I was told repeatedly that one was not allowed to travel freely in Cuba. I traveled for many reasons, but above all, to reassure myself that I was free. I had no inclination to go anyplace where I might not be.

Washington, D.C. 1995

A brother and sister who attend school with the daughter of President Clinton plan to spend their summer vacation beaching and cycling in Cuba. The children hold a press conference to display a letter received from the U.S. government. It informs them that if they violate the law which prohibits U.S. citizens from going to Cuba, they may be fined up to $100,000 and/or receive a prison sentence of up to ten years.

In the decades since the revolution I had begun to imagine Cuba not as a dangerous place but a boring one, and stopped thinking about going there until I read in the *Washington Post* that two American children might be charged and imprisoned if they dared go to Cuba. The article sent images of the island floating through my head. I discovered that even the most precious of them, saved from my childhood fantasies, were fuzzy.

Costa Rica, 1995

It is November when I land in Costa Rica, a stopover between numerous other destinations on a trip through Latin America. The monitor shows a flight departing for Havana in just two hours. I have no reservations and no visa, just a smoldering resentment that my own country should threaten its citizens with imprisonment if they dare visit Cuba, and a desire to match childhood dreams against modern reality.

When the airline clerk tells me that there is a seat available, and she can issue me a visa on the spot, I promptly take possession of both. Thirty-five years, I think as I board the plane, is a long time to wait for a flight.

Cuba, At Last

Just before landing I ask my seatmate if he knows of a guest house in Havana. He throws out his arms. "All Havana is a guest house!"

I discover what he means when I reach the city. No matter where I go all I have to do is ask someone, "Do you know where I can rent a room in this area?" I am immediately invited to the person's home, or their parents' home, or the home of a friend, and offered a room, or sometimes the whole house, with or without meals. The price named is usually reasonable, but occasionally is so little that I insist on paying more.

I realize that this is a "new Cuba," in some respects changed from what visitors might have experienced a few years earlier. Yet these are not "new Cubans." These are people who were born in Cuba, have stayed, and continue to call it home. These Cubans, who knew Cuba before and know her now, are the ones who are opening their doors with such a wide welcome, enthusiastically showing me what they and their country are all about.

Anna's Place

My first night is at the two-story home of Anna, a retired school teacher. A chunky, dark-haired pair in their mid-thirties are introduced as Anna's son Marco and his wife María. Marco is a civil engineer with the government. María makes shell jewelry which is sold at the *Palacio de Artesaniá*. I am not their only guest. There is also Fresa, a vivacious black twenty-year-old from Santiago de Cuba who is having a fling in the capital with Paul, a cherubic Swiss man who wants to marry her, and Luna, a dancer with copper-colored hair to the small of her back, who belongs to a Cuban salsa group soon to tour Europe.

We have barely made our introductions when the volume of the big TV is turned up and conversation ceases. I wonder what has drawn their attention so expectantly to the big screen: perhaps a televised speech by Castro? It turns out to be a Brazilian soap opera which I soon discover is as much an institution as Monday night football in the States or Hockey Night in Canada. When the soap opera ends an hour later, Anna shuffles off to the kitchen to make coffee. I talk with Marco and Maria about their work, while Luna buffs long fingernails painted copper to match her hair.

Paul sits on the sofa with Fresa squirming in his lap like a restless child. "Marry me!" he murmurs into her neck.

"I'm going to marry the Italian," Fresa says indifferently.

"Darling, don't say that!"

Luna cuts a languid eye at Paul. "The Italian isn't as rich as you, Paulo, but at least he knows how to *act* rich. Just look at you!" She waves disdainfully at his rumpled jeans. "You're so simple. You don't look like a man with money."

"Money means you can do what you like," Paul protests. "I happen to like simplicity."

"If you like being simple, you should have been born Cuban," says María sourly. "What a life!"

"What's wrong with life in Cuba?" I ask.

"Everything that can be wrong with a country that's had to cope with Spanish imperialism, the Batista dictatorship, an invasion by the U.S., a fifteen-year-long contra war, and an embargo that's lasted thirty-six years," says Marco bitterly.

"The counter-revolution didn't last fifteen years; only twelve," corrects Anna. She sets tiny, half-full cups of coffee before us and looks at me. "Isn't that right?"

"I've read that Washington supported counter-revolutionaries, but I didn't know it went on that long," I admit with some embarrassment. "I don't know that part of Cuban history."

"You should go to the *Museo del Pueblo Combatiente*. There are maps showing where all the attacks took place, and photos of the Americans captured, and the names of the patriots who were killed."

"Go to the *Museo de Artes Decorativas*," suggests María. "It's more interesting. Such beautiful things!"

"Let's go to dinner," Paul suggests. "Do you want to go with us, Rosa? I'm going to propose to Fresa, and she's going to say yes." He wraps his arms around her slender waist and squeezes hopefully.

"Maybe yes, maybe no," she says, squirming out of his embrace.

"Oh, Fresa, don't be such a tease," María admonishes.

Fresa flips her short skirt up and moons María with tiny buttocks barely covered in white lace.

"No need to show off," Maria sniffs. "We know he brought you those bloomers."

"You want them?" Fresa makes as if to pull them off.

María flushes as she and the rest of us register the improbability of her double-sized bottom fitting into Fresa's small panties.

"I can buy my own."

"No, she can't," Fresa says to me. "They don't sell underwear in Cuba, except in the dollar stores."

At my look of surprise, Luna explains, "Because of the embargo."

"I have dollars," says María haughtily. "And it's not just the embargo. It's Fidel's fault. He should resign, for the good of the country. Otherwise the U.S. will never stop harassing us."

"A new leader won't change Washington policy," argues her husband. "Unless the new one is a puppet. Is that what you want – an American puppet running Cuba?"

"What I want are new bloomers. And shampoo."

"I'll leave my shampoo," Luna offers. "I can get more in France."

Anna sits down heavily and takes a tiny sip of coffee. "Things might get worse if Fidel goes. I remember when they were worse."

Fresa is nestled in Paul's lap now, eyes closed and frowning slightly like a bored child on the verge of falling asleep. Suddenly she lifts her head, turns brilliant dark eyes in my direction, and asks petulantly, "Why is the United States doing this to us? What have we ever done to you?"

In the days to come I will find myself listening to dozens of conversations about whether Castro should resign and whether things would change for better or for worse if he did. I come to dread the subject because sooner or later someone will turn to me as Fresa has just done and ask more or less the same thing. And I will sit there feeling like a fool, because how do you answer a question like that?

Deisy's Place

One day I go out to a Havana suburb called Santa Fé. I like the laid-back feeling of the area and the nearness of the ocean so I do what I have done before: ask a teenager strolling by if he knows where I might rent a room. He takes me to his friend Deisy's almost-two-room flat. It is in a pleasant neighborhood, spotlessly clean, yet something like a slum. Many of the smaller homes have no running water. They do have bathrooms and showers, but water for both is carried by bucket from a tap in the courtyard and heated, if hot water is desired, on a two-burner kerosene stove.

Deisy is in the process of building her own home. One room and the bath are finished. The second room is still a cement shell. She explains that most land in Cuba is in the hands of the government and although in theory it can be bought, the bureaucracy is so slow that few bother. It's easier to buy from an individual. This privately-owned lot is already covered with tiny houses; there is no land left. So Deisy has done what many city-dwellers do: she has bought a roof.

I asked what it cost. She smiles wryly. "Did you notice that I don't have a TV?" I had noticed, as hers is the first Cuban home I have seen without one. "A color TV and a VCR, that's what I paid for this roof."

One evening a crowd gathers in the street half a block from Deisy's place. I ask what's going on and she explains that it is a Block Meeting, organized by the Committee for the Defense of the Revolution.

"Don't they spy on people?" I ask, repeating what I had often heard in the States.

She looks at me uncomprehendingly. "I don't know. Would you like to go?"

We stroll down to where the crowd is gathered. Small children dash around the legs of adults who are either listening to complaints or voicing their own over a microphone. Someone objects to the frequency with which the electricity goes off. A Committee member explains that it can't be helped; the embargo has caused oil shortages which make it impossible to generate enough electricity. Someone in the crowd calls out that the embargo may be responsible for the shortage, but not being told *when* the outages are going to occur is a matter of bureaucratic laziness. Others shout agreement.

Another person takes over the microphone and begins to complain about trash in the neighborhood, and how people aren't picking up after themselves like they used to. I am surprised by this; Cuba is exceptionally clean.

I can't make out what the next speaker is saying because a teenager across the street has turned on a boom box. I look around for Deisy and see her among the teenagers, dancing to the disco music.

Deisy is no teenager. She's twenty-nine, recently divorced, and extremely pretty. It is not long before a neighbor whispers to me that Deisy is a prostitute, more or less. "She goes to discos," the neighbor gossips, and when I don't take her meaning, she adds, "She goes with *foreign men.*"

This may well be true, for Deisy has no visible means of support, yet has a variety of "luxury items" like soap, shampoo, coffee, and underwear; things that can only be bought with dollars. But I like Deisy. There is a lioness quality about her that goes beyond the strong limbs, golden tan, and tawny hair. After bringing up a bucket of water to wash breakfast dishes and the tile floor of her tiny house, she spends the rest of the day giving herself a manicure or chatting with friends who drop in, seemingly content to be here in this small room doing virtually nothing. Toward evening, when a lioness might get up and pace the cage, Deisy borrows bicycles from a neighbor and we cycle down to the sea to watch the sunset. Then we stop at a food stand in somebody's front yard for fresh orange juice and manioc pizza. By the time we get back to her place it is dark. Deisy puts on a pair of white jeans and brushes a fresh sheen into her tawny hair. She says she is going out for a while, and I know she is off to prowl the disco jungle.

One evening Deisy's sister stops by the apartment. The sister's husband, Efrain, is as dark as Deisy is fair, a darkness that goes beyond complexion. I know, even before I answer the seemingly-benign question he puts to me about how I like Cuba, that no reply will please him because I am among the many things that make him angry. But I must reply. The place is crowded with Deisy's friends; they have stopped their chatter to listen.

"I love Cuba. Well, the country I don't know that well yet but the people are great, very helpful and generous."

"Of course you *love* Cuba." He emphasizes the words, mocking me. "*You* can leave whenever you like. Not like us, trapped like rats in this goddamned rathole all because of one power-crazed bastard."

This is the beginning of a harangue that goes on for five, ten, twenty minutes, putting an end to conversation and drowning out the music emanating from Deisy's portable cassette player.

When he finally winds down I ask, reasonably enough, "If you don't like it here why don't you leave?"

"Because I don't want to spend another two years in a room the size of this one with twenty other guys and no place to shit but a hole in the floor! You know what that's like? Like this!" He squats in front of me and pantomimes a man defecating. "El Salvador, Guatemala, Nicaragua, Haiti — anyplace would be better than this hellhole!"

If Cuba is hell to him, who am I to say otherwise? But neither here nor anywhere else would I let that statement go unchallenged.

"I've just come from Nicaragua. There are sixteen thousand homeless children in Managua. In Guatemala there at least one hundred thousand, and the police are murdering them because they bother the tourists. And massacres in the countryside — the last one not a month ago. I don't know Cuba well but I don't see soldiers sticking guns in people's faces nor any kids living in the street."

He leans over me, leering darkly into my face. "Tell you what, Cuba-lover. You come live here. I'll go where you come from and live in the street. Gladly."

He stomps out of the house. The others sit with their eyes glazed over, not surprised by the outburst, merely bored. They've heard it all before and, for some reason I don't understand, are remarkably tolerant.

"Why *does* he stay?" Knowing how many Cubans have emigrated to Miami over the years, I am truly puzzled.

His wife, a slight woman with soft brown eyes, answers the question, speaking slowly so that I understand every word. "His father was an officer in Batista's army so theirs was a good life before the revolution; at least, that is how Efrain remembers it. When Castro took over his father fled to Miami. Later his brother went, too. But his mother didn't want to leave Cuba and said Efrain was too young to go. When he was a teenager he applied for a visa but was refused because he hadn't fulfilled his year of military service. In his twenties he tried again and again was refused because, they said, his brother had not fulfilled his. So Efrain served another year in the army to meet his brother's obligation. By then we were married and had children and for a time there was no possibility. When the Muriel boatlift happened, Efrain again applied. For whatever reason, his papers were not processed. Before he could get out, the boatlift ended. And so he tried to escape illegally. The boat had only cleared the mouth of the harbour when he was caught. He spent two years in prison." She said, very gently, "It has made him crazy."

Deisy and the others nod and murmur agreement. "*Loco, sí.* It was prison that made him so."

I cannot bring myself to feel sympathy for this disagreeable man. Yet how different are we, really? Had I spent two years in prison for any reason, would I be any less angry? Any less *loco*?

Effie's Place

I bus to the southern coast of Cuba, to a small colonial town called Trinidad. An older woman named Effie rents me an entire apartment for ten dollars a night. Each morning she brings bread from the bakery, fresh-squeezed orange juice, and coffee made from beans roasted just moments before. At night she prepares the vegetarian meal I request, and tells me I am the first foreigner she has met who does not want lobster or shrimp, which are caught daily from a nearby reef.

Some days I bicycle out to the reef and wander along a palm-fringed beach that looks just as I knew it would, except there is no José to build a fire. I swim and dance alone, then lie on the sand and enjoy the colors of the sea, as brilliant as those he conjured for me those many years ago.

I don't mind being alone, but hardly ever am. Here, even more than in Havana, I am a diversion, a foreign experience for people who never expect to travel. The first to cluster around me as I walk Trinidad's cobblestone streets are what, even to my Cuba-inexperienced eye, are the less ambitious, the layabouts. Mostly women, they drift by with their none-too-clean children and do a kind of indirect begging, showing me their ration books and pointing out how little is available. See? It's been more than a year since panties were available, and seven months since they had soap. Mostly it's soap they want. Soap is available at the dollar stores, but who has dollars?

By now I know who has dollars. Mainly prostitutes, and people like Effie who manage to rent an occasional room or make a meal for the odd foreigner who chooses to stay in town rather than at a resort on the beach. Dollars also accrue to men who have a car or motorscooter to rent, and those who sell their illegally caught shrimp and lobsters to tourists at bargain prices.

Once the Cuban government forbade people to possess dollars, thinking it could corner the market on whatever foreign exchange came into the country. Now it attempts to do the same thing in a more effective and less restrictive way. It has moved certain items — items which people can live without but don't want to — from the ration stores to the dollar stores. In every dollar store I find Cubans briskly exchanging Yankee money for consumer goods they can't buy anywhere else.

It is Effie who teaches me the intricacies of shopping in Cuba, allowing me to trail along as she shops for my vegetarian meals. She explains that the system is meant to ensure that when there are shortages (as there always are), whatever is available is equitably distributed. But there's no use our going to the ration store; she has already used her coupons for this month. We stop by a government-run store where no ration cards are needed, but it only seems to have surplus farm produce, which this month happens to be sweet potatoes. We buy several, then go to the dollar store for coffee. Later we bicycle out to a farm to buy cucumbers, onions, and tomatoes. Effie says that in the past farmers were only allowed to sell to the government. Now they can sell to anyone.

On the way to the farm we stop at the home of a man who has a supply of black-market rice. I ask him why, now that private commercial enterprises are legal, he doesn't sell openly? He laughs. "If I did I'd have to pay taxes!" I figure out later that he might also have to explain to the authorities how he came by the rice in the first place. Effie tells me that he knows someone who knows someone who works at a government rice storage facility; the rice was stolen from there.

Bicycling back from the farm, Effie points out a vast tract of tilled land which she says used to be the ranch and sugar cane fields of her father. It was confiscated after the revolution. The farm house she grew up in, if I should want to see it, is down that road. It's a museum now.

I ask if she wants to go there but she says she does not; it makes her sad to see it. She describes what she remembers of her mother's bedroom with its lace-canopied four-poster bed. Her mother recreated the bedroom in their house in town where they lived after the farm was confiscated. Her mother had preferred living in town, but her father, whose life had been devoted to turning that wild land into one of the finest farms in the area, was very bitter. He lived ten years after the revolution and was in constant pain. It was the bitterness, Effie explains; it poisoned him.

As she speaks of her parents, now dead, there is sadness in her voice but none of the pass-on-to-the-next-generation hatred I recall from Southern families who claimed to have lost their wealth in the Civil War. Effie must be about sixty, which means she would have been twenty-something at the time of the revolution. How does she feel about it?

She pedals steadily beside me along the country road, which has almost no traffic. "We were twelve children," she says. "My family was one of the wealthiest in this area. At that, my father could only afford to send two to university. My two eldest brothers were the ones chosen. They live in Miami now, and are even richer than our father was. But we never hear from them. They hold it against the rest of us who stayed. They think we chose to support the revolution."

"And did you?"

"Me? I chose nothing. I was the youngest girl. It fell to me to look after my parents in their old age."

There is a long pause, filled with the white noise of our bicycle tires hissing on the pavement. At last she says, "I have six children. Every one of them, and now three of my grandchildren, have gone to university. Even the girls." Her eyes are distant. I can't tell whether she is looking into the past or the future.

Suzanna's Place

Old men sit under a vine-covered arbor in the plaza playing chess. One invites me to play but I'm not skilled enough for this company. I wander up the cobblestone street toward my apartment.

Children on an outing with their teacher skip by in a wavy line. November is a month devoted to field trips, and everywhere I've encountered groups of children: in museums, on farms, even at marimba band practices. They seem to be having a good time, although teachers tell me that they do not go as far afield now as they used to because of the gasoline shortage; they are limited to places that can be reached by walking. I watch the children until they turn the corner. Three of them peek back at me and wave.

I pass an ancient crone who sits all day in a window seat next to a life-sized wood carving of the Virgin. She always smiles when I pass and circles her ear with her finger in the universal sign for "crazy." I stop to speak to her. She doesn't seem senile so I ask what she means by the sign. "Fidel," she smirks. "He's loco."

The manager of a nightclub steps out onto the sidewalk and invites me in for an espresso even though it's mid-afternoon and the place doesn't open until evening. I haven't time, I tell him. I'm leaving in the morning and still have to pack. Too bad, he says, but do stop by this evening. A good Afro-Cuban band is playing; it's a memory I'll want to take back.

I am distracted by a black woman and a Latina on the sidewalk ahead of me, shouting insults at each other. They clash in a tangle of slapping and hair-pulling. I find myself hemmed in by the suddenly-gathered crowd. The Latina has the other's thumb in her mouth, and is biting hard, while the black woman has her thumb in the Latina's eye, gouging until I think it's going to pop from its socket and fall at my feet. Why doesn't someone separate them?

I step forward and jerk them apart. The Latina, who is the more aggressive of the two, flies at me. Her hands reach for my hair and without an instant's reflection, I backhand her in the face. She goes back on her heels and loose cobblestones do the rest. To the crowd it appears that with a flick of my wrist I have knocked her flat on her behind.

"Why did you hit *me*?" she wails in disbelief. "She's the one who's running around with my husband!"

"Then go home and fight with him!"

Onlookers roar with laugher, but I am horrified. I can't believe I hit her, let alone knocked her down. Amidst congratulations, I hurry away.

Back at the apartment I try to pack, but can't forget the startled humiliation in the woman's dark eyes. Finally I wrap a pair of black bikini panties in a silk scarf and go out into the street.

Sitting on the curb near where the fight occurred is a plain-faced little girl of about eight with strawberry blonde hair and a sprinkling of freckles across her nose. I remember seeing her in the crowd, and ask if she knows the name of the Latina woman, or where she lives.

The child looks up at me with large green eyes. "Are you going to hit her again?"

"No. I want to tell her I'm sorry. I have a present for her."

"What is it?"

"*Bloomers*," I reply, finding humor in the peculiar name Cubans have for panties.

"*Bloomas!*" She takes my hand in the unself-conscious way children often do here and leads me through an alley and along a narrow street where the residents' stares inform me that foreigners rarely come.

"What is her name?" I ask.

"Suzanna," she says, letting go of my hand and scooting through the open door of a small house. In the dim interior I see Suzanna sitting in a chair. An older woman is beside her, holding a wet cloth to the eye that was gouged.

"Look." The child points at me. "It's the American lady."

Suzanna looks as astonished to see me standing there as she looked when I hit her.

"I came to apologize. And to bring you a present." I hold out the scarf-wrapped packet.

I can see she doesn't know what to make of it, but she comes forward slowly and takes the gift. We smile tentatively at each other.

"Come in. Sit down." She waves at a worn green velour sofa.

I sit on the sofa feeling uncomfortable under their stares but knowing this was the right thing to do. Suzanna sits facing me in the straight-backed chair. She strokes the blue silk scarf with slightly trembling fingers.

"How did you know where I lived?"

"The little girl showed me."

"Keri. She's my daughter."

"Oh. I saw her there at the, uh ... You know, I didn't mean to hit you. It just looked like you were going to hurt each other. Your eye ..." Her eye looks terrible.

"I don't care," she says sullenly. "That whore's been chasing my husband for months."

"Who's chasing who?" the older woman mutters sourly. "If it's not her it's some other woman, and more than one."

I shrug. "You can't fight them all."

Keri nudges her mother. "Open the package."

Suzanna unties the scarf and holds up the bikinis with a delighted gasp. Even with the swollen eye, she is an attractive woman.

"You might have to put on your new bloomers and go look for another man," I joke, imagining that the notion will bolster her ego.

Suzanna laughs, but not with her eyes. What comes from her throat ends in a choking sound that's closer to a sob.

"She'd leave him if she could," the older woman tells me. "But he says he'll kill her if she does."

Fresh in my memory are reports of three women murdered in Canada in recent months, and others in the U.S., too many to recall their stories, whose husbands said they would kill them if they left, and who did exactly that. Horror overwhelms me.

"I know there's a Women's Center in town. Can't you go there?"

"I'm afraid," she says in a voice that's hardly even a whisper. Tears drip down onto the black bikinis lying in her lap.

All I can think to say is, "I'm sorry, Suzanna."

Keri moves close to her mother. Anything else that might be said is there in the child's unsmiling eyes.

Canada — 1996

Anti-Castro Americans have applied for advertising space on Toronto buses and subways. The ad depicts a Cuban couple behind bars while tourists frolic on the beach, its caption: "Your Paradise. Their Hell. End the suffering. Don't visit Cuba."

Toronto transit officials refuse the ad, calling it distasteful. The anti-Castro group announces that it will use billboards to get its message out to the public.

The ad fills me with rage and despair. The woman in the picture reminds me of Suzanna, and my own younger self. The bars I could see never held me long. What confined me was what I believed: lies that conned me into giving up freedoms I might have had.

I go to my map-covered wall and run a hand across the world. Little by little my dark mood lightens. There will always be lies but there's always truth; it's just a matter of figuring out how to get there from here.

When I go back to Cuba next year, I'll take some Americans with me.

LEAVING HOME

Malibu Beach 1994

I sit on an expanse of blue carpet, staring out at panoramic ocean view. This is Andrew's Malibu home, perched on a hill less than a mile from where mine was. It survived the fire because he stayed and fought it all night alone, at times surrounded by the flames.

When I asked him why he stood his ground, he didn't say, "Because it was my home." He said, "Because it was my fire."

Andrew is the president of Earth Trust Foundation, an organization I've worked with as a volunteer off and on for a couple of years. I don't know him very well, don't know that a year from now, when I'm living in another country, he will invite me to become director of Earth Trust's social justice programs. We'll work together in the modern way, by phone, fax, and e-mail, and will become close while remaining, as we are now, semi-strangers.

He is a tall man, just slightly stooped, as if to make his height less intimidating. There is about him a quality of understated strength, like this house, which he designed. He's watching me with eyes that are a lighter blue than the ocean, more like the sky on a warm summer day.

"Are you on your way to Canada?"

"No, not yet." I haven't said why I'm here, but I think he knows. Although I love the mountains of British Columbia and the man who awaits me there, the days just now are short and cold. Letting go of the notion that Malibu is home, letting go of this sunlit sea and traveling north will be the hardest trip I've ever made.

"I have a place down on the beach where you can stay if you like."

The place is half a mile from the Budwood, a single room with a deck that juts out over the waves. One must walk along the sand to reach it and at high tide there's no leaving without getting shoes full of seawater.

The view at this bend of the coast is south toward Catalina Island, which seems to be resting on the horizon. But I'm more intrigued by what's close at hand. At dawn it's pelicans that capture my attention, skimming in pairs just above the waves. Then I look for a glint of morning sun on the nose of a little seal patrolling up and down the shore. It might be any time of day that a school of dolphins circles by. Sometimes I go out in a kayak and find them suddenly all around me. I never see the big sea lions in the water, but late afternoon finds whole families sunning on the off-shore rocks. I watched these animals all the years I lived at the Budwood, but never knew or loved them quite so much as I do now.

In the room there is a bed, a chair, and a jury-rigged desk to hold my computer. This is enough, or perhaps too much. A pencil would serve as well for all the writing I'm doing. Mainly I sit on the deck and watch the shoreline, hoping to glimpse my animal neighbors.

On the night of the lunar eclipse I go to bed early because it's cloudy and the moon is hidden. Near midnight I wake and discover that the sky is clear. I have a sudden need to be at the Budwood. I pull on my jeans and rush out, almost colliding with a man on the steps. It is Bond, who has had the same urge, coming to ask if I want to go with him.

We climb the mountain to a point above where we used to live and watch earth's shadow move across the moon. In this eerie light the burned land seems more lunar than the luminous balloon hanging above us. We hold hands like two lost children, knowing that the place we once called home is more than light years away.

The people who lived on the Budwood, whose presence made me know that I had come home whenever I returned from wherever I'd been, are now scattered all over L.A. Aino lives in Laurel Canyon, Pamela and Richard in Mandeville Canyon, Jacqui and David in Santa Monica Canyon. The horse is stabled in Topanga Canyon, and Bruce and Bond live nearby, at the mouth of Pena Canyon.

Some years ago I had a dream in which we all, horses and riders, were struck by a wave bigger than the mountain and were washed over the precipice into a canyon. I recall the sensation of being knocked from the saddle, followed by floating in blackness. I remember wondering if the world still existed, and if so, in what form.

I still pick up my mail from the Budwood box, which by some fluke was left intact. Usually I run down the beach to get there but today the tide is high so I walk along Pacific Coast Highway toward the mailbox. I have gone perhaps a hundred yards when I look up and see a wall of black water as high as my head sweeping down a canyon toward the highway. Dammed by houses on the ocean side of the highway, it forms into a lake that spreads out in both directions and stops at my ankles. What prevents it from washing over me is that the walls of several houses give way. The muddy water gushes through living rooms and out onto decks and cascades down to the beach.

A cream-colored Cadillac caught on the canyon road swirls like a leaf into the middle of the highway. A woman, looking amazingly calm, climbs out the window and wades through the lake of waist-deep mud. Within minutes there are a dozen emergency vehicles on the scene and a swarm of media helicopters overhead. Looking along the highway, I see that at least twenty houses have been inundated by the mud. Behind me several others are undisturbed, including my own flimsy room which is perched on a rise so slight I had never noticed it.

I walk back and sit on the deck. In the distance I see the spout of a grey whale migrating north, from Baja to the waters off British Columbia. I think about where it has been and where it's going, and where I've been and where I'm going.

It occurs to me that when a person is in their fifties as I now am, it's time to stop asking what one wants to do with one's life, and start asking what one wants to have done. Answers to the first question always seemed terribly contingent on other people: whether bosses approved my work, whether editors liked my writing, whether family and friends encouraged me. But somehow I feel that answers to the question of what I want to *have done* rest wholly with me.

Before my thoughts have carried me any further, the pen I've been fiddling with begins to make a list.

1. Build a house.

This, definitely, is something I want to have done, mingling my own sweat and skills with those of that Canadian man who mellowed me out, because he is, I know, the only one I'll ever live with again.

2. Write a book.

Gloria Steinem once said that frequent interruptions, inherent in the caretaking roles that women commonly choose, force them to shorter forms like poems and journal entries. That's probably true but I'm not a caretaker anymore. I have time now, and there is a book I want to have written.

I study the horizon for awhile and try to think of something else. A list just two items long seems hardly worth making. There should be at least three things I want to have done that I haven't done already. I'm sure there is. But that third thing, whatever it is, I can't bring to the surface of my mind.

Having no schedule to keep, I often sit out on the deck until the wee hours, watching the play of moonlight on the waves. It is February and none too warm. The chill finally drives me indoors to bed. I have barely drifted to sleep when I am awakened by a jolt so hard I think a car must have crashed into the house. The crash is followed by a sickening sway that rocks the bed from side to side. It's an earthquake, of course. Earthquakes never scared me up on the Budwood, but now my heart is pounding. This house is lightly built, only a summer place. I should go outdoors but the deck, perched on skinny poles, is even flimsier. On the beach I'd be safe from falling debris but that first hard jolt means the epicenter was not far away. If it was offshore there could be a tidal wave.

I have never experienced such a long-lasting earthquake, never had this much time to think of and reject alternatives. The cat scoots under the bed and I figure that's as good a place as any. We lie there together while the shaking continues, then stops, and a while later, come the aftershocks which go on for days. The Malibu fire took out three hundred homes. This quake destroys twenty thousand.

In the grey dawn, with a terrified cat crouched in my lap, I write,

Six-point-six is a number
That shatters lives and ways of living,
Every number to the tenth power more force.
Or is it only squared; is that enough
To cancel so many cubes called home?
I was never good at numbers and anyway
By now too numb to feel six-point-six
As more than another shock
After shock.
It caught me hiding under myself
Preparing to run from a place I love
Can one get clear of that in time?
Or is there only reaching out
Catching hold of even moving things?
Waves rising on the beach
Snow falling in the mountains

A few familiar faces.
Are these enough to steady me
Until this quaking stops?

Some days I can't bear to go up to the Budwood. Other times I can't stay away. I had to come today, though it hurts to be here. I avert my eyes from the rolling grey hills which Jacqui says remind her of a great grey elephant down on her side. It's an image that has stayed with me because, naked of vegetation, that's how vulnerable they seem. The land is deep in ash and there are no tracks. Since the fire no wildlife has passed this way. It wasn't that the deer couldn't outrun the fire, some said afterwards; it was that the miles-long wall of flames sucked the oxygen from the air and suffocated fleeing animals before they could escape.

Between the human and divine orders of terror, there are not enough safe places in this world. Suddenly I know that this is one of the things I want to have done. A sanctuary for wild things. For jungle cats.

The thought carries me to Hopi and then to Jo. The earthquake has made cracks in trails where she on horseback always went flying ahead. Most of those trails are impassable now but it doesn't matter. It has been years since we rode here together. In that time we've followed many paths, sometimes she in the lead, sometimes I. We've come to trust each other.

The last time I visited her she told me she was pregnant. The thought of her risking childbirth made me anxious. I covered it up by teasing, "Does this mean you have to get married?"

She and her lover (after six years of their living together, can I still call him that?) had laughed and hugged each other and said definitely not; their relationship was too secure to require the pseudo-cement of that particular convention.

"What'll you do for a name?" I challenged.

"Easy." Jo flipped me a self-satisfied smile. "If it's a boy it will be Aiden Joseph Doyle the Twenty-Fourth. I'd never have the nerve to break a chain like that."

"And if it's a girl?"

She feigned surprise that I should even ask. "Why, it'll be a Jordan, of course."

What it was was a miscarriage, probably because she was working too hard and not attending to her health. She said it was no big deal; that they might try again in the future. I wish they'd adopt but it's not my call. Jo hasn't been my child for a very long time, but a woman who shares my dreams. She'll love the idea of a jungle cat sanctuary.

I pause under a blackened eucalyptus tree where Jerry once hung a swing for the pleasure of his (mostly beautiful) women friends, and where some many years later Jacqui and David's toddler dangled, her plump legs growing longer by the day. I built a sandpit for that child, brought sand from the beach and poured it into a cement basin formed by hand. In the wet cement I imbedded a tile decorated with a hummingbird. Maya, who wasn't yet two, pointed to the picture of the bird on the tile, then to a hummingbird feeder hanging nearby, and babbled some infant gibberish to let me know she knew what kind of bird it was.

I scuff through the ashes and find the hummingbird tile. There are no birds here now. Wherever they went, I hope they found eucalyptus trees to nest in and flowers always blooming.

A rumbling of earth startles me out of myself. I brace for another aftershock but the ground underfoot doesn't move. Then I see it's only a landslide, crashing into a wild canyon a few hundred yards away. It is followed by silence, then, from the opposite side of the gully, "Yip, yip, yip!" Three little coyotes rush down the slope, not away from the slide but to the canyon bottom where, in a cloud of dust, the earth is resettling itself. They must be as crazy as I am to be so drawn to the unpredictable.

The cabin I first stayed in when I came to the Budwood was small. Now it's even smaller, just a pile of twisted metal and cracked cement, furnished with the rusting wires of Bond's once-elegant piano. What gave off music to his touch now leaves my fingers stained with grime.

I wipe them on my jeans and walk up the path to the big house where I and three other families lived. The units, like our lives, were separate but constantly overlapping; fuses blown in one putting out lights in another, or parties at one spilling over into the next. On my old patio, pots that once held geraniums, jasmine, and aloe vera lie about in broken shards. It's easy to see what Bond meant when he said, the morning after the fire, "Our lives have been turned into archeology."

The only thing that hasn't changed is the view across the bay. Planes lift off from LAX headed for cities all over the globe, and boats on the spreading blue ocean below set sail for distant ports. This is something I found here and something I must take with me: this constant reminder that the whole world is real, and there are many ways to get there.

My Mazda, parked at the beach below, stands out like a bright red toy against the ocean blue. A fog is blowing in. I should be on my way.

As I walk down the driveway I try to imagine the mountains of British Columbia where I'll be in a couple of days. But the ocean is still too much in view; it blocks the mental image. I suck in a breath of moist salty air and look back one last time. The hills have already disappeared in mist, blowing in from the sea.

I put a Grateful Dead tape in the cassette player, volume cranked up high, and pull out onto the foggy highway, headed north.

EPILOGUE

The Rainforest

It was suggested by some who read this book in manuscript that it needed some "culminating event" to tie its themes together and show where all these experiences were leading. I wanted to resist the advice, to argue that my life isn't that tidy. For that matter, I'm not sure anybody's life comes together in a single "culminating event." But I confess to being involved in something that could be interpreted that way, something which margays and travel and Third World suffering and a lot of other threads tangled through this story may have been leading to. The problem is that I'm still in the middle of it, and can't be sure where this thing and I are going. I'm not even sure where it began.

I think it was after I settled in British Columbia, after Derek and I built our house in the mountains; after Andrew hired me to direct Earth Trust's social justice program, and I started traveling again.

The new job took me back through some of the same territory I'd traveled before but this was a different, more focused kind of travel. I evaluated rural community banks that Earth Trust had supported in Nicaragua (now the poorest country in the hemisphere after Haiti), and urban ones in El Salvador (now the most violent next to Guatemala). I went to see about funding a Guatemala group that wanted to do organic gardening in a Mayan village where, in 1982, all males over the age of six were murdered by the military. These people used to keep their livestock in a communal pasture but now the field is empty. That's where the slaughter of men and boys took place, and the women, who were forced to watch, won't go there any more.

Earth Trust also sent me to Ecuador to see about an organic garden project on the northern coast. Local people, descendants of shipwrecked and runaway slaves, have survived there for two centuries by gathering shellfish from the mangroves. But in the past few years the mangroves have been scooped out by earth-moving machines to form mile upon mile of man-made lakes. The shrimp being cultivated in these lakes are for export only; they belong to the multinationals.

These marimba-playing descendants of African slaves also ate fruit from the forest and dug for yucca root which they pounded into a kind of tortilla. At least that's what they did before the road came. The road was built for big refrigerated trucks to take out the shrimp, and for even bigger logging trucks to take out the trees. From the coast, roads penetrate the rainforest twenty or thirty kilometers at a time. Where roads go the loggers go, and the forest falls. The people of this region, who only know hunting and gathering, don't know where to turn.

I found a Columbian biologist, María Victoria Arboleda, working there, teaching a group of women how to enrich the thin tropical soil with compost and to plant in raised beds so their vegetables don't drown in the torrential downpours. An orchard had been established, and the women wanted to try raising poultry. I liked these strong black women. Some of them reminded me of Luz, with whom I once shared a jail cell. Luz was from this region. I thought their project worth supporting so came back to Canada to organize the funding.

When Jeff heard about it he phoned. "Ecuador!" he exclaimed. "I can't believe you went back to Ecuador!"

I admit there is some irony in the fact that Ecuador is where my special project is happening. Not with the Africans on the coast but with the Secoya tribe which lives in the eastern part of the country, an area called Amazonia because all its great rivers drain into the Amazon.

I met the Secoya leader, Elias Piaguaje, one rainy afternoon in Quito. Elias is a soft-eyed, always-smiling man with short brown legs and short black hair. Elias said petroleum companies were seeking permission to do exploratory drilling in Secoya territory. He said that there are but 350 of his people left and unless they can get some outside help they are doomed. I told him about a dream I had of creating one safe haven in the world for little jungle cats.

Elias smiled. "The Secoya hold title to forty thousand hectares. Half of it we need for hunting and farming and wood for our houses and canoes. If the rest was left in virgin forest, and designated as a reserve, well, that might save some endangered wildcats and also help save the endangered Secoya."

This is how I come to be trotting through the rainforest behind a barefoot Secoya man who is wearing a purple dress. Behind me are two Americans from the Center for Endangered Cats. One is seriously out of shape, his sweatband drenched in perspiration. The other is struggling under a heavy pack.

Their lack of Third World travel experience was apparent the moment they got off the plane. As we whisked them into a taxi, María Victoria explained to the one called Bo that he'd have to ditch the camouflage outfit he was wearing because it's illegal to wear para-military garb in most South American countries, and extremely dangerous. But there was nothing to be done about his pack, which must weigh close to a hundred pounds. I urged them to travel light, but Bo said he'd tolerate the weight; he prefers to be prepared.

María Victoria and Elias bring up the rear. She keeps stopping to examine some fascinating plant or insect and Elias, smiling his enthusiasm, explains its nature from the Secoya point of view. They've caught up to us only because it's getting dark and hard to see things. I'm worried about the Americans. The trail is slippery with mud and crisscrossed with roots. Bo keeps stumbling with that heavy pack. If he sprains an ankle, it'll take us forever to get him out of here.

I trot ahead and ask our little guide in the purple smock, "How much further to this cabana where we're supposed to spend the night?"

"One hour," he says cheerfully.

"You said that when we left the village," I point out.

"One hour walk," the old man repeats.

"But that was an hour and a half ago. It's dark already."

He bobs his head with indignation at this challenge to his sense of time. "One hour only. For young men without packs."

"Ah. And how long for *us*?"

"For you, four hours."

He presses rapidly on, whacking at vines with his macheté to clear a path which only he can see.

"We're not going to make it," I tell him. "We'll have to camp here in the jungle."

He shouts something in Secoya back to Elias who comes forward to join him. Their machetés swing furiously. In less than ten minutes a large lean-to has been constructed, with a floor of palm fronds laid over the muddy earth. Bo eases his pack to the ground, digs out a camp stove, and starts to cook supper. I pitch the tent I've brought for María and myself and tumble inside, too tired to think about food.

"I'm getting too old for this sort of thing," I mutter to María Victoria.

"Well," she teases, "it's not too late to become a suburban housewife." She sits with her feet protruding from the tent as she unlaces muddy hiking boots. She wiggles into her sleeping bag, and adds, "If you go out to pee in the night, don't get too close to the trees. Most of them are defended by ants. The ones called Congos can really hurt."

How in such dense forest does one keep from getting close to a tree? From the ant's perspective, exactly how close is too close? Did I ever have the steadiness to be a good suburban wife? The questions turn muddy in my brain and float away on a river of sleep.

By morning the rain that battered the tent all night has stopped. Bo's voice filters through the nylon.

"Rosa? Are you and María Victoria awake?"

"Sort of," I mumble.

"Coffee's ready."

I zip open the flap and accept the steaming coffee with a smile of undiluted gratitude. Never again will I tease him about that heavy pack.

María Victoria stirs and pushes a curtain of long black curls away from her face. Bo peeks in at her wistfully, and I know he'd like to have spent the night beside her.

"What about you, María Victoria? Would you rather have tea?"

"Umm, yes, thank you," she murmurs sweetly.

When Bo goes back to the camp stove to get the tea, I whisper, "A man who serves you tea in bed — what more do you want, María Victoria?"

She gives my braid a tug. "Mind your tongue, *bruja*. Matchmaking is a dangerous game, and we've got work to do."

We crawl out laughing and find the others already having breakfast. Sunshine splashes through leaves still glistening wet from last night's rain.

"You like it?" Elias asks, waving a hand at the towering, vine-hung trees around us.

"Yes, I like it."

"The *tigrillos*, they like it here, too."

"I know."

We'll meet with other Secoya leaders when we get back to the village and negotiate a deal. We'll provide training in sustainable agriculture to make the lands they've already cleared more productive so they don't have to keep slashing and burning the forest. We'll help them build a lodge down by the river so trekkers headed for the Amazon will stop and spend a few dollars. We'll create a center for the study of all the jungle cats native to this region — oncillas, margays, ocelots, jaguarundis, pumas, and jaguars. But especially the little ones that no one knows much about except that their habitat is being destroyed and there aren't many of them left.

In exchange, the Secoya people promise that this forest will be kept as it is and the jungle cats who dwell here will be protected "for all time."

Bo and I will go back and raise the money. María Victoria will start the gardens. Jo will come with me next time, and we'll scour the country for captive margays. When we find one locked in a filthy small cage or strangled at the end of a chain, we'll persuade its captor to let us have it, and bring it here, and let it go free.

There you have it: a love of margays and a connection with my daughter and a quest for personal freedom and a conviction that the world will keep getting worse unless we all keep doing things to make it better. Maybe all of that was leading up to this, or maybe not. Before this became a book it was, and still is, a life. It might be premature to call this project its "culminating event."

Anyway, how do I know we can raise the money to create this, the world's very first, margay sanctuary? Will future generations of Secoya honor commitments made by their elders to protect the jungle cats that share their rainforest? Even if they do, will petroleum companies drilling in Amazonia so poison the environment that nothing can survive here? Will there be future generations of Secoya people? Or jungle cats? Or us?

I LOVE ...
The road, the river
the air that takes me
like a kite cut clean
over the edge
of my own dreams.

The child who took a grain
from me, and pain, and made
a woman pearl; some alchemy
of mind
and music of the spheres.

The sea; its luring moonpaths
its terrible sweet caresses
its thunder
and seductive song
eternal and alive

Land forms that soar
and plunge and promise
escape, for an eternity
from days of endless, flat
predictability.

A man whose mind
moves in weightless ways
into mine and over new terrain
and doesn't seem to mind
being sane.

Writing, words letting go
taking wing and leaving
space inside my head
for things I thought
I didn't know.

Any vision, turned solid
from first light inside my head
to something good,
something true
to itself, to me.

And jungle cats in hiding,
giving, taking life,
guiltless natural gods
never ever conceding
the numbered days of Eden.

ACKNOWLEDGEMENTS

Books are like children; they require the support of a community of caring people to come out right. Since before it was born, this book has had such a community. I especially want to thank:

— friends, more than I can name, who encouraged me, saved my letters over the years, and kept insisting that these adventures should be recorded somewhere other than on backpack-crumpled notepaper.

— those who critiqued, edited, and proofed the manuscript: Jackie Drysdale, Sara Jefferson, Almeda Glen-Miller, Louise Drescher, Lynne Phillips, Barbara and Bruce Robinson, Richard Hertz, Grace Hampton, Wendy McCleskey, Jerry Ziegman, my cousins Lori Rees and Gaylon Monteverde, and my daughter Jona Sun.

— my publisher, Lesley Choyce, whose comments on creative non-fiction convinced me that this type of book has merit;

— and Derek, friend, lover, computer guru, and editor. He made sure that my writer self (which like my keys, I've often misplaced) didn't get lost.

Rosa Jordan
The Monashee Mountains
British Columbia, 1997